Randall L. Patton

SHAW INDUSTRIES

THE UNIVERSITY OF GEORGIA PRESS   ATHENS & LONDON

Randall L. Patton

SHAW INDUSTRIES

A HISTORY

06   05   04   03   02   C   5   4   3   2   1

Library of Congress Cataloging-in-Publication Data

Patton, Randall L., 1958–
    Shaw Industries: a history / Randall L. Patton.
        p. cm.
Includes bibliographical references and index.
    ISBN 0-8203-2364-0 (hardcover : alk. paper)
    1. Shaw Industries—History. 2. Rug and carpet industry—
Georgia—History.   I. Title.
    HD9937.U54 S486 2003
    338.7′677643′09758—dc21   2002007873

British Library Cataloging-in-Publication Data available

CONTENTS

This book is in many ways a follow-up to my earlier volume (with David Parker) titled *Carpet Capital: The Rise of a New South Industry*. While *Carpet Capital* attempted to tell the story of the growth of the carpet-manufacturing district in northwest Georgia, this book focuses more closely on a single firm, Shaw Industries. As the twenty-first century opened, Shaw remained the largest manufacturer of carpeting in the world, the leading company in the "carpet capital of the world," Dalton, Georgia. Though the company was clearly in transition in the late 1990s, and many of the firm's longtime top management personnel had begun to retire, the original CEO, Robert E. Shaw, remained at the helm as chairman of the board.

This book attempts to place the story of Shaw Industries within the appropriate historical contexts, but it is primarily a company history. The company funded this history in large part as a way to try to preserve something of the "institutional memory" of the firm at a critical juncture. Though the company's old records were not extensive, I had access to minutes of board and executive committee meetings. I also conducted more than two dozen interviews to supplement an already extensive body of oral histories on the carpet industry housed at Kennesaw State University. The company placed no restrictions on my editorial control of the manuscript. I hope that this book serves the two main purposes for which it was intended—to help preserve the history of one of Georgia's most important post–World War II corporations and to help provide some insight into the evolution of southern industry in the Sunbelt era.

I should add a note on the relative coverage of some of Shaw's divisions. Cabin Crafts receives more attention than any other Shaw acquisition or discrete division. This does not reflect any additional significance attached to that acquisition by Shaw management. In fact, management questioned the extended treatment of Cabin Crafts. Rather, the coverage reflects the author's editorial decision. Cabin Crafts' long history and its position of leadership in both the old bedspread industry of the 1930s–50s and the new carpet industry of the '50s and beyond made that firm unique. It was also through the Westcott/Cabin Crafts connection that the Shaw family became involved in these industries.

On a similar point, the presence or absence of particular names within the manuscript should not be interpreted as overly significant. Shaw Industries personnel are notoriously reluctant to claim individual credit for accomplishments. This is laudable, but it sometimes obscures the roles of key individuals. The author apologizes in advance for any glaring omissions of key personnel.

While a number of people were very helpful, sole responsibility for mistakes and misinterpretations rests, of course, with the author.

I would like to thank everyone at Shaw Industries who helped with this project, particularly Julius Shaw, Todd Callaway, Camilla Moore, Connie Corbin, Ben Laughter, and Carl Rollins. Retired vice president Warren Sims, the company's unofficial historian for many years, was also particularly helpful. I would also like to thank my readers who reviewed the manuscript for the University of Georgia Press. They offered many good suggestions that improved the manuscript.

Finally, I must thank my family for helping me get this project done. My wife, Karen, was as always my closest adviser and best reader. My sons, Randall and Matthew (six and three years old, respectively), helped more than they could know. I always enjoyed taking a break from the project just to play. They helped remind me of the bigger picture.

SHAW INDUSTRIES

The Rise of Northwest Georgia's Carpet Industry

Shaw Industries is the largest manufacturer of carpet in the world and the biggest textile company in the United States. Headquartered in Dalton, Georgia, Shaw ranked 473rd on the 2000 *Fortune* 500 list of the nation's largest businesses, with revenues in excess of $4 billion. Shaw topped WestPoint Stevens, Springs, Burlington, and other diversified textile firms as well as its rivals in carpet manufacture—Mohawk and Beaulieu. Shaw Industries employed more than 30,000 people in 2000, making it the largest manufacturing employer in Georgia.

The roots of Shaw's success can be traced directly back to the formation of Star Finishing Company in the Sunbelt South era of the 1960s, or further still to Clarence Shaw's father and his Star Dye Company, founded in 1946. Indirectly, the Shaw story extends even further back. Shaw Industries emerged within a northwest Georgia industrial cluster that had its origins in the mid-1890s. Shaw built on the accomplishments of its predecessors and benefited from the experience of earlier firms and entrepreneurs in northwest Georgia's tufted textile complex.

Ultimately, Shaw could trace its origins back to the beginnings of carpet manufacture in the United States in the early nineteenth century. All along the way, entrepreneurs faced a changing environment at every level—local, regional, national, and international. Robert E. and J. C. Shaw, the brothers who founded the company; their father, Clarence Shaw, who started the small business that preceded Shaw Industries; the founders of Cabin Crafts, a pioneer firm in northwest Georgia's drive to become the world's "carpet capital"; Harry and Julian Saul, the driving forces behind Queen Chenilles (later Queen Carpet Company); and the Doerr family, who created the Philadelphia Carpet Company in the 1840s—all of these businessmen made choices, crafted strategies, reacted to changes in the marketplace or the business environment, and created institutions of long-term value. And most of them did it in the American South, a region long noted for its industrial backwardness and poverty.

This story focuses on Shaw's management and the evolution of corporate strategy in response to changing conditions over time. The Shaw story begins with Clarence Shaw and Cabin Crafts. Cabin Crafts played a large role in the creation of first the bedspread and then the carpet industries. Cabin Crafts eventually became a part of Shaw Industries (in 1987). Running parallel to the Cabin Crafts story is that of Clarence Shaw, who created Star Dye Company, a firm that provided dyeing and finishing services to the bedspread and small-rug makers of the Dalton district in the 1940s and 1950s. The focus then shifts to Bob and Bud Shaw, Clarence's sons, who dramatically expanded their father's business by forming Star Finishing Company. Star Finishing moved boldly into the dyeing of carpet, something Clarence Shaw had always resisted. Bud Shaw formed a carpet manufacturing company in the 1960s. The Shaw brothers came together in 1967 to purchase the Philadelphia Carpet Company. Through the Philadelphia Holding Company, Star Finishing and Philadelphia Carpet came together to form the core of the corporation that would become Shaw Industries in 1971.

Shaw Industries was formed in the late 1960s, in the midst of an unprecedented economic expansion that lifted all carpet producers and made failure difficult. The Shaw Industries business strategies were forged in the recessions that followed the boom. Demand ran ahead of supply from 1950 through the mid-1970s. "It was hell-bent-for-election" during those years, Bob Shaw recalled, as sales increased so quickly and generated so much cash that "you didn't need any controls." At least "not until the recession came, and you had to figure out who you were and why." By the end of the 1970s, success no longer came easily. The decades after 1973 presented great challenges to American manufacturers in virtually all fields. Managers throughout every segment of the U.S. economy had to ask searching questions about their industries and individual companies. No company answered those questions better than Shaw Industries in the 1980s and 1990s.

The President's Emergency Council labeled the South "the nation's Number One economic problem" in 1938. During the heyday of the civil rights movement in the 1950s and early 1960s, observers increasingly viewed the South as the nation's number one moral problem (or number one international embarrassment). By the early 1970s, however, economic issues had come to the fore once more as politicians, journalists, and business leaders marveled at the Sunbelt phenomenon—they observed a South that had become the nation's number one economic opportunity. The region not only seemed to be "catching up" to national norms but appeared to be on the verge of surpassing the performance of the nation's older manufacturing regions—popularly dubbed the Rustbelt.

Not surprisingly, academics, journalists, and politicians began seeking the source of this remarkable transformation. Early efforts produced more heat than light in congressional debates over disproportionate federal expenditures. In the 1980s, James C. Cobb highlighted the "selling of the South"—the region's crusade to attract outside investment. Cobb noted that the progress achieved by the cheap sale of the region's resources, both human and environmental, had been far less spectacular than advertised (and had created new problems as well).[1]

Gavin Wright located the source of the South's persistent underdevelopment in its isolated, regional labor market. The key to the South's advance toward national norms in the second half of the twentieth century, Wright argued, lay in New Deal programs that undermined the low-wage, isolated labor market. Policies such as the minimum wage "operated to slow the growth of employment in low-wage industries in all parts of the country, an effect whose greatest impact was felt in the South." The textile industry was clearly the most important regional industry affected. The South was a net loser in migration from the early twentieth century until the mid-1960s. Outmigration tended to come from the extremes—that is, it was heavily concentrated among the most poorly educated and the best educated. Migrants to the South, Wright observed, "were highly educated by southern standards." Many of the outmigrants "faced hostility, unemployment, and a host of social problems." Wright posed his tentative answer to southern development as a question. Was the southern advance toward national norms "southern economic development," he asked, "or was it the replacement of one economy by another, the two having in common only the coincidence that they both occupied the same geographic space?"[2]

Elaborating an answer to Wright's question, Bruce Schulman has more recently argued that "the South's progress from national economic disgrace to rapid growth region proved not so much a *transformation,* although considerable transformation occurred, as the *importation* of a new regional economy." He pointed to the pivotal role played by the federal government in "prim[ing] the region for growth." In Schulman's view, the South became a "blank slate . . . because political and economic forces wiped it clean." Federal "wage policy, farm and industrial development programs," the interstate highway system, and "equalization grants assailed the colonial South and helped erect a new political and economic order." The Cold War national security state and its attendant military-industrial complex dominated the region's growth agenda from the 1950s through the 1970s. "Unique among American sections," Schulman wrote, "the Sunbelt South . . . has been a planned region."[3]

Implicit, of course, in this analysis is a theme as old as the field of southern history—continuity versus change. The historical literature of the post–Civil War American South is replete with various visions of a New South, and much ink has been spilled trying to fix the key turning point or change in the central theme of the region's past. Schulman has suggested that the South's development trajectory changed dramatically after World War II as a result of federal intervention.

The histories of the carpet industry and of Shaw Industries seem to indicate that, at least in the northwest corner of Georgia, Sunbelt prosperity grew from deep roots in the region's industrial past. It also had much in common with similar industrial concentrations in other parts of the United States and the world. Companies such as Shaw Industries, the nation's leading textile manufacturer and world's largest producer of carpets, did not emerge on a "blank slate" (nor could they have). Although there was much that was new about this industry when it originated in the 1950s, it was constructed on a preexisting foundation. Schulman's "blank slate" concept has much explanatory value and seems to describe accurately much of southern development in the post–World War II years. Of course, there are exceptions to any broad generalization, and this book attempts to add some nuance to the story of post–World War II southern economic development by focusing on the story of one of the leading, though little-known, companies created during the Sunbelt era. Although new industries and new government policies certainly helped define the southern economy after the war, the slate was not wiped clean in every locale—especially northwest Georgia.[4]

As World War II drew to a close, the economic future of the South was a subject of intense discussion and debate. Some advocated greater federal spending and regulation to promote economic growth. Others sought to induce northern capital to move to Dixie. This "selling of the South" approach involved offering tax breaks and other incentives to encourage outside industries to relocate to the South. A few continued to preach the possibility that southerners could lift themselves by their own bootstraps.

"Development of the South is Possible with Own Capital." So ran a headline in the *Dalton Citizen* in January 1945. The story summarized a speech at the Dalton Merchants Association, but it could well serve as a capsule version of the history of northwest Georgia's tufted textile industry. Few stories better exemplify the bootstrap approach to industrial development than this localized manufacturing district. From Dalton's industrial revolution of the 1880s through the city's emergence as the world's "carpet capital," local people and locally generated capital have played the most important roles.

The tufted textile industry clearly has much in common with other localized industrial "agglomerations" throughout the United States and the world. Economist Paul Krugman has observed that "the most striking feature of the geography of economic activity . . . is surely *concentration*." Krugman found that the carpet industry was the ninth most geographically concentrated industry in the nation (among more than a hundred industries). Segments of the textile sector, including carpet, made up half of the top twenty localized industries.[5]

The story of Shaw Industries and the carpet industry highlights the dangers of making too-broad generalizations. Certainly Dalton and other small communities in northwest Georgia share common elements with the rest of the South. Yet the area also shares common elements with Silicon Valley, the automotive district of southern Michigan, and a host of other such agglomerations. The history of carpet manufacture in northwest Georgia is "a very typical one," according to Krugman.[6]

The carpet industry perfectly illustrates Krugman's contention that "the long shadow cast by history and accident over the location of production is apparent at all scales."[7] It is also evidence of the lasting impact of the southern crusade to build a regional textile industry. Carpet manufacture was the last segment of textile making to be captured by southern firms, and it happened in a completely unexpected fashion. Accidents abounded, yet the general textile-manufacturing foundation laid by two generations of southerners after the Civil War formed the context within which such "accidents" could occur.

American carpet manufacture has always been highly localized. Prior to World War II, the industry was centralized in a few towns in Connecticut, Pennsylvania, and New York. During the first century and a half of carpet manufacture in the United States, dating from the 1790s, Americans made carpets and rugs the way that European firms made them and in a fashion similar to the way that other textile goods were produced. Carpets were woven on looms—first handlooms, then power looms—from wool. A number of innovations in the late nineteenth and early twentieth centuries improved the speed and versatility of looms. New industries pushed textiles down toward the bottom of the value-added scale.

At the beginning of the twentieth century, the textile trade that had led the industrial revolution increasingly became a target for downtrodden regions trying to "catch up" with the industrialized world. The South launched a mill-building crusade to bring the cotton mills to the cotton fields. In this drive, the

South largely succeeded. Entrepreneurs built local mills, and some northern firms relocated to the South in search of cheap labor and low taxes. Southerners started at the bottom of the quality chain, creating mills to produce the coarsest grades of cloth and other products, and then slowly and painfully worked their way up the quality ladder. By the 1920s, the South was home to the lion's share of the American textile industry, most of it owned within the South.[8]

The carpet and rug segment of textiles established a position near the top of the value-added rankings within the textile sector. Carpet manufacture remained exclusively a northern industry as late as World War II. Southerners had captured other segments of the carpet trade, all of which were much higher volume operations, but the top of the value chain eluded them. A handful of northern manufacturers—Bigelow, Mohawk, Alexander Smith and Sons, Philadelphia Carpet Company, and a few others—dominated a stagnant carpet market. Per capita consumption of carpets actually declined in the first five decades of the twentieth century. Carpet had the unenviable distinction of being a relatively expensive product on the eve of the greatest mass-consumption boom in history. By the early 1950s, trade journals and carpet mill executives wondered aloud about the future of the industry. No revolutions in loom productivity appeared to be on the horizon; wool prices crept upward.

Manufacturers searched for ways out of the logjam. They slashed capacity, idling looms. They initiated huge advertising campaigns. Predictably, they moved operations to the South, as other textile firms had done earlier. By 1958, more than 60 percent of carpet-producing looms operated in Dixie. Mohawk, Bigelow, Alexander Smith, James Lees, and other woven carpet firms opened mills in the South and shuttered northern plants. It would seem, then, that the story of northwest Georgia's rise to become carpet capital of the world was intimately linked to the flow of carpet capital from North to South. Surely those northern firms settled on the Dalton area as a likely southern locale that offered cheap labor and low taxes. Perhaps a few southern firms also adopted the loom technology used by established firms and became effective competitors, too, repeating the southern pattern. The fact that one of those old northern firms—Mohawk—is now headquartered in northwest Georgia seems only to confirm this all-too-obvious chain of events.

But it did not happen that way. Northern firms scattered carpet-weaving plants across the old Confederacy from Glasgow, Virginia, to Liberty, South Carolina, to Rabun Gap, Georgia, to Greenville, Mississippi. They studiously avoided Dalton until the very recent past. While some of these plants still produce some carpet, the transfer of market dominance in carpet manufacture from a local (though slightly larger than the northwest Georgia district) agglomeration in the Northeast to a local agglomeration in the foothills of the Appalachian Mountains did not happen slowly or as a result of capital migration.

A combination of purposeful action, fortune, and accident combined to create the tufted textile complex of northwest Georgia. The Dalton area came to dominate carpet manufacture because local people developed a new technology that supplanted weaving. The new process, tufting, proved to be many times more efficient than weaving in producing floor coverings.

The new technology of northwest Georgia's carpet industry traces its origins back to the 1890s. At age fifteen, Whitfield County native Catherine Evans Whitener revived an old handicraft tradition by making a tufted bedspread in 1895. Whitener gave her initial spread to a relative as a wedding gift. She began receiving requests from other friends and relatives for similar items, and soon she was selling these handmade bedspreads. Whitener began with cotton sheeting, applied a design to the sheet using a stencil and meat skin, and then filled in the design by hand with a needle and heavy yarn. She left the yarn ends high, in "tufts," and clipped the ends to create a fluffy, chenille effect. Finally, she washed the spread in hot water, partly to clean it but mostly to shrink the sheeting to lock in the yarn tufts. Whitener taught other area women the craft, and slowly a cottage industry grew.[9]

Whitener and her colleagues had originally supplied their own raw materials and handled their own marketing. Stories abounded of women packing up bundles of bedspreads and sending them off to northern department stores like Wanamaker's and Macy's with notes asking for payment if the spreads were sold. Legend holds that no such package was ever wasted, and by the 1920s demand had outpaced the limitations of purely home manufacture. Spread houses and an extensive putting-out system emerged, with merchants stamping designs onto spreads at a central location and then using individuals known as "haulers" to distribute the stamped spreads and yarn throughout the countryside for tufting. These spread houses and individual residences turned U.S. Highway 41, the Old Dixie Highway, into "Peacock Alley" for miles near Dalton, the center of the booming trade, as bedspreads with colorful designs such as the famous peacock adorned clotheslines along the roadside. Tourists snapped up the spreads, and demand grew.

By the early 1930s, several companies were experimenting with converted sewing machines to speed up production. Cabin Crafts pioneered in the application of technology to the tufting process by patenting a needlepunch gun device that could insert raised yarn tufts into a piece of backing material. This gun was used in conjunction with hanging hoops over which a sheet could be stretched. Operators (always women, most with experience in hand-tufting) filled in a pattern as they had with needle and yarn before, only much faster. Glenn Looper, a Georgia Tech graduate and Dalton, Georgia, resident, is generally credited with the first successful adaptation of a tabletop sewing machine, but many others probably developed the same technique roughly simultaneously by about 1937. The key adaptation was the addition of a "looper" (named for its function, not for the fortuitously named ostensible inventor). The looper was a metal hook (made originally by converting old hacksaw blades) attached underneath the sewing machine that grabbed the yarn as it was inserted into the sheeting by the needle. The looper pulled the yarn, creating a raised yarn tuft. The sharp blades also cut the tufts to create the chenille effect. These converted sewing machines (secondhand Singer models purchased from the garment trades in New York) greatly speeded the process of stitching in the pattern and eliminated entirely the necessity for cutting the yarn tufts by hand.

The emergence of the tufting machine combined with early New Deal minimum wage regulations (contained in the National Recovery Administration's tufted bedspread code) spurred the industry to move toward centralized production. Many of the spread houses, which originated as places to stamp spreads and house inventory, expanded to become factories. Tufting "mills" had also developed a variety of other products using the new technology, such as bathrobes and covers for toilet tanks and seats. Most importantly, manufacturers began covering the entire surface of a piece of cotton backing material with raised yarn tufts to create small rugs. Manufacturers locked in the tufts by covering the backs of the rugs with latex (often simply using paint brushes in the early days).

While tufted textile manufacture represented the future in northwest Georgia, the past and present were still symbolized by traditional textile enterprises such as cotton mills. One of Shaw Industries' founders, J. C. (Bud) Shaw, first began working with carpet fibers at Dalton's Crown Cotton Mills in the 1950s. It is difficult to overestimate the significance of Crown in the industrial history of Dalton. Crown was created in the 1880s as a part of the "New South" industrialization movement and became a dynamic engine of industrial growth for Whitfield County. The county's manufacturing value-added per capita exceeded the state average by 50 percent by 1900.[10]

Crown's mere existence probably helped spur the development of the handicraft industry in the surrounding rural countryside. Surplus yarn was available cheaply from a local source. Cotton sheeting could be purchased locally

and at low cost as well. Crown continued to grow along with the home manufacture of bedspreads. During the 1920s, most likely, the balance began to shift.
After World War I the textile industry entered into a prolonged depression.
Ironically, by the time the South achieved its goal of capturing the nation's textile industry, the tired old industry no longer appeared worth having.

By the time the rest of the nation and other industrial sectors sank into the
Great Depression in 1929, northwest Georgia's tufted bedspread cottage industry helped thousands of families make ends meet. And, against all odds, these
novelty items continued to sell in spite of the depression. While the total value
of manufactured goods declined for Georgia and the nation in the 1930s,
Whitfield County's total volume rose. Crown Cotton Mills suffered stagnation,
and local businesses closed their doors. Tufted textiles thrived, however. No
good data exist for tracking tufted textiles as a distinct industry in the 1920s and
1930s (the census did not track this small new industry, and no effective trade
association kept such statistics until much later), but inferences can be drawn
from anecdotal evidence and aggregate census manufacturing numbers. The
total volume of manufactured goods and the per capita value of those products
rose in Whitfield County between 1929 and 1939.

Local legend has long held that the tufted textile industry helped northwest
Georgians weather the depression better than other sections of the South. Census records support the assertion. In 1929, on the eve of the Great Depression,
Whitfield County ranked seventh among Georgia counties in terms of the per
capita value of manufactured products (about $502). By 1939, Whitfield had
risen to third among Georgia counties. While per capita value in Whitfield had
grown only slightly (to about $528), manufacturing suffered in the remainder
of the state, with the value of shipments falling in most counties. Total manufacturing volume in Whitfield increased from $10.4 million in 1929 to almost
$13.8 million in 1939, a trend that ran counter to the national and state eco-
nomic tendencies—total value of manufactured goods declined in the nation
and in Georgia during the depression decade. Had Georgia matched Whitfield
County's per capita manufacturing numbers, the state would have ranked
eleventh among all U.S. states in 1939 (instead of thirty-second). Whitfield also
ranked third in the state in value-added per capita, and Georgia would have
ranked ninth nationally (ahead of Pennsylvania, just behind Massachusetts) in
this category had the state matched the tufted textile district's $263 average.[11]

No one could have guessed it in the 1940s, but entrepreneurs in the northwest corner of Georgia were poised to take the final step in the southern con-
quest of American textile manufacture—the carpet trade. The acceptance of
small tufted rugs emboldened area manufacturers, who began experimenting

with larger rugs after World War II. Even as traditional carpet makers opened weaving plants in the South, Cabin Crafts, Barwick Mills, and a handful of other maverick southern firms developed a new method of manufacture. The new mills, as it happened, won an overwhelming victory. Most of the old weaving mills moved tentatively into tufting in the 1950s, but none embraced it as fully or enthusiastically as the new mills. And none were as successful. Dalton area entrepreneurs had no investment, financial or emotional, in old plants or equipment.

This story is fleshed out in chapter 1, but a brief summary helps to set the stage. During the 1930s, new firms in the Dalton bedspread district and machine makers in nearby Chattanooga began adapting the small, lightweight tufting machines to produce heavier and larger products. After World War II, Chattanooga's Cobble Brothers and Dalton's Cabin Crafts engaged in something of a race to build a machine capable of inserting heavy carpet-grade yarn into a wide piece of backing material. Both firms succeeded by 1950. Cabin Crafts built some of its own machines, but Cobble Brothers became a major supplier to the new carpet tufting industry of the Dalton district.

In all of these developments, southern textile entrepreneurs and mechanics, especially from the hosiery segment, played the leading role. Cabin Crafts, a firm founded by three men from Dalton and nearby Chattanooga (Bob McCamy, Fred Westcott, and Lamar Westcott), played a significant role in building the bedspread industry, pioneering new tufted products, and initiating the production of tufted carpeting. The three founding partners all had extensive experience in the hosiery business. Shaw Industries can also trace its roots back to Cabin Crafts. Georgia Tech textile engineering graduate Clarence Shaw, the father of Shaw Industries founders Robert E. (Bob) Shaw and J. C. (Bud) Shaw, had worked in hosiery mills in Dalton and Nashville before getting into the tufted textile business.

Over time, tufting companies developed wider and wider machines for tufting. By 1950 several companies were producing room-sized rugs and broadloom carpeting on tufting machines. Eventually, carpet and rug production became the chief focus of northwest Georgia's tufted textile industry, eclipsing bedspreads, robes, and other small goods. The production of these small tufted goods had never reached $100 million. By the early 1960s, however, tufted carpet had swamped woven goods, claiming an 80 percent market share. The total carpet market (now primarily tufted) exceeded $1 billion in 1963 and surpassed $2 billion within a decade. Tufted carpet made up more than 90 percent of U.S. carpet production at the end of the twentieth century, and northwest Georgia produced more than three-quarters of the nation's carpeting. This $10 billion-plus industry formed the backbone of the region's economy and contributed to the rapid growth of the entire state.

Woven manufacturers often scoffed at the new process, but consumers readily substituted tufted for woven carpets and increased their purchases. The American Carpet Institute, which represented primarily the northern woven carpet companies, published a report in 1958 that starkly revealed the bottom-line differences between the rival processes. Sixty-nine woven plants produced almost 83 million square yards in that year. Productivity stood at about 1.7 square yards per person-hour of labor. By contrast, ninety-two tufting mills turned out more than 113 million square yards of carpet. Tufting mills employed fewer than 10,000 workers, while woven mills employed more than 15,000 workers. Even though tufting statistics include "scatter rug" production, the productivity advantage was clear. Tufting mills averaged almost 6 square yards of product per person-hour.

With the advent of carpet tufting machines, eager prospective manufacturers entered the field to compete with established woven carpet companies. Dalton-area firms such as Cabin Crafts, Barwick Mills, Coronet Carpets, and a host of others began marketing tufted carpets made from all types of fibers—cotton, wool, rayon, and staple (chopped and spun) nylon. Wool was expensive; the other fibers all had particular weaknesses. Yet even with these inferior fibers, tufted carpet surpassed woven goods in total sales during the 1950s. In 1957, the DuPont Company took a fresh look at an old research project that had been deemed not sufficiently profitable in the early 1950s—a new type of nylon fiber called "bulked continuous filament," or BCF. Simply put, DuPont scientists developed a method for giving greater bulk and resilience to nylon without having to go through the tedious extra steps of chopping, carding, blending, and spinning. The marriage of the tufting machine and BCF nylon secured the future of tufted carpet manufacture.

BCF nylon was especially good in loop pile constructions. For cut pile styles, nylon staple worked better. Nylon staple—extruded from plastic pellets and then chopped, carded, blended, and spun like natural fibers—better replicated the look and feel of wool in these constructions and tended to be higher priced within the low-price universe of tufted carpets. Staple nylon's big drawback was a problem with pilling—bits of fiber would pull loose and become entangled in little balls of yarn sticking to the carpet (much like, for example, pilling of a sweater). BCF did not present the same problem since the fiber ran in a continuous line throughout the carpet. BCF nylon was also cheaper than staple nylon (because several steps of manufacture were removed) and therefore found its greatest use in low-end products or in carpets for high-traffic

areas. DuPont continued to refine its staple nylon fibers, and while BCF products were important to the budding new industry, staple nylon fibers retained
a significant market share as well. Staple nylon was particularly used to create
carpets with a bright sheen or luster. Attractive products with a sheen could be
made only in cut pile constructions (with the yarn loops cut). Such carpet resembled handwoven Oriental fabrics. This would be important for Shaw Industries in the 1980s, when the company invested heavily in buying existing
yarn-spinning mills. Some of Shaw's best-selling products in the 1980s would
be classified as "luster fabrics."[12]

DuPont's fiber research played a key role, but the chemical giant was
spurred into action by the rapidly growing demand for carpeting. The inexpensive plain carpets produced by the tufting process proved popular with
consumers. Per capita carpet sales (combined woven and tufted), which had
remained stagnant for decades, rose from 1.97 to 2.81 square yards during the
1950s. Tufted carpets accounted for all the gains, and woven volume actually
declined during the 1960s. During the 1960s—the decade that Bob Shaw has
called "the gold coast"—the pace of growth quickened exponentially as per
capita sales increased by more than 300 percent to 8.46 square yards.

The established carpet makers tried to reverse the fortunes of weaving and
wool with an advertising campaign in the late 1950s. The American Carpet
Institute (ACI), the trade association that represented the old firms, nearly
doubled its advertising budget to $1.25 million from 1955 to 1958. Individual
companies also promoted traditional woven goods with new advertising. The
ACI campaign tried to project the idea that "home means more with carpet
on the floor." The trade association and many individual companies tried to
sell the idea of carpet in general and to educate consumers about the quality
advantages of woven wool products. The industry's largest producer in the
late 1950s was Mohasco. The name *Mohasco* symbolized a merger between Mohawk and Alexander Smith, two prestigious firms. Mohasco's public relations
director explained his firm's strategy in just these terms. "As the largest company in the industry, we feel that it's our duty to sell the concept of carpet—the
generic of carpet," he contended. Unless consumers were "sold on carpet
per se, it doesn't matter how much we advertise the Mohawk line."[13]

In retrospect, it appears that the ACI and firms such as Mohasco made a
huge mistake. The ACI sponsored a research study in 1961 that starkly summarized the new market reality. More than 40 percent of consumers who purchased carpet within the previous six months could not even offer a guess as to
the brand name. Of those who offered a response, fewer than 40 percent mentioned a manufacturer. Most consumers could not distinguish between tufted

and woven constructions by sight. When consumers were asked what factors influenced their purchase decision, they ranked color, style, price, and durability as the most important variables. Carpet buyers almost never mentioned method of manufacture or type of fabric.[14] The campaign to sell the "generic of carpet" only added fuel to the tufted carpet fire, since consumers clearly had little knowledge or interest in details such as construction and fiber.

In this environment new firms multiplied rapidly to take advantage of the booming market. The number of tufted carpet mills nearly doubled in the five years after 1958, from 88 to 167. By 1977, perhaps 400 mills produced tufted carpeting nationwide, but a majority of them were headquartered within a fifty-mile radius of Dalton, Georgia.

This was the local context within which Clarence Shaw, his sons, and a host of other entrepreneurs in northwest Georgia operated. While the industry grew from deep roots and owed much to the vitality of an industrial district, the general post–World War II economic boom—the global phenomenon Eric Hobsbawm has labeled "the golden age"—certainly created the conditions that helped spawn the tufted carpet industry. The explosive growth of the new industry resulted in part from a fortunate conjuncture of events and trends. Mansel Blackford and Austin Kerr echoed most business and economic historians when they observed that the release of "pent-up demand," which accumulated during the World War II years, helped produce "an unprecedented prosperity for Americans and the firms that supplied them goods and services." U.S. gross national product grew 52 percent in the years 1945–1960, while per capita GNP rose 19 percent. Growth accelerated in the 1960s as real GNP rose 46 percent and per capita product increased 29 percent in a single decade.[15] The tufted carpet industry directly benefited from the rising incomes and purchasing power that characterized the postwar period.

Pent-up demand was augmented by government policies throughout the industrialized world in the golden age. Pursuing a broadly Keynesian approach, the United States and Western European nations focused on stimulating demand and promoting economic growth. Federal policies that encouraged the housing construction boom and helped boost real incomes for middle-class and working-class consumers played a significant role. All over the developed world, Hobsbawm wrote, "the commitment of governments to full employment and—to a lesser extent—to the lessening of economic inequality . . . for the first time provided a mass consumer market for luxury goods which could now become accepted as necessities. The Golden Age democratized the market."[16]

The economic boom of the 1950s and 1960s was sparked by pent-up demand, but it reflected another long-term trend as well—mass production. Motivated by spectacular examples such as Henry Ford's Model T, American industry adopted the strategies and techniques of mass production to satisfy the growing mass demand. The mass-production model emphasized the routinized, continuous manufacture of roughly standardized goods at the lowest possible cost. After World War II, American industry improved on Ford's original model. While Ford had insisted that Americans could purchase any color Model T they wanted as long as it was black, General Motors and other automobile firms found ways to introduce shades of novelty—more colors, slight alterations in shape and style—into assembly-line, continuous, mass-production processes. These goods could then be offered at low prices to the emerging mass market, increasingly dominated by middle-class and working-class consumers.[17]

This trend toward mass production and standardized goods affected the textile industry as well. "Demand homogenized steadily in apparel and furnishings textiles" as the ornamental designs that dominated the trade before the 1920s declined in favor of simpler constructions—this represented the triumph of the mass-production model in textiles. This trend persisted at least through the 1960s. This was good news for the new tufted carpet industry. Tufting produced solid-color carpets and simple patterns much more cheaply than weaving. Moreover, as Philip Scranton has observed, the homogenization trend was accompanied by a seemingly contradictory demand on the part of home furnishings and apparel buyers for "a wide stylistic variety" within these newly established boundaries.[18]

The carpet industry, like the bedspread industry that preceded it, was characterized in its early years by a decentralized production process. Almost no mills in the 1950s produced their own yarn, and only a small handful did more than a very small amount of their own dyeing. Some manufacturers used predyed yarns, but that practice carried substantial risks. The laundries that had grown up to serve the bedspread industry began shifting toward dyeing carpets. Local mechanics began developing large tanks, called *becks,* that could be used to dye carpeting after the tufting process. The rise of specialized finishing companies using this postproduction dyeing process allowed tufting companies to spread their risk. A great host of manufacturers contracted with a smaller number of finishing companies to add the final crucial element—color—to their products. Manufacturers were able to build inventories while delaying color decisions until the last possible moment; finishers could spread their risk among many manufacturers. Beck dyeing, as practiced by Star Finishing and other dyeing and finishing companies in the Dalton district, made it possible to mass-produce thousands of yards of quite similar carpeting in a continuous fashion and then to batch-dye pieces fairly quickly in a wide array of colors to satisfy consumer whims. Printing added even more "stylistic variety" to what amounted to a very simple, inexpensive, mass-produced commodity—low, level-loop, lightweight carpet.

A third characteristic of the postwar U.S. economy accompanied rapid growth and mass production. The gap between center and peripheral firms widened, and big business seemed to reap the lion's share of benefits in the golden age, particularly in manufacturing.[19] The irony of the mass-production economy was this: the equipment necessary to process a high volume throughput, or continuous stream of materials and products, at low unit costs generally required frightfully high initial investments and startup costs.

Small manufacturing businesses suffered in this age of "Fordism." Surveying small business in 1980, Harold G. Vatter found that "manufacturing was the only major small-business sector, outside of farming, in which the number of firms in operation failed to increase. . . . Relative crowding out of individual, small entrepreneurship from manufacturing was the apparent record of the U.S. economy in the quarter century after World War II." In other words, the age of mass production and mass consumption was dominated by big business.[20]

The tufted textile industry certainly represented an exception to this pattern. Vatter acknowledged that there were exceptions to the overall decline of small business and entrepreneurs within the manufacturing sector. "Small manufacturing, highly sensitive cyclically, thrives on rapid economic expansion, withers under contraction."[21] While small business in most areas of manufacturing declined in the "golden age" in spite of the long-term rapid growth, tufted carpet indeed thrived.

Loom technology dominated textiles, including rug and carpet production, through the 1940s. Research and development by established firms focused on incremental improvements to the existing technology; no one had made the technical leap necessary to break free from the loom as a means of producing rugs and carpets. Northwest Georgians created a new consumer goods industry from scratch, complete with an anomaly: inexpensive machines capable of mass production. The tufting machine represented a far smaller capital investment than Detroit's assembly lines (the prototypical mass-production technology), yet those machines opened new avenues for quick, inexpensive processing of yarns into rugs and carpets.[22]

Shaw Industries and the carpet industry of the Dalton district emerged from the interplay of all these factors. Owners and executives in this industry made choices within a shifting historical context. The carpet industry was not unique in this; all individuals and firms make their own history, in a sense, out of the raw materials at hand. The tufted textile industry, the mass-production/ mass-consumption economy of the postwar era, and the restructuring of American business in the post–golden age years after 1973—when the energy crisis, inflation, and nagging unemployment emerged as dominant trends in the U.S. economy—formed the setting within which entrepreneurs sought their fortunes, built companies, and sometimes created institutions in the northwestern corner of the Empire State of the South.

CHAPTER ONE

Beginnings

After the Civil War large areas of the American South began to participate more fully in the world of commerce and business. Commerce and industry came to characterize a "New South," a busy, enterprising South. The region had never been devoid of enterprise, but the entrepreneurial spirit seemed to touch an ever-increasing proportion of southerners in small towns.[1] Northwest Georgia was no exception. In Dalton, Georgia, local business and civic leaders made an "industrial resolution" that resulted in a large new cotton mill in 1884. By the early twentieth century, an enterprising woman named Catherine Evans Whitener had begun the process of creating a new industry—tufted textiles—in the region when she started making tufted bedspreads. Cartersville (in Bartow County), located about forty miles south of Dalton, boasted its own entrepreneurial heritage. Jacob and Moses Stroup and Mark Anthony Cooper developed iron manufacturing in antebellum Bartow County. Bartow residents participated in the home manufacture of tufted bedspreads in the early twentieth century, though not on the scale of Dalton-area residents. In 1940, B. J. Bandy, the first man to make a million dollars in the tufted bedspread business, established in Cartersville perhaps the largest tufted textile mill in the industry. In Cartersville and Dalton, as in innumerable small southern towns in the late nineteenth and early twentieth centuries, many small-business owners sought material progress for their towns and profit for themselves.

Clarence Shaw was a product of this New South. Clarence's career in many ways paralleled that of the South, and northwest Georgia in particular, in the twentieth century. Indeed, in tracing Clarence Shaw's path, one encounters the most significant trends, individuals, and institutions associated with northwest Georgia's tufted textile industry. The Cabin Crafts company of Dalton played a leading role in shifting the production of tufted bedspreads from the home to the factory and, later, in the transition from manufacturing bedspreads to manufacturing small rugs and then carpeting. Cabin Crafts and its founders also played a key role in connecting Clarence Shaw and the Shaw family with the tufted textile business in Dalton. Shaw's Star Dye Company served dozens of manufacturers of tufted bedspreads, robes, and small tufted rugs ("scatter rugs") in the Dalton area. Though Clarence's sons would later expand this modest beginning into a corporation the elder Shaw could not have imagined, Star Dye played a crucial part in the evolution of Shaw Industries.

Julius Clarence Shaw, known to most as Clarence, was born in Cartersville, Georgia, in 1897. The Shaw family had been in northwest Georgia since the expulsion of the Cherokees in the 1830s and were prominent members of the business community in the Cartersville area. At one time, Clarence Shaw's father, Levi, owned seven stores in Bartow County. Levi proudly announced in 1913 that he sold "everything but liquor and lightning rods." Levi sent Clarence to college at Georgia Tech.

Clarence majored in textile engineering at Tech, but the Great War interrupted his studies and left him with a lasting legacy—the loss of most of his hearing. He was in the navy in World War I and was standing nearby when one of the ship's guns exploded, nephew Elbert Shaw related. "The vibrations caused him to lose his hearing." Elbert vividly remembered Clarence's hearing aid—a constant companion for the rest of his life. It "had a big round, flat microphone with a cord to wear around the neck." Clarence Shaw talked to his nephew in later years about going to the ship's doctor. According to Elbert, upon hearing the news that he had lost his hearing, Clarence said, "Well, my first inclination was to sit down and cry, to think that here I am, a very young man and I'm not going to be able to hear. I had a little talk with myself and I said, 'Clarence, you've got this handicap, but that just means you're going to have to work twice as hard as anybody else just to stay even.'" That statement stuck with Elbert throughout his life.[2]

Cotton prices plummeted in the early 1920s. Many stores operated cotton gins, and most customers depended on cotton for their income. Consequently, Levi Shaw's fortunes sagged considerably. Clarence's son J. C. (Bud) Shaw later recalled that his family "went broke" during the cotton crisis. Seeking to make his own way, Clarence became fascinated by the prospect of quick payoffs during the Roaring Twenties. For a time he abandoned his training in textile engineering and moved to Florida to participate in the real estate boom. When the Florida land bubble burst in 1927, Clarence Shaw moved to Dalton. Bud Shaw recalled that Clarence "went broke in Florida and came back and started pursuing some of his background, which was textile engineering. He went to work for Westcott Hosiery Mill."[3]

George Lamar Westcott, founder of the Wescott Hosiery Mill, was born in Chattanooga, Tennessee, in 1894. After graduating from the prestigious Baylor Prep School, he studied at the Philadelphia Textile Institute. He earned high marks, especially in yarns and knitting procedures, and was awarded a scholarship in his final year. After completing his course of study in 1917, Lamar Westcott returned to the South to apply his textile training. Possibly with his brother Fred, he established the Westcott Hosiery Mill in Dalton on the eve of the U.S. entry into World War I.[4] Fred R. Westcott graduated from the McCallie School (another prestigious Chattanooga prep school) and the University of Virginia. The Westcott brothers spent much of their lives collaborating in business ventures. In 1932, Fred and Lamar joined with Robert McCamy, a former superintendent at the hosiery mill, to form a tufting company called Cabin Crafts.

Jack Turner worked with all three founders of Cabin Crafts from the late 1940s through the mid-1960s, as he moved from accountant up to president. Turner remembered Fred Westcott as "a very unusual fellow. He was probably the most talented of the three. He was a tremendous merchandiser and had a real feel for style and design. . . . Fred and Lamar were about as different as two brothers could be. Lamar was a very stable sort of person. After you got to know him, you could always predict what he would do. I worked primarily for him. It wasn't very difficult because after being there for a little while I could almost think just like he thought. With Fred it was just the opposite. You never knew what he was going to do, how he was going to react to a situation. He was very unpredictable, and a little bit unstable, but a very, very smart man." Bob McCamy "was a pretty solid, steady-as-you-go" sort of person.[5]

According to local legend, Fred and Lamar Westcott were partners at the hosiery mill, but Jack Turner recalled things a bit differently. As he remembered the story, Lamar Westcott had been the sole owner of the Westcott Hosiery Mill and had employed both his brother Fred and Bob McCamy, as well as Clarence Shaw. Soon after Lamar sold the mill to Real Silk, the stock market crashed, and the Great Depression set in. In cost-cutting moves, the firm soon "disposed of Fred and Bob, let them both go." Real Silk also disposed of Lamar Westcott's dyer, Clarence Shaw, who then moved to Nashville, Tennessee, in search of hosiery-related work.[6]

"We moved away because the Westcotts had sold out to Real Silk," Clarence's son Robert (Bob) Shaw remarked. "Washington Hosiery, the company Dad went to work for in Nashville, was still in the dyeing of hosiery, so he went up there." Clarence Shaw was living in Nashville when his second son was born in 1931, but Bob was born in Cartersville. "It was one of those things; in those days when you were having a baby, you went home to grandmother." Soon after his birth, Bob and his parents returned to Tennessee, and they lived in Nashville for the first ten years of his life.[7]

While Clarence Shaw left the Dalton area for his job in Nashville, Bob McCamy and his wife, like hundreds of other Dalton families, began their own bedspread business, or spread house, during the depression. A Dalton native, McCamy was born in 1904. He attended Georgia Tech until his father's death, at which point he was obliged to return home and go to work. McCamy's chief talent lay in organizing production and manufacturing. Fred Westcott joined the McCamys in their spread house soon after, bringing his expertise in design and marketing.

Like other spread house owners, the McCamys purchased raw materials and stamped designs on sheeting. However, the McCamy operation worked a bit differently from older spread houses. While many such companies employed haulers to deliver raw materials to workers in the countryside and pick up tufted bedspreads, the McCamys worked with tufters who could pick up the materials and return the spreads themselves. "The women would come by on Monday morning and pick up the raw materials and sheeting," Bob McCamy's son, Julian, recalled, "and return with the finished goods on Friday afternoon." These women either lived in town or had access to a car. Bob McCamy paid the workers and marketed the spreads. Julian's mother named the business Cabin Crafts, because it reflected the handicraft nature of the work—it was truly home manufacturing, or a "cabin craft." The McCamys used the Cabin Crafts name for probably a year or more before the formation of a new corporation with the same name in 1932.[8]

Fred Westcott joined the McCamys in the Cabin Crafts operation in 1931. A year later, Jack Turner related, "Lamar Westcott joined them and brought some capital to the business, and they incorporated in 1932 (June 1) in the depths of the Depression." The initial capitalization of the business was $10,000. Although Lamar may have sold the hosiery mill out from under relatives and friends in 1929, in the long run his decision had allowed him to raise the capital that made it possible to establish Cabin Crafts as perhaps the largest spread house in the business. Lamar Westcott also patented a needlepunch gun for use in tufting bedspreads, and that tool was a key to Cabin Crafts' ability to centralize production of tufted bedspreads in a factory setting.[9]

Fred and Lamar Westcott and Bob McCamy each had areas of expertise. All three had technical knowledge and a talent for identifying potential improvements in machinery. Beyond that, Lamar specialized in finance, Bob focused his attention on manufacturing, and Fred devoted much of his time to style and marketing. From early on, Lamar worked only half-time for the company, ably performing his financial duties but spending much time traveling and working for civic and community organizations. Fred served as CEO of Cabin Crafts for most of the rest of his life, though he took time out to serve as a marine officer during World War II. After West Point acquired the company in 1946, Fred remained chairman of the separate Cabin Crafts board of directors until his retirement in 1963. Bob McCamy served as vice president for manufacturing until the mid-1950s, when he took over as president.

Modern Floor Coverings characterized Fred Westcott as an "American inventive genius," and the label was difficult to dispute. Fred "was dedicated to style and quality." Under his direction, Cabin Crafts developed the most extensive marketing program in the tufted textile industry, both in bedspread days and after the advent of carpeting. He employed designers such as Joe Platt, who "created set designs for the movie *Gone With the Wind*." Indeed, Cabin Crafts bedspreads and area rugs adorned those movie sets. Fred Westcott gathered ideas from a variety of sources in the home furnishings marketplace. He also sought advice and developed close ties with prominent buyers for major department stores, including Elaine McAlister of Macy's. Despite those ties with buyers, Charles Powell, longtime friend and colleague, recalled that Fred Westcott always rejected the often-repeated suggestion that salesmen have some input into product design. "That's one way to ruin the line," Westcott told Powell.[10]

Powell remembered that working with Fred Westcott was not always easy. Fred had little tolerance for "yes men" and encouraged employees to express dissenting ideas. He reputedly fired several employees over the years for refusing to disagree with him on any major issue. Arguing had its potential price as well, however, recalled Powell. "Arguing with Fred wasn't easy. He was a dynamo—and quick tempered. I don't know how many times I was fired and then rehired the next morning. He was a quick decision maker. When we had a line that didn't sell—and we had those—he'd close it out fast. Failure was as much a fact of life to him as success."[11]

Fred Westcott worked tirelessly to improve the Cabin Crafts products and performance. "Once he dragged a visiting buyer over to the mill at midnight to work out an idea," Powell recalled. "They stayed until 3 A.M. The next morning, Fred was at the door at 7 A.M. ready for breakfast. He never slept on ideas. He'd get up in the middle of the night to write them down, working into the morning and then putting in a full day at the plant. Hobbies? He didn't have them, except for reading and the theatre. . . . He hated anything that got in the way of business, including shopping and getting his hair cut." Fred Westcott also loved to travel, though his travels often had a business connection. He rarely returned from any trip without new ideas for products and styles.[12]

Each of the three founders of Cabin Crafts tended to stick to his area of expertise, Julian McCamy remembered, and that led to a good working relationship. While Fred Westcott devoted his energy to marketing and Lamar devoted his to finance, Bob McCamy developed Cabin Crafts' manufacturing capabilities and operations. The company plants reflected McCamy's attention to detail and his determination that "whatever you did, you did right." McCamy constantly sought to upgrade company machinery and facilities. The firm's creation of its own machine shop and internal machine-making capability and the construction of the magnificent new Springdale manufacturing plant in 1954 exemplified McCamy's approach.[13] His stability helped balance Fred Westcott's creative energy, while Lamar Westcott's financial acumen helped the firm prosper during the depression. No doubt Lamar and Bob had to rein in Fred on occasion.

Two of the three Cabin Crafts founders shared a religious faith that helped shape their views on business affairs and their firm's relationship to the community. "Fred never went to church regularly anywhere," Jack Turner observed, "though he later joined the Episcopal Church. He wasn't much on religious affairs." Lamar and Bob, on the other hand, were members of the Board of Elders of the First Presbyterian Church of Dalton. Lamar served for nine years on the church's World Mission Board, and Bob served on the local church's Building Committee. These shared beliefs were evidenced in at least three ways. The personnel policies of Cabin Crafts reflected the founders' commitment to treating employees with respect and concern but avoided the overt paternalism practiced by many of the South's textile mills (there was no mill housing, for example). The Westcotts also practiced stewardship, the idea that those who acquire great wealth have a responsibility to invest it wisely. Stewardship demanded a significant level of community service and philanthropic activity. But it also demanded constant attention to business, finding ways to cut costs and improve efficiency, and succeeding in the competitive environment. Successful competition protected the interests of employees, shareholders, and the community that benefited from Cabin Crafts' stewardship. Finally, a strong work ethic infused company leaders. In the case of Bob McCamy and Lamar Westcott, that work ethic may have developed in part from their Presbyterian-Calvinist faith. For Fred Westcott, the work ethic apparently grew from some other internal source, some inner wellspring of creative energy and commitment.

Cabin Crafts quickly gained a reputation as the highest-quality producer of tufted bedspreads and by 1940 emerged as the leading company in this infant industry. The tufted textile industry remained a loose agglomeration of manufacturers, suppliers, and service providers; however, most firms did not pursue vertical integration. With rapidly rising sales but no clear idea of when the boom might turn to bust, mill owners preferred to contract with small firms for services such as dyeing and laundering. Cabin Crafts' chief commission dyer, Dalton Spread Laundry, had difficulty with rugs, as did most laundries. The poor quality of the dyeing became a serious matter in 1941, and the Cabin Crafts management began to search for alternatives.[14]

Clarence Shaw's sojourn in Nashville, ironically, had led him toward a greater involvement in tufting. Bud Shaw remembered something of his father's work in Nashville. Though Clarence worked primarily as a hosiery dyer, for a time he did some work on the side as a troubleshooter for a local dry cleaner. Eventually he came into contact with a Nashville firm engaged in producing scatter rugs. "Dad and I would go over to a place called Tennessee Tufting Company. Dad was dyeing hosiery, but the tufting company would mess up scatter rugs that they were trying to dye, and Dad's job, since he knew something about dyeing, would be to straighten up what they messed up." Apparently the dyers at Tennessee Tufting "knew how to dye them, but they didn't know how to bleach them and then redye them" if a mistake were made. "So if they'd made a mess out of it, either they sold it as off-goods" or they called in Clarence Shaw and "bleached it or scoured it and reprocessed it."[15]

The Cabin Crafts founders turned to Clarence Shaw in 1941. Fred and Lamar Westcott, disenchanted with the dyeing work done for their company by Dalton Spread Laundry, knew about Shaw's work in bleaching and redyeing rugs for Tennessee Tufting. Lamar suggested that Dalton Spread Laundry hire Shaw to help improve the dyeing and laundering of scatter rugs and bedspreads. In fact, Westcott wanted Shaw to oversee and improve the dyeing operation at Dalton Spread Laundry. Since Cabin Crafts was the laundry's largest customer, the owners were eager to comply. "It was Mr. Westcott who called my father and brought him back to Dalton," Bob Shaw recalled. By the end of the 1930s, Cabin Crafts "was the leading producer of tufted bedspreads," and "Dalton had become the bedspread center of the world. It had gone from a cabin business to a machine business. Now they needed the technology of dyeing, and Mr. Westcott remembered my father, who had been superintendent of the dye house at the hosiery mill. He brought dad back here in 1941—it was a week before Pearl Harbor, so it's easy to remember. I was ten years old."[16]

So Clarence Shaw returned to Dalton and began managing Dalton Spread Laundry's dyeing operations. Cabin Crafts converted to war production in 1942, and Dalton Spread Laundry did more work on defense products than scatter rugs during the war. As often happened in the tufted textile district of northwest Georgia, the employee decided to strike out on his own. In the latter days of World War II, Clarence decided to buy a small company called Star Dye, operated by the Wynn family. In early 1946, Shaw obtained a new charter for Star Dye Company.[17]

"If W. C. Martin had not been childless, Shaw Industries would not exist as it does today." This offhand remark by longtime Shaw family friend and Shaw Industries vice president Warren Sims about the origins of Star Dye reveals much about the contingent nature of industrial development in a small-town environment and about the familial relationships that characterized the tufted textile industry of northwest Georgia. "W. C. Martin was the uncle-in-law of Mrs. J. B. McCarty. Martin was a lawyer but also the president of the First National Bank of Dalton. He was very successful, financially." Martin and his wife "didn't have any children, so a great deal of his estate went to Mrs. Mc-Carty. She was the wife of John Brown McCarty, who ended up in business with Julius Clarence Shaw in Star Dye Company. John B. McCarty furnished the money, and Mr. Shaw furnished the management and the talent." If Martin had had direct heirs, John McCarty would not have had the capital to invest in Star Dye.[18]

Warren Sims recalled growing up in Dalton near the Shaw family. He went to school with both Bob and Bud Shaw and came to know Mr. and Mrs. Clarence Shaw well. "Clarence Shaw was a straight-laced, conservative, dedicated Christian," recounted Sims, and "his wife was even more so. . . . They taught those boys about ethics, morals, and stewardship" in both religious and civic terms.[19]

Clarence Shaw was a staunch Presbyterian (though Levi had been a Baptist), and the Protestant work ethic seemed deeply ingrained in the family. Bob Shaw clearly learned lessons about the value of work and productive behavior from his father. "Dad was a great believer in work. We'd play high school football on Friday night," and then the next morning "we'd go down to Piggly Wiggly and sack groceries for twelve hours."[20]

Clarence Shaw instilled that Protestant work ethic in his sons, but he also taught them about stewardship. Elbert Shaw recalled that his uncle was among the most generous people he had ever known. "He taught me a lot about giving." Elbert remembered "a black gentleman who worked for Shaw Industries in the 1970s, and he was also a minister. He had not worked for Clarence Shaw but had known him in the 1950s." This man told Elbert the following story: "One day the floor in our church was just falling in. I went over to Mr. Clarence Shaw's and asked him if he could help us with that floor. He said, 'How much money do you need?' And he just gave it to us."[21]

Clarence Shaw was also deeply involved in his own church, the First Presbyterian Church of Dalton. "He told me once that they needed an educational building for the church," Elbert Shaw remembered, "and he was elected to be in charge of raising the money for it. He said that he wrote the names of each church family on a little card and called all the men of the church together. He told them, 'Now we've got to raise [so many] thousand dollars for this. I want each one of you to take three cards of people to call on. I have only one requirement. Leave the ten hardest nuts to crack to me.' And he had a way of cracking those nuts. He could be a very strict person but had so much love inside him."[22]

No one at Star Dye Company came to know Clarence Shaw better than Buddy Sewell. Born on July 27, 1928, in Dalton, Sewell went to work for Star Dye in 1946, just weeks after the company started operations. "We dyed bedspreads; of course, we also bleached bedspreads; we dyed scatter rugs, and we dyed chenille robes." Sewell came to work at Star Dye as a result of an ultimatum from his father. "Mr. Shaw was the manager down at Dalton Spread Laundry, and my dad was the foreman down there." When Shaw bought Star Dye, "he hired my daddy to run the night shift. Back in those days we just worked two twelve-hour shifts. I had quit school, and Daddy said, 'Now you're going to work, or you're going to go to school,' so I went to work" at Star Dye. "They found the hardest job in the place for me to do, that night." Running the extractor was a tough job, and Sewell drew the assignment, perhaps as a punishment from his father for quitting school. The extractors removed most of the water from bleached or dyed rugs, bedspreads, and other tufted products. "You would take maybe 150 or 200 pounds of these rugs or bedspreads and pack them in this centrifugal extractor, and it would almost weld them against the side. Your job was to put them in there, then once they had extracted the water out, then you had to claw them out. Oh, your fingers would bleed."[23]

Starting a new business could be a risky proposition. Clarence Shaw and John McCarty took risks to get into the tufted textile dyeing business, and employees such as Buddy Sewell's father likewise risked something by coming to work at a new business. "I remember my dad came home one night and told my mother," who worked at the American Thread Mill, "that he was going to go to work for Mr. Shaw over there. Of course, she was nervous about it, you know, it being a new business. He had a pretty fair job at Dalton Spread Laundry. He said, 'I'll be making $42 a week salary, plus I'll get a dollar and a nickel for all the hours over forty hours.' Of course, things brightened up then because that was pretty good money in those days."[24]

Buddy Sewell soon moved from running the extractors to the vats, "where we dyed the small rugs and bedspreads," and from there to the dryers. After proving himself by running the dryers at night, Sewell moved up to the day shift, still running the dryers. From that position, he got his first exposure to the technology and chemistry of dyeing. "The dye room was right next to me, so the guy in there taught me to weigh dye." Soon after, "I made it big time—I got to the trucks." Sewell started driving a truck, making local deliveries and pickups. Within just a year or so, Sewell had moved around and had learned the complete operation at Star Dye.

Shortly after moving to his truck-driving position, Buddy Sewell got married. He still recalls Clarence Shaw's reaction. "I pulled in with a load one day, and Mr. Shaw called me" into his office. "He told me . . . I mean, he didn't ask you what you wanted to do, he told you what you wanted to do, but he told you in a nice way. So he put me to weighing dye" because "he had fired the first-shift dye weigher. From there, he started teaching me dyeing. I don't know why, he just did." Sewell's history of good work combined with his recent marriage convinced "Mr. Shaw," as Sewell still referred to Clarence more than forty years later, to take Sewell under his wing in a sort of apprenticeship.[25]

Clarence Shaw had long been accustomed to working under difficult conditions and with makeshift tools and supplies. "He was an old hosiery dyer," Buddy Sewell stated, "and a very good dyer. He worked back when you made your own bleach and this kind of stuff, you couldn't buy it." Sewell described what was charitably called "the lab" at Star Dye in the 1950s. In the lab "we had an 18-by-18 square pot. It had a . . . waterline and a steam line running to it. As beakers, we had quart milk bottles. And we had three graduated cylinders, a 25, a 50, and a 100. And that was our lab. My job was that every time that I got caught up, I stirred that pot. . . . that was my lab experience. You would be standing back there with the sweat just popping off of you because it would be hot with that steam coming up because you had to heat it up." The heat of the lab taught "you pretty fast to do it right the first time if you possibly could."[26]

Buddy Sewell echoed the sentiments of others when describing Clarence Shaw. Though Shaw did not practice the thorough-going paternalism of the

Crown Cotton Mills, which had a mill village, he apparently developed paternal feelings toward his employees and often expressed them.[27] Sewell's stories put some flesh and blood reality into the vague term *paternalism*. "Mr. Shaw was an exceptional man in that he had a great loyalty for the people who worked for him. I never did anything—when I bought a car, when I married, when I bought my first house, when my first child was born—without speaking to him about it. I was called into the office." Shaw would always begin his remarks with "'Now Bud, I'm going to talk to you just like I would Bob and Bud.' And I would sit down and get fatherly advice. Of course, like Bob and Bud," Sewell wryly observed, "I didn't listen. I mean, I listened, but I didn't hear."[28]

Clarence Shaw valued loyalty from his employees and returned it in kind. Perhaps he saw himself as something of a protector of those who depended on him. For example, when a man tried to sue Buddy Sewell for an alleged bad debt in the early 1950s, Shaw reacted in typical fashion. "Mr. Shaw called me into the office and asked me about it." He first tried to ascertain the facts of the case. "I told him, 'There's nothing to it, I paid that bill some time back.'" Satisfied with Sewell's explanation, the two "got into his GMC pickup truck. He was hard of hearing, and you could hear that old motor—we could always tell when he left the plant. Anyway, we went up to this place, went in and talked to this guy, who was about drunk. What had happened," Sewell explained, was "this guy had bought the store from his son and he was going to sue me for a bill that had already been paid. So they got into it about it, and Mr. Shaw told him, 'By damn, I'll spend $500 to see that he doesn't pay this bill.' I sat there just trembling, I didn't know what was going to happen." The creditor eventually backed down and gave in. "That was the type of man he was. He would stick up for you."[29]

Clarence Shaw defended all his employees, Sewell recalled, as if they were family. "One of our customers called one time and had Miss Fannie crying." It was "something about deliveries." She was the secretary and "didn't have any control over anything like that. Mr. Shaw called him up, and man, you talk about getting a tongue lashing; now he got one. We lost the business for about a week. That's just the way he was. If you had called him up and got on him, he probably wouldn't have said much."[30] But Shaw reacted instinctively to protect his people.

"Of course, if you needed dressing up, he'd do that," Sewell insisted. Frugality was a Shaw virtue, and Clarence expected it from his employees. "I remember one time—we had gotten a Coke box in. Cokes in those days were a nickel apiece, but you had a one-cent deposit on the bottle. We got pretty lax around the plant, leaving bottles here and there." But "Mr. Shaw was very thrifty. I was going around the corner one day with a sack of dye, and I saw these bottles" sitting in his path. Shaw was standing to the right of the bottles. "So I just jumped them and went on. I was at the dye becks coming back, and he said 'Bud, come here.' He told me how much those bottles cost" and "made me pick them up."[31]

John Kirk, another Star Dye veteran, confirmed Clarence Shaw's managerial attributes. Kirk began working for Star Dye in 1949 at the age of seventeen. "He would chew you out if you needed it," Kirk said. "But he did it in a different way" from most mill owners in Dalton. "He would take you aside and give you a dressing down, but he wouldn't do it in front of everyone." In other words, Shaw allowed workers to maintain their "honor" before fellow workers.[32]

John Kirk worked first, as Buddy Sewell had, on the extractors. He eventually worked at most jobs within the plant. Kirk "liked to work on cars" and demonstrated a talent for working with machinery. Mr. Shaw moved him into the maintenance department in the late 1950s. From then until his retirement in the 1990s, Kirk spent his days keeping Star Dye/Star Finishing/Shaw Industries machinery and equipment running.[33]

Clarence Shaw insisted that things be done his way around Star Dye. He had little interest in employees using their own judgment and preferred to make most decisions, even small ones, himself. Like many entrepreneurs, he liked to be in control of his own destiny. Buddy Sewell remembered a Star employee who was "running the washers, and something messed up. So Mr. Shaw came around there and was talking to me; he wasn't mad, he was just talking to me," and the washer operator "told him, 'Well, Mr. Shaw, I thought . . .' And Mr. Shaw said, 'Now wait a minute, dammit, if you're going to think, buy your own laundry.' I never will forget that."[34]

That sort of management style worked in a small firm like Star Dye, where the scale of operations allowed one talented individual to run the entire show. Clarence Shaw enforced a kind of discipline among his workers. He even laid off Buddy Sewell for sleeping on the job at one point. "I had gone to sleep sitting on a bundle," as Sewell remembered it. "My daddy was on vacation, and I was working at night. I sat down and went to sleep. I woke up the next morning." A fellow worker who bore a grudge against Sewell's father ratted him out. "And so Mr. Shaw . . . laid me off. He said, 'You take off till your daddy comes back.' Daddy came back, and of course he dressed me out real good, and I went back to work. But in those days, I wasn't worth killing. I was like all young people, there to get by with as little as I could. After I married, my attitude changed, and Mr. Shaw evidently saw that, and he took an interest in me, in seeing that I became a dyer."[35]

John Kirk agreed that Clarence Shaw enforced discipline but contended that he was lenient in his own way. He recalled that Mondays often included a ritual. "Mr. Shaw would go down to the city jail and get a few of his hands out," workers who had perhaps enjoyed the weekend a bit too much. The term *weekend* was a bit exaggerated anyway—Kirk recalled working a twelve-hour shift, six or seven days a week. Alcohol was not absent from working-class life in the Dalton tufting district, and local mill owners often tolerated a bit of overindulgence. "Mr. Shaw never fired anybody for being drunk on the job," Kirk recalled, "but he sent a few home for the day."

Clarence Shaw, like countless small business owners throughout the South, became a protector, a patron, in a sense a father, to his employees, or at least to his "good workers." Douglas Flamming has studied the subject of paternalism in the Dalton industrial district.[36] Flamming's study of Dalton's Crown Cotton Mills, its mill village, and other labor policies helped redirect the study of paternalism in southern industrial history. The very word *paternalism*, he noted, had been so overused as to be rendered meaningless by the 1980s. By giving the term a more precise definition, Flamming made the concept more useful in historical analysis. He defined paternalism as a set of "official company policies which provided nonwage benefits to workers, sought to create a distinctive corporate culture, and regulated the living environment of the millhands and their families." Flamming argued that while "southern culture may well have embodied traditions of patriarchy, elite beneficence, and a highly personal style of business management," the development of company paternalism "did not depend on any of these cultural mores." Instead, Flamming argued that corporate paternalism evolved, in part, as a response to a regional labor market crisis and, in part, as a regional manifestation of welfare capitalism, a national phenomenon of the early twentieth century. Employers associations promoted the adoption of profit-sharing arrangements, the construction of recreational facilities and health clinics, and other measures to discourage workers from joining unions.

Clarence Shaw clearly exhibited some traditional southern "cultural mores," but personnel policies at Star Dye Company could not have been labeled paternalistic, at least not under Douglas Flamming's definition. In this personal style of management, Clarence Shaw shared much in common with other managers in the Dalton district. Cabin Crafts, Barwick Mills, and other area firms practiced a similar style of management with a personal touch while avoiding full-blown paternalism.

The workforce at Star Dye was exclusively white and almost all male, according to John Kirk. It was not until the 1960s that Star Finishing hired

African American and female workers in the plant. Star Dye was hardly unique; in a small southern town in the 1950s, a segregated workforce was commonplace; few mills hired African American laborers, and none hired them in large numbers. The southern textile industry, in particular, had a historic aversion to hiring black workers. As late as 1960, blacks made up only about 3 percent of the southern textile workforce. Most jobs in southern textiles had traditionally been reserved for whites only. That custom held fast in the Dalton area until the mid-1960s. Even then, there was relatively little public protest in the Dalton area around the issue of integrating the mills. Whitfield County's black population hovered at or just below 5 percent throughout the twentieth century, while in surrounding counties the proportions were even smaller.[37]

Buddy Sewell and John Kirk remained valued employees, and Clarence Shaw continued to take a personal interest in the young men and their families. Clarence Shaw allowed Sewell to take the equivalent of paid family leave when his wife became ill in the mid-1950s. "My wife got sick, and we had two children. In those days, the doctors would come to your house. Sometimes they would call" Sewell at work and tell him, 'Buddy, you're going to have to come home.' Dr. McGee would come out to the house and give her a shot, and I would have to watch the children." Even though Sewell took time off from work, "Mr. Shaw paid me just like I was at work every day. We didn't punch a time clock; a woman wrote your time down. Many times he would come back into the dye room, or back where I'd be stirring the pot, and he'd stick $20 or $30 in my pocket. Tears would be in his eyes, and he'd say, 'Here, Bud, I know you can use that.' You can't forget things like that."[38]

The familial atmosphere pervaded Star Dye in other ways, as evidenced by the company's annual Christmas party. Buddy Sewell recounted: "We used to have a Christmas party every year, and we got a bonus twice a year, according to what your job was, how long you had been there. At the Christmas party, you got a large basket, a gift from the company, your wife got a gift, your children got a gift, and Santa Claus was there. So it was a real big to-do." For the party, the secretary would shop with a list of the children's ages and buy gifts according to their ages. "Now you can imagine what a job that was. Mr. Shaw got such a kick out of it. He would stand up there" during the party, and "there would be tears in his eyes. He was very tenderhearted. He was one fine man. I've been offered a lot of jobs with a lot of other companies over the years, for a lot more money through the years. But I always had that feeling that I'm going to stay because I know I'm going to be all right here, and the fact that I owe so much." In fact, Buddy Sewell spent his entire working life at Star Dye, Star Finishing, and Shaw Industries. He retired in 1996 with fifty years of continuous service.

John Kirk retired in 1994, after forty-five years of service to the only company he had worked for as an adult.[39]

Star Dye remained a small operation throughout Clarence Shaw's life. He ran the business in an ultraconservative manner, especially in the area of finances. Warren Sims, a vice president at Dalton's First National Bank in the 1950s, remembered Clarence Shaw as one of the bank's best customers. While Bob and Bud Shaw learned much from their father, Sims reported that Clarence "was just the opposite from Bob and Bud" in financial terms. "He wouldn't buy anything if he didn't have the money in his pocket." Clarence Shaw's Star Dye account was the second-best account at the First National Bank of Dalton because of that. They were not necessarily the biggest business, but as far as depositors go, Star Dye maintained huge cash balances—checking account balances. He was insistent on that."[40]

The office accommodations at Star Dye also reflected Shaw's disciplined, conservative approach. Buddy Sewell remembered that Shaw demanded no luxuries around the plant. "His office was no bigger than this," said Sewell, indicating most of the area of the small dining room in his home. "He had a secretary in there. She had a desk in there. He didn't have a desk. He just had a wooden chair that would lean back. There were a couple of filing cabinets in there, and then he had a cabinet where he kept his manuals, and that was his office. It didn't get any bigger until after Bob came."[41]

Clarence Shaw's business philosophy revealed his innate conservatism just as much as his personal style did. During the 1950s, the tufted textile industry of the Dalton district expanded from the manufacture of small rugs to capture the national market for room-sized rugs and wall-to-wall carpeting. While a few of Dalton's laundries moved with the industry, Clarence Shaw steadfastly refused to expand into this new product area. Both his sons urged him to move into dyeing and finishing large rugs and carpet, but Clarence preferred the safety of well-known markets to the risk of pursuing new horizons.

Cabin Crafts, by contrast, played a key role in the transition from bedspread and small-rug production to carpet manufacture in the Dalton area. Unique among tufted textile manufacturers, Cabin Crafts pioneered in building its own tufting machinery. Bob McCamy, W. M. (Bill) Sapp, and Bob Hackney played key roles in the evolution of Cabin Crafts' machine-making capabilities. Sapp, a Dalton native, attended the city's public schools and graduated from Georgia Tech with a degree in textile engineering. Hackney, another Dalton native, had no formal training but was widely reputed to be the Dalton area's most talented mechanic in the tufted textile trade. Julian McCamy remembered Bob Hackney as a "quiet, introspective man" and indicated his father had great respect for Hackney's abilities. Sapp served as the chief engineer at Cabin Crafts, while Hackney supervised the firm's unique machine shop. Both worked closely with Bob McCamy, the firm's vice president for manufacturing and operations.[42]

Otis Payne observed and participated in all the crucial work of the Cabin Crafts machine shop during the transition from bedspreads and small rugs to carpet. Payne was born in Dalton, Georgia, in 1915. His father died of pneumonia when Otis was five, and the young boy's family moved to the Crown Cotton Mills village. Payne's mother took a job at the mill to provide for her family. They lived in a mill house right in front of the main entrance. Payne, like hundreds of thousands of southerners from the late nineteenth through the mid-twentieth centuries, grew up in a mill village. "I went to work in the Crown Cotton Mills when I was fourteen [years] and six months old; that's how old you had to be [under Georgia law]." He worked in the mill until World War II began. Payne started off sweeping the floors at Crown and put in some time in the machine shop, but he spent most of his years there in the carding room. He displayed an early talent for mechanical work and by 1941 was helping to overhaul old machines and install new machinery.[43]

Along the way, Payne took courses to improve his skills. He and two friends drove to Chattanooga twice a week for three months to complete a course at a vocational training school. Payne learned to run lathes, milling machines, and other typical machine-shop equipment. He later took courses in drafting and molding. Cabin Crafts also offered extension courses in the company's machine shop. These courses were not limited to employees of Cabin Crafts but were open to all. Payne still remembered his course project, a drill press.

By the late 1930s, Payne had begun working in the bedspread industry on the side. After work he and a friend would visit local mechanic Shirley Crook, who was converting Singer 3115 sewing machines, surplus equipment from the New York garment trades, for bedspread tufting. Payne watched, learned, and pitched in to help. "We used the complete head" of the existing machine, Otis recalled, but they took out the bobbin and made a cutting attachment for it. They used a bigger needle, had to make a new throat plate, and put a bracket on each end to make a complete unit. Payne and others engaged in converting these machines made looper attachments with knives from converted hacksaw blades. Eventually, machinists in the industry were able to buy steel, make dies, and cut their own loopers and blades to specifications (see figure A).[44]

As the United States geared up to serve as the "arsenal of democracy" in 1940 and 1941, Otis Payne found employment through a friend with a group of machinists at a government munitions plant in Gadsden, Alabama. The plant

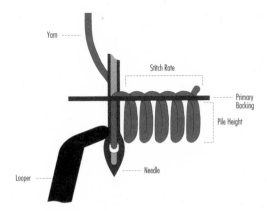

Yarn

Stitch Rate

Primary Backing

Pile Height

Needle

Looper

Figure A: Tufting process

made 105-millimeter artillery shells for the war effort. The company continued to ask for draft deferments for Payne throughout the war, a testament to his skill. The draft board put him at the top of the draft-eligible list "I don't know how many times, but the company would get me a deferment," Payne remembers. "We were making parts to keep up the production machinery; you couldn't buy parts back then; you couldn't even buy a key for a chuck." Payne and his colleagues learned to use scrap metal of every sort, and the necessity for making machine parts from scratch taught creativity. That creativity served Payne well after the war.

When the war ended in 1945, Payne returned to his native Dalton and took a job at Cabin Crafts. He joined the small crew in the machine shop and "started making parts" in that department. The largest bedspread tufting "machine that they had at that time—why, I could carry one in each hand." Two- and four-needle machines were the largest they had at that time. Payne's first major assignment was the construction of about a half-dozen skip-stitch candlewick machines. These machines would insert "two stitches, skip two inches, then make two more stitches," and then repeat. Over the next few years, the Cabin Crafts machine shop produced six- and twelve-needle machines. Payne recalled getting an order for three hundred needlepunch guns, the company's signature technological innovation from the early 1930s. The needlepunch gun had been the key to much of Cabin Crafts' success in accelerating the production of bedspreads and custom rugs. Faster than sewing by hand, the needlepunch process still required a fair amount of skill and a steady hand. "We never did finish the three hundred, but we made over two hundred of the things before we quit making them. . . . we made as many as they could use and kept them running."

By 1946, Bob Hackney had been placed in charge of the Cabin Crafts machine shop, and the company began to shift its emphasis from bedspreads to larger rugs. Jack Turner spoke for many when he recalled Hackney's talent. Hackney "was a mechanical genius, very limited in his educational background," and "he didn't have any college at all. He was able to read and write, but he had no formal training in engineering. He could look at almost any piece of machinery and sit down and draw you a picture if you needed one, almost to scale, and tell you exactly how it worked."[45]

According to Otis Payne, Bob McCamy pushed for wider, heavier machines to produce heavier tufted goods—larger rugs and carpets—and Hackney used the machine shop's resources to produce the machines McCamy wanted. During the late 1940s, numerous manufacturers experimented with ways to make room-sized rugs on tufting machines. Most of these early efforts revolved around sewing smaller rugs or pieces of rugs together.[46] At about the same time, the Cobble Brothers company was working on wider tufting machines as well. Joe Cobble had already patented a machine capable of tufting the entire width of a bedspread in a single pass in 1943, but the machine did not go into production until after the war. The Cabin Crafts machine shop worked on a wide bedspread-tufting machine as well, using parts purchased from Cobble. The Cabin Crafts machine went into production in the late 1940s, just in time from Payne's perspective. Cabin Crafts' increasing emphasis on machine making was cutting into the firm's capital reserves. It became difficult to finance the construction of ever-larger, experimental tufting machines. The new wide bedspread machine cut production costs and produced revenues that helped finance the development of heavier rug-making machines. Even with these profits, Cabin Crafts struggled to keep up with Cobble Brothers and maintain the firm's distinctive edge in the tufting industry's machine technology.

The Cabin Crafts founders—Lamar and Fred Westcott and Bob McCamy—sold most of their company to the West Point Manufacturing Company in 1946. West Point, long a major player in the southern textile industry, had deep pockets and access to capital markets that Cabin Crafts could not yet tap. Funds raised from that sale helped finance further work on Cabin Crafts' prototype of a carpet-tufting machine. The West Point Company kept the Cabin Crafts founders on as managers, and Lamar Westcott assumed a seat on West Point's board. Cabin Crafts operated with near autonomy as a subsidiary until the mid-1970s.[47]

Julian McCamy recalled opposing the sale of Cabin Crafts, the tufted textile industry's pioneer firm, to West Point in 1946, though he was only a teenager. He also indicated that his father had been less than comfortable with the sale, but the two Westcott brothers convinced him to go along. "Neither Fred nor Lamar Westcott had any children, so they had no one to pass the company on to." Bob McCamy did have an heir, but Julian was still much too young and unproven. And the founders wanted West Point's access to capital markets to help with their expansion plans.[48]

Bob McCamy, Hackney, Payne, and the Cabin Crafts machine shop crew knew that Joe Cobble, already in the field with wide bedspread machines, was working on a carpet machine as well. Otis Payne and his colleagues knew Cobble "was fixing to make a big rug machine," but he had to cast all the parts for the machine. "It takes a considerable amount of time to make patterns" and do all the other work necessary to make special parts from scratch. The Cabin Crafts mechanics took Cobble's bedspread machine parts, readily available, and adapted those parts to produce a machine capable of producing 12-foot-wide rugs in a single pass. Cabin Crafts bought a dozen needle-bar housings, cams, and connecting rods; in other words, they bought "all the working parts from Cobble," Payne remembered, "and we built the rest of it." McCamy and Hackney contracted the production of one large metal housing piece to a Chattanooga metal-working firm and used spare and scrap metal available locally to make the rest. The key was in adapting the needle bars. Cabin Crafts mechanics took large hollow-point needles from needlepunch machines used to tuft small rugs and fitted them into the bedspread needle bars from Cobble. "It was a loop machine, and we made the attachment that goes in under the bottom," and then "we had a 12-foot machine." This occurred in late 1949 or early 1950.

"When we went to run it, we didn't have [backing] materials wide enough to make a 12-foot rug out of." This was all very expensive, and Cabin Crafts began to run out of money. According to Otis Payne, it was at this point that Cabin Crafts went in with West Point and "got the financing. That's when it really started to get going." Actually, West Point had acquired Cabin Crafts in 1946, but the association was not immediately obvious. What Payne probably remembered was a key contribution from one of West Point's other textile mills. The textile giant's Langdale, Alabama, mill came up with a process for double-weaving 12-ounce cotton duck—the most popular backing material for rugs—on 60- and 80-inch looms. This enabled Langdale to make 10- and 15-foot-wide backing material.[49] West Point's financial commitment to Cabin Crafts probably increased at about this time as well. The West Point connection—both in financial backing and in the supply and support of raw materials—proved significant in the evolution of Cabin Crafts as an industry leader.[50]

Payne and his colleagues went on to build five carpet machines "before

Cobble got to making them enough [so] that you just could buy them," probably in 1951 or 1952. Payne's early model is remarkably similar to the basic tufting machine in use today, although the modern machine operates with much greater speed (see figure B). By getting a jump on Cobble and other firms in the industry, the Cabin Crafts machine shop provided a crucial boost to the firm's entry into carpet production. Cabin Crafts, Barwick, and Mose Painter, for example, had produced broadloom carpets from strips made on narrower machines and sewn together in the late 1940s. Cabin Crafts almost certainly produced the first *seamless*, tufted broadloom carpeting in 1950 on a machine "cobbled" together with parts purchased from the Chattanooga machine maker and scrap metal.

As Cobble began mass-producing tufting machines for the booming carpet trade in the 1950s, Cabin Crafts quietly stopped production of its own machines, but the innovative company continued to make good use of its machine shop and talented mechanics. The Cabin Crafts machine shop was responsible for a number of inventions and innovations that increased the efficiency of various machines, solved particular problems, or created new effects. Inspecting tables, turntables for lift trucks, and a host of other devices were built in the machine shop. The machine shop modified needlebars on existing tufting machines, for example, so that the entire needlebar could shift an inch and a half. Bob McCamy came up with the idea as a way to cover up some of the inconsistent dyeing that plagued the industry, but the innovation opened more creative possibilities as well.[51]

The early attempts at patterns ran into another problem. The cotton ducks and other backings used in early carpet manufacture were less than ideal; they shrank after dyeing and drying and stretched with wear. Patterned carpets with such backings would obviously be a disaster as designs shifted with the backing material. Roger McNamara, a new Cabin Crafts employee freshly recruited in 1955, immediately began pushing for a new innovation that would help with this problem—a second backing, preferably with jute. Jute secondary backings did not shrink or stretch and gave tufted carpets much greater dimensional stability.[52]

The machine shop, like Cabin Crafts generally and other carpet firms, often lost talented people to competitors. Sidney Felker, a protégé of Otis Payne's who began work at the Cabin Crafts machine shop in 1959, recalled that there was a time in the 1960s when it was quite difficult to find and keep talented mechanics. The proliferation of carpet mills created jobs for machinists and put a high premium on people such as Payne and Felker.[53] The Dalton district

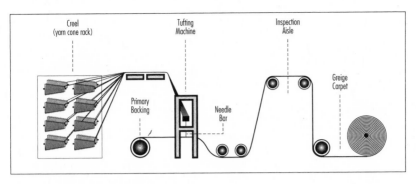

Figure B: Tufting from creels

has long suffered from a labor shortage, in both the skilled and unskilled segments of the carpet industry.

One of those talented machinists who left Cabin Crafts in the 1950s was Grover Gowin. He had worked in the company machine shop during the early critical years of making tufting machines in the early 1950s. E. T. Barwick hired Gowin away from Cabin Crafts, and Gowin helped set up a machine shop for his new employer. After just a few years with Barwick, Gowin started his own machinery firm and made a fortune developing and manufacturing dye becks. When Bob and Bud Shaw moved into carpet dyeing, their Star Finishing Company used new Gowin becks for its initial startup in 1960.[54]

Cabin Crafts used its internally developed machine-making capabilities and West Point's capital to become the acknowledged leader in medium- and high-quality carpeting during the 1950s. The construction and expansion of the company's new Springdale plant in Dalton exemplified the firm's commitment to efficiency and constant modernization. Completed in June 1954, the new facility became the company's fourth manufacturing facility in Dalton. Designed by the company's chief engineer, Bill Sapp, the Springdale plant had all the features needed by tufting manufacturers. The building, occupying an 85-acre plot on the edge of Dalton's city limits, had a single story, making it easier to move large, heavy rolls of carpeting. The floors were concrete, again reducing the problem of carpet weight for storage. New additions in the late 1950s and early 1960s created what Sapp called the best "laid-out tufted carpet mill in this country. Everything is on one floor—no ramps, no stairs. Material flow is virtually in a straight line," he noted. Cabin Crafts was one of the first tufting mills to integrate forward to dyeing and finishing, and the Springdale plant included dye becks and latex coaters.[55]

Cabin Crafts focused on the high-end market for carpets and emphasized style, quality, and brand-name recognition. To a greater extent than any other tufted manufacturer, Cabin Crafts was able to build a recognizable consumer franchise. The company produced a wide array of textured carpets, and the Cabin Crafts designers constantly experimented with new combinations of cut-and-loop patterns, sculpted designs achieved with shearing machines, and a variety of colors. The firm also pioneered in using synthetic fibers.

Cabin Crafts played a leading role in promoting tufted textiles throughout the world. Both Fred and Lamar Westcott loved to travel, and Fred developed a hobby of returning from international trips with new ideas. Cabin Crafts, in partnership with West Point, owned carpet mills in England and Italy by the early 1960s and had developed extensive licensing arrangements with floor-covering firms in South Africa, Australia, New Zealand, Sweden, France, and Canada. Under the licensing agreements, Cabin Crafts allowed these foreign companies to use its patents on a variety of tufting machines and techniques in exchange for access to design ideas from around the world. Cabin Crafts played a key role in the transfer of tufting technology to international enterprises. As Fred Westcott put it, "We don't import merchandise. We import and export ideas."[56]

Cabin Crafts and Barwick Mills were the only two firms from the Dalton tufted textile district to be welcomed into the American Carpet Institute (ACI) before the mid-1960s. Cabin Crafts' reputation for producing high-quality products earned the recognition of the declining carpet aristocracy, evidenced by Fred Westcott's election to consecutive terms as chairman of the board of ACI in 1962 and 1963.[57]

Lamar Westcott retired from Cabin Crafts in 1954, though he continued to serve on West Point's board for several years. Fred Westcott and Bob McCamy both retired in November 1963. The founders entrusted Cabin Crafts to West Point veterans Virgil Hampton and Jack Turner. Just a few years after these retirements, West Point moved to integrate Cabin Crafts more fully into the parent firm's operations. Cabin Crafts, for more than twenty years an independent subsidiary with its own board of directors, became an operating division of West Point in 1967. The old company was now known within West Point official circles as "the Carpet and Rug Division."[58] Dalton residents, of course, knew this community fixture only as Cabin Crafts. In the 1960s the Dalton district began to lose the first generation of tufted textile leaders, those people who had managed first the transition to factory production in bedspreads and then the shift toward carpet production.

As the Cabin Crafts founders neared retirement in the late 1950s, Clarence

Shaw became gravely ill with lung cancer. Cabin Crafts and Star Dye had never had much of a relationship. Bud Shaw recalled that Cabin Crafts developed its own in-house dyeing facilities in the 1950s, but these were not extensive enough to fill all the company's needs. Cabin Crafts still contracted with outside firms such as Dalton Spread Laundry for dyeing and finishing services, especially with bedspreads and small rugs. Star Dye "never got one dollar's worth of business from Cabin Crafts," according to Bud Shaw. Competition was as much a characteristic of the Dalton carpet industry as cooperation, and perhaps more so. "Business was business," commented Bud, though the precise reasons for Cabin's reluctance to use Star's services remain unclear.[59] However, Clarence Shaw's illness had a ripple effect that would draw Cabin Crafts and the Shaw family closer together in the early 1960s, at least for a short time.

New leaders and new companies, formed in the 1950s and 1960s, took center stage during the 1960s. All those new firms, in a sense, built on the foundation created by Cabin Crafts. Star Dye had a role to play in the emerging carpet industry as well, though none would have guessed it in the late 1950s. Clarence Shaw's passing brought new leadership to the company and the family's fortunes. His sons Robert E. (Bob) Shaw and J. C. (Bud) Shaw adopted a different, more aggressive strategy. In the 1960s, the new Star Finishing Company hitched its wagon firmly to the booming broadloom tufted carpet industry and held on for the ride.

CHAPTER TWO

Making the Transition

Bob Shaw returned to Dalton when his father became too ill to manage the business. A lifelong smoker, Clarence Shaw developed lung cancer in the late 1950s. Clarence continued to direct the business as long as he was able and continued to advise Buddy Sewell on technical matters. "When he got sick," Sewell recalled, "and he hurt so bad, I used to have to go up to his house if I ran into a problem and needed some answers. He would be in the bed. You could just see him wasting away. But it was something I had to do, because he wanted me to do it." Increasingly, Bob took over direction of the company.[1]

Julian McCamy married Clarence Shaw's daughter, Eleanor. McCamy, son of Cabin Crafts cofounder Bob McCamy, recalled that the Shaw family used the pending wedding as an incentive to keep Clarence on his feet and active as long as possible, as a way to keep him from giving up. After giving his daughter away, Clarence Shaw retired to his bed and passed away within a few months.

Buddy Sewell remembered that Bob and Bud Shaw both worked at Star Dye during college summer breaks. "Bud just worked a little while one summer, and he wouldn't come back. But Bob came in pretty often." Bud Shaw recalled that he and his father had a difference of opinion and came to a mutual decision that it would be best if he worked elsewhere. Bob continued to work intermittently at Star Dye. Ever the avid golfer, Bob worked hard in his father's plant but generally made strategic escapes one or two afternoons a week during his stints at Star Dye. "I worked right beside him," Buddy Sewell remembered, "pulling tumblers and this kind of stuff, up till it come about tee time," at which time Bob would take off.[2]

Reflecting four decades later, Bob Shaw captured the essence of the business he took over in 1958. "It was a little business. In fact, when Dad died, it was a $300,000-a-year business. He was very conservative. He had gone broke during the depression, and he never went into debt from that point forward." Most of the folks who had gone through the depression "didn't after that time. He had put together maybe a hundred thousand dollars in the company, and that was the forerunner of Shaw Industries."[3]

Both Bob and Bud Shaw urged their father to expand into carpet dyeing and finishing in the 1950s. Bud Shaw elaborated on the same theme in explaining his father's conservatism. "Cotton went to a nickel a pound in '22, and my family went broke because we were in that business: gins, lumber mills, things of that nature, but primarily cotton. Dad saw that, that was right after he came out of World War I." After graduating from Georgia Tech and spending a brief time in textiles in Greenville, South Carolina, the elder Shaw was swept up in "the Florida land rush of the '20s, and wham, bam, down it goes." Shaw went back into textiles, but the Florida land bust was followed by the Great Depression. "You know, we get out of that," Bud Shaw recalled, and "we go into World War II and then all of a sudden you don't have any raw materials available to make the product out of." After that extended age of uncertainty, "then all of a sudden the south wind seems to be blowing at your back just a little bit in '46, '47, but let's remember the experiences that he had after World War I—a depression. So his question automatically is, 'What is this? Now that we've had these heydays where we've created all this debt, now shall we go back and have a repeat of what happened right after World War I, or is this south wind going to continue blowing at our back? Shall the cold north wind blow again, or shall the south wind blow?'" Quite understandably, Clarence Shaw always feared a sudden shift in the winds of fortune and managed his affairs accordingly.[4]

Clarence Shaw had resisted Bud's suggestions in the 1950s that he move into broadloom carpet dyeing. Bud tried to convince his father "to expand a whole heck of a lot," but the elder Shaw refused. Bud gave his interpretation of his father's position. During the early to mid-1950s, Clarence Shaw "had three other children to educate," and he had just "gotten his stake, Star Dye Company, and he ran that on a very, very conservative basis." In retrospect, Bud acknowledged that his father "was very wise to do it" his way. Clarence avoided the great risks that would have accompanied the leap to carpet finishing.

Bob Shaw had a similar explanation and elaborated on his father's situation. "Dad never believed that carpet should be dyed in a beck," Bob recalled. "He always believed that carpet should have been dyed continuously, which we're doing now. He was just thirty years ahead of his time. He just didn't believe in wrapping a piece of carpet around a reel. We're still beck dyeing today, fifty years later. More than that," Bob continued, by the mid-1950s, "my father was in his late fifties and had two of us in college and had two girls getting ready to go to college. It wasn't so much that he didn't want to go into it; I think he felt that his house was paid for, his business was paid for, and he could see his way clear to educating four children."[5]

The smaller tufted goods that Clarence Shaw had built his stake on—bedspreads, robes, and scatter rugs—began to decline in importance at about the time he became ill. The total dollar value of tufted bedspread shipments slowly declined from $52 million in 1952 to about $48 million in 1964. The signature product that had helped build Harry Saul's Queen Chenilles—the tufted bathrobe—fell even more sharply, from a high of $11 million in 1952 to just over $4 million in 1964. As it happened, Clarence Shaw's conservative strategy would not have worked for much longer, as Bob and Bud Shaw well knew.[6]

As the market for small tufted goods declined, consumer demand for tufted carpeting more than compensated. The U.S. carpet industry shipped 71 million square yards in 1958, about 60 percent of it tufted. This was phenomenal growth for a product—tufted carpet—that had not existed in 1949, and for an industry that had been virtually stagnant for decades. It was little wonder that, as Max Beasley of the Cobble Brothers tufting machine–making company recalled, many observers believed that "every year was the last big year for tufting." Surely, the fad would run its course, just as the mania for tufted spreads and robes had. To the surprise of those doomsayers, the tufted carpet industry grew at an even faster rate in the 1960s. The introduction of BCF (bulked continuous filament) nylon in the late 1950s helped push carpet sales to new heights during the following decade. By 1968, total carpet shipments exceeded 395 million square yards, with more than 90 percent of it of the tufted variety. Out of more than four hundred industrial groupings ranked by the U.S. government, only three experienced higher growth rates than carpet in the 1960s—computers, televisions, and aircraft. Total industry sales exceeded $1 billion in 1964 and approached $2 billion by the end of the decade.[7] If the growth of tufted carpet during the 1950s had seemed miraculous, the boom of the 1960s defied description.

While the industry faced a bright future in the early 1960s, the specific fortunes of Star Dye and its employees appeared much cloudier. Uncertainty permeated the atmosphere around Star Dye Company in the weeks and months that followed Clarence Shaw's illness and eventual death. Buddy Sewell remarked that when Bob Shaw took over at Star Dye, all the employees "were a little bit shook, you know, because Bob was a little rowdy when he was young. So we were a little concerned. . . . He was a rounder." Sewell recalled that Bob came in one day with a golf club in his hand and two golf balls. He led Sewell "out back in the parking lot, and he teed those things up and knocked those boogers right straight up Main Street. Man, I just flew back" into the building.

"He was a corker. But he was sharp." And the vultures were circling, in a sense, as many tried to take advantage of young Bob Shaw after he took command at Star Dye. "All the guys in town got in on top of him, then," Sewell recalled; "they figured his dad was gone, now was the time to kill him. But it didn't happen that way."[8] Bob and Bud Shaw soon acted to take advantage of the booming carpet market by de-emphasizing Star Dye's traditional business in small rugs, robes, and bedspreads and moving into carpet dyeing.

Bob and Bud Shaw followed different paths to their involvement with the carpet industry. Bob Shaw attended the University of the South in Sewanee, Tennessee, for a while. He worked in sales for suppliers to the carpet industry. Bob first sold yarn for Bibb Manufacturing Company and later worked for the F. H. Ross chemical company (headquartered in Chicago), selling dyes to the carpet trade in northwest Georgia. As indicated in Buddy Sewell's brief characterization, Bob Shaw had yet to find his niche when his father became ill.

Bud Shaw followed a clear career path in his early years. He showed an entrepreneurial streak early in life. He and a friend got a franchise to deliver the *Atlanta Constitution* in Dalton early in their high school years. Bud also worked during the summers as a soda jerk at the Bradley and Bandy Drug Store. He worked from 5 A.M. to 9 P.M. during his high school summers, delivering newspapers and mixing milk shakes. He recalled earning about $75 per week between the two jobs. Bud then attended and graduated from Georgia Tech with a degree in textile engineering, with a double major in organic chemistry and management. Clarence Shaw helped his son obtain summer employment with the city of Dalton in 1950 as a surveyor. Bud helped in the surveys that expanded Dalton's city limits. He later worked at the American Thread Company before taking a job at Crown Cotton Mills.

Bud Shaw recalled believing that David Hamilton, Crown's CEO, "was really going to take Crown and go." Hamilton put Shaw in charge of the company's new synthetic yarn unit. In that capacity, Bud worked with a subsidiary of an established carpet firm to develop yarn for the new tufted carpet industry. "I had been working at Crown Cotton Mills in conjunction with Hartford Rayon Company, a division of Bigelow Sanford Carpet Company," Bud Shaw recalled. He and George McGrath of Hartford Rayon "worked on a solution-dyed process for dyeing rayon." The two "started making rayon and yarns out of solution-dyed material instead of natural, and then what we'd do is take colors A, B, and C and twist the three together to produce a tweed yarn. This was a pretty nice variation." Despite such efforts, Crown was unable to exploit fully such innovations for the carpet industry.[9]

Bud Shaw's experience at Crown was frustrating. According to both Shaw and Warren Sims, "Crown should have been Shaw Industries." In other words, they believed that with Crown's capital, accumulated technical expertise, and prime location, Crown could have become a major supplier to the carpet industry. Crown might then have moved into carpet manufacturing, with the right sense of timing, and perhaps become an industry leader. That was precisely what Shaw Industries did in the 1960s and 1970s. Why not Crown? Sims attributed it to conservative management. David Hamilton and the Crown leadership had built a substantial business by the 1950s. Like Clarence Shaw's leadership at Star Dye (though on a larger scale), Crown's management moved into a closer relationship with the emerging carpet industry, but not as aggressively as they might have.

Perhaps Hamilton and his colleagues at Crown fell victim to the "entrepreneurial conservatism" that may have afflicted southern textile mill managers. According to one scholar of southern textiles, "the ease with which these entrepreneurs could enter cotton manufacturing . . . came at a price." Entry into cotton manufacturing "required relatively little in the way of flexible and rapid adjustment to a dynamic environment," and "the diversion of entrepreneurial energies into textiles would in the long run exert a deleterious effect" on the South's "industrial development." The South's capture of an older industry with well-worn market grooves encouraged an "entrepreneurial conservatism" that inhibited innovation.[10] The cotton textile market, in brief, may not have been as dynamic as the carpet market, but it was a time-tested market. Tufted carpets might be a flash in the pan. The carpet trade emphasized close attention to shifting consumer tastes in color and style. Color was the single most important element in a consumer purchase decision, yet color choices varied widely with the fashion markets. Crown had little experience with such volatile markets.

Still, Crown moved tentatively to take advantage of the booming market for carpet yarn in the mid-1950s with its synthetic yarn division. Crown pressed further into the carpet field in the early 1960s by creating Texture-Tex Yarns as a wholly owned subsidiary. But as Crown's original cotton mill in Dalton struggled with outdated equipment, the obvious solution was to move that facility toward supplying the carpet market. With Crown in desperate need of new equipment, why not take the opportunity to move in that direction? Bud Shaw believed that organized labor at Crown represented a major stumbling block.

Crown's workers had successfully organized in the 1930s. Douglas Flamming has argued that the labor unions—first the United Textile Workers (UTW) and then the Textile Workers Union of America (TWUA)—filled a vacuum created by the decline of company paternalism in the late 1920s and 1930s. During the 1940s and 1950s, Crown's managers and workers built a solid working relationship. By the 1960s, that relationship had soured. When Crown attempted to introduce new high-speed equipment for producing rayon yarn, including carpet yarn, workers objected to the increased pace. Crown experienced a brief boom in the mid-1960s, but Hamilton and his managers became increasingly exasperated with their workers. Turnover rates shot up as Crown lost workers, especially younger ones, to the new carpet mills. Union rules, Bud Shaw recalled, made it difficult to introduce new processes and rearrange work assignments. Older workers overwhelmingly voiced concerns that the new workloads associated with the rayon process were too intensive. Crown's workers also developed a habit of protesting against company policies by going outside the established grievance procedure with impromptu work stoppages.[11]

The handwriting was on the wall by mid-1966 when Crown organized Texture-Tex. The new subsidiary, though located only ten miles from the original Crown mill, "neither retrained nor hired Crown's older, union millhands." Crown decided to cut its losses, both in terms of the outmoded plant and equipment at the Crown mill and with regard to its organized labor force. Crown did what northern textile mills had been doing for decades—it escaped labor problems by moving. "Running away from labor problems," Flamming observed with dark humor, "did not necessitate a very long journey." Crown ultimately decided to expand the operations of Texture-Tex by building a new plant in Valdosta, Georgia, the first time that Crown's management had built a new production facility outside the Dalton area. Crown management decided to shut down its older mills in 1969.[12] Perhaps labor difficulties played a larger role than entreprenurial conservatism in Crown's decisions.

Frustrated with Crown's inability or unwillingness to move aggressively into the carpet market, Bud Shaw sought other opportunities. As a "by-product" of Shaw's work with rayon at Crown Cotton Mills, though, he "was offered an interest in Rocky Creek Mills in Statesville, North Carolina." Rocky Creek Mills was an operating division of Marion Manufacturing Company, which in turn had a close relationship with J. P. Stevens; Stevens was the selling agent for Marion. Marion's Rocky Creek division was beginning to produce yarn for the carpet industry, and Bud Shaw's experience in this field made him an attractive candidate. The deal was enticing to him because it offered him part ownership and a chance to run a business that was nearly his own business.[13]

Bud Shaw and his family packed their bags and moved to Statesville, North Carolina, in 1957. "I remember moving a lot," Julius Clarence Shaw III said of his memories of his childhood in the family of a talented textile manager. Julius Shaw, currently Shaw Industries vice president for investor relations and corporate communications, was born October 2, 1953, while his father was working at Dalton's Crown Cotton Mills. "Dad would go in almost every Saturday," Julius recalled. "Rocky Creek Mills was out, literally, in a pasture with a cattle barn right in front of it. . . . So as Dad would go in to work a couple of hours on Saturdays, I would spend a lot of time playing at that barn."[14] While Bud Shaw was living in North Carolina, he maintained part ownership of Star Dye and still had an interest in expanding the family's involvement with the carpet industry.

Bob and Bud Shaw moved decisively to enter the carpet-finishing business with the formation of Star Finishing Company in 1960. "Dad got sick in the late 1950s, and I came back, really, to close out a family business," Bob Shaw remembered. Star Dye "was the forerunner of Shaw Industries. We incorporated Star Finishing in August 1960, in a little building over here, just 22,000 square feet. We were something like a $3 million business by 1966." The vultures, needless to say, stopped circling.[15]

Bob and Bud Shaw incorporated Star Finishing initially as a subsidiary of Star Dye, according to the October 5, 1960, edition of *Home Furnishings Daily*. The trade journal identified Robert E. Shaw as "general manager" of the company. According to Bob Shaw, "new plant operations [would] consist of dyeing and processing broadloom carpeting." *Home Furnishings Daily* also reported that "M. S. Morrison, a 25-year veteran with DuPont, is leaving his present job to serve as plant manager of Star Finishing Co." Thus Star Finishing made its first appearance in the trade press. Stuart Morrison received "an interest" in the company as well, Bud Shaw recalled. Morrison had extensive experience in the techniques of dyeing broadloom carpeting, acquired in his last years with DuPont. He later served as a vice president of the firm and, according to Warren Sims, "became one of Bob Shaw's right hands at Star Finishing." Morrison's expertise as a chemist and experience with DuPont served Star Finishing well.[16]

Other companies formed to dye and finish broadloom carpeting in the Dalton district in the late 1950s and early 1960s. Star faced several competitors including older firms such as Rogers Dye and Dalton Carpet Finishing and newer entries such as Constellation, Advance, and Foremost. These firms used similar equipment; indeed, Gowin becks were standard fare for carpet dyeing operations in the 1960s. Many were better capitalized than Star. Bob Shaw recalled that Star Finishing had been started with about $100,000, essentially the legacy of Clarence Shaw. Star Dye put up $50,000 and Bud Shaw's Rocky Creek Mills also contributed $50,000 in capital. Constellation, a new firm managed by Shaw family friend Rollins Jolly, started with an initial capitalization nearly ten times that—about $1 million, "underwritten by a private stock company composed of local people," according to *Textile World*. Bud Shaw and his brother were keenly aware that they "were behind some other finishing companies" at the outset.[17] Carpet dyeing required greater capital investment than tufting. Yet Star Finishing outpaced its competitors in less than a decade, becoming the largest commission finishing company in the industry by 1967.

The process of making large rugs and carpets by tufting was less than a decade old when Clarence Shaw passed away in January 1959. Carpet dyeing was an even newer process, and it took courage to risk most of the family's accumulated wealth by entering such an unproven field, all the more so considering that Buddy Sewell was the only Star Dye employee with any experience or even modest training in broadloom beck dyeing. Sewell remembered those early days at Star Finishing when Bob Shaw moved full-scale into dyeing broadloom carpeting. Just before Clarence Shaw died, "Bob went on the other side of the driveway and built a bigger office. He had an office for himself and the secretary. And he built a little lab at the end of it. So I got away from stirring that pot [and] got my own steam table, which had twelve holes in it, and I could be running twelve beakers at the same time. I had some pipettes and all this other stuff that I needed. We bought a little washer. We were uptown then," Sewell recalled. Becks were not used in the dyeing of bedspreads and were rarely used for small rugs. Small tufted goods were generally dyed in open vats, stirred with paddles. Star Dye, in fact, had only one six-foot dye beck when Bob took over, and it was not large enough for dyeing broadloom carpet.

How, then, did Buddy Sewell come by his knowledge of beck dyeing? The Shaw family's relationship with the Westcotts and Bob McCamy was crucial here. "What Bob [Shaw] had done was send me over to Cabin Crafts—we had a good relationship with Cabin Crafts at that time—and I stayed over there about three or four weeks, coming in every day with them, just getting the feel of everything" in the carpet business. "Bud Newman was the dyer at Cabin Crafts, and he was very helpful" to Sewell. When they started up Star Finishing, Buddy Sewell was "the only guy that knew how to dye carpet. I had 'em by the throat."[18]

Buddy Sewell had learned to dye cotton rugs and robes first and then had to shift to dyeing nylon and other synthetic fibers. The processes were quite different. With cotton, he explained, "if you're going after a brown shade or a beige shade, you start with a brown dye, and you shade it in with a blue or a violet or whatever. But with nylon, you work with three primaries mostly (red, yellow, blue). You don't do that on cotton. You start with browns, with a gray,

47

a green. We had several greens, several grays. And believe it or not I can still re-member formulas from back in 1950." At Cabin Crafts, Sewell sharpened and learned to adapt the skills and methods he had learned from Clarence Shaw.[19]

John McCarty's family also played a role in educating Bob Shaw about the tufted textile industry he was entering. John McCarty was a silent partner in Star Dye and had no expertise in the industry. His brother, Frank, on the other hand, had helped create the industry. Frank McCarty had owned his own scatter rug–making company, McCarty Chenille, in the 1940s. E. T. Barwick bought the small business in 1949 and kept Frank McCarty on to manage pro-duction. McCarty helped get Barwick Mills up and running, managing the new giant's growing production capacity in the 1950s. Frank McCarty also helped establish E&B Carpets in the early 1960s. At his brother's request, Frank shared his extensive knowledge and experience with Bob Shaw as well.[20]

Cabin Crafts and other local and family connections provided important technical assistance at the inception of Star Finishing. This was part of an on-going pattern of close connections between the Westcott and McCamy fami-lies and the Shaws. Indeed, while Clarence Shaw was seriously ill, he had arranged to have Bob McCamy—who had just become his daughter's father-in-law—consult regularly with Bob Shaw so that McCamy might check the young man's progress and advise him. Cabin Crafts then essentially trained Buddy Sewell in carpet dyeing. Not surprisingly, Bob Shaw had fond memo-ries of Bob McCamy and the Westcotts. "The Westcotts were friends of the family: Lamar and Lulu, as we called them. They were Presbyterians, we were Presbyterians. They brought my father back to Dalton. I don't think anybody visualized the bedspread industry becoming a $10 billion business. I replaced Lamar Westcott on the board over at Berry [College in Rome]. They had one child, who they lost." Lamar Westcott "came to believe, as he said, that he was responsible for me. So Mr. Westcott and I were very good friends." The West-cotts and Bob McCamy served, as Warren Sims characterized the relationship, as mentors for many young men who came of age in the Dalton area in the 1940s and 1950s.[21] The relationship should not be exaggerated, however. For much of the 1960s, 1970s, and 1980s, Cabin was chiefly a Shaw competitor.

Most of Bob and Bud Shaw's contemporaries have noted their excellent sense of timing, and certainly the time was right to initiate a business such as Star Finishing in the 1960s. The new company came along at the right time to ride the carpet boom of the 1960s. Buddy Sewell observed that "it seemed like if you got started in the early 1960s, all you had to do was just keep punching and hold on." Bob Shaw characterized the period in much the same way: "We were just hanging onto the carpet industry. What the tufting industry was doing was making a floor covering that was affordable for the masses. We got caught up in what I call the 'gold coast.' Everybody in Dalton was looking for gold."[22]

The increasing number of prospectors drew Bob and Bud Shaw's attention in the late 1950s and early 1960s. The booming carpet market attracted entrepreneurs, both locally and from outside the area. The number of companies engaged in the production of tufted carpet nearly doubled between 1958 and 1963 (from 88 to 167). The rate of increase slowed somewhat, but by 1972 the number had doubled again to 333, a majority of them in Georgia. In this decentralized, unintegrated industry, few of these mills had any internal dyeing and finishing capacity. Most of the handful of mills with dyeing facilities did not have enough capacity to handle all their finishing needs on a regular basis. Many of these firms operated with pre-dyed yarns to reduce the need for finishing services. Opportunity for entry into carpet finishing obviously increased in this period. Companies that offered such services could help small manufacturers achieve a degree of flexibility they had not previously known. Finishers and tufters could share the risks in this rapidly growing industry.[23]

Walter Hemphill played a key role in helping Star Finishing get off the ground in the crucial early years. Hemphill was a native of Marion, North Carolina. He served in the navy during World War II and went to work for Marion Manufacturing Company immediately after the war. "I got involved in a training program for industrial engineers at Marion Manufacturing. Later, we bought a company called Rocky Creek Mills. I inherited that also for the industrial engineering work. It wasn't long after that until Mr. Bud Shaw came to Rocky Creek Mills as the plant manager. That was the beginning of my connection with the Shaw family. I continued to do the industrial engineering for Marion and for Rocky Creek—for Bud, you might say—over a period of two or three years."[24]

Hemphill became involved with Star Dye and Star Finishing through the Bud Shaw connection. "We got involved through Rocky Creek Mills with Star Dye Company in Dalton to build a carpet dye house to dye broad-width carpet. Bud and Bob Shaw were both very instrumental in seeing that there was a need, because broadloom [tufted] carpet was new at that time [1959–60]. With Star Dye already having been in the scatter rug–dyeing [business], it was a natural for them to be interested in expanding into broadloom." Early in 1962, Bob Shaw asked Hemphill if he "would consider moving to Dalton to help start up the dye house. In May 1962, I came over to talk with Bob Shaw, and over a period of a month or two we decided that I would come to work as a consultant to see what we could do to help get the plant up and running."[25]

Hemphill remembered Star in its embryonic stages as a fairly small establishment. "At the time I came, we had about 45 employees. We had one lady in the front office," Willie Mae Dantzler, who "was Bob Shaw's secretary, payroll clerk, and receptionist all wrapped up in one."

Hemphill remained on the payroll at Marion Manufacturing for another year, though he was working in Dalton. "At the end of the year, we decided I'd better stay another year because we [Star Finishing] were already in our third expansion," he recounted. "At the end of the second year, it was decided that I needed to make a decision either to stay here [in Dalton] or go back to North Carolina. I decided to stay here, and I've never regretted that."[26]

Walter Hemphill attributed Star Finishing's success and rapid growth to two things. "The timing was right. There was tufting being done, and there was a dire need for dyeing and finishing, and there weren't that many dye houses available at that time, so the ones that were in business were busy—and I mean busy. The other thing was that we set out from the beginning to be the best. We had the technical know-how, the manufacturing know-how, management know-how. It became a team effort very early on. There was no one person, other than Bob Shaw, who ran our company. The rest of us worked as a team, and I think that carried forward." Hemphill recalled the technical team at Star: "Stuart Morrison was the chemist, and a good one, a real professional. Buddy Sewell was superintendent of dyeing, and I just fit in where I could. That got us off and running. We kept expansion going all the time. In 1964, when we decided I would stay here on a permanent basis, Mr. Morrison was made vice president of technical services, and I became vice president of manufacturing for Star Finishing. Stuart handled all the technical problems, and I handled all the other problems, including personnel. We worked as a team for the years that followed that."[27]

The teamwork did not always come easily. Sewell, Hemphill, and Morrison came from differing backgrounds. Morrison had a quarter-century's service with one of the nation's largest and most prestigious companies, as well as extensive professional training as a chemist. Hemphill brought his own experiences from Marion Manufacturing, a more traditional southern textile firm. Buddy Sewell had deep connections to the Shaw family. He had served as an apprentice to Clarence Shaw and had learned to dye rugs and smaller tufted goods from one of the acknowledged masters. He was a quick study and learned to dye carpet by observing the Cabin Crafts operation. For all his experience, he had no formal education in textile technology. The three men had a difficult relationship at times but managed to cooperate effectively most of the time. All three brought important skills and talents to Star Finishing.

From the beginning, Bob Shaw took risks in order to do business on a large scale. He was never afraid to expand with this booming industry, and Star Finishing profited by his commitment to expansion. "We built a reputation early on as being a quality dye house," Hemphill observed. "We were big enough to turn the goods around and get them back to the customer in a reasonable time so that he could service his customers on the other end."[28] Star Finishing started out leasing the building, equipment, everything. "We wound up with twenty-four becks in Plant 1; I think we started off with four becks. It was leased, building and everything. So we had it all hung out there." The move was certainly a risk. Bob Shaw chided an interviewer in 1999 who mistakenly assumed that he had purchased dye becks and other equipment to begin Star. "No," Shaw corrected with a chuckle, "we didn't *buy* equipment, we *leased* equipment. The whole company was started on $100,000. We leased becks, and we leased the dryer from some small machinery manufacturer [Gowin]. We leased the building from Bob Mathis. It was 22,000 [square] feet. When we got into business, we got them to build us another 22,000 feet. Then we were getting too big, and we had to buy the building to expand."[29] Walter Hemphill helped preside over a swift expansion of Star's production capacity. Star Finishing also became Dalton Utilities' "biggest customer on water and electricity. We began to make our mark in the city, you might say."[30]

Star provided technical assistance to manufacturers, "especially with the color lines," Walter Hemphill recalled. "And we would match anything—a leaf or piece of cloth or anything. Of course, Buddy Sewell and Stuart Morrison were doing most of this." According to Buddy Sewell, customers usually came in with color ideas. The carpet mill owners would hire designers such as Dusty Rhodes. "They would bring you a color line of maybe eighteen colors. You matched them up in the laboratory and then took them to the big machines [dye becks], and hopefully" the colors came out right. Dyeing was an inexact science in those days, and mistakes were common. Star soon established a reputation for quality work, but initially the company depended on the patience and loyalty of good customers. "There were a lot of people who stood by us in those early years," Sewell continued. "They gave us chances. A lot of the carpet, you know, we just didn't do a good job [when] we were getting started. And they forgave us."[31]

Not all of Star Finishing's early customers were so forgiving. Indeed, even after Star worked through its early difficulties, John Kirk recalled, some area manufacturers continued to try blaming Star for their own mistakes. In such a decentralized industry, the wholesalers and retailers who bought most carpet from manufacturers had difficulty in assigning responsibility for poor-quality goods. Manufacturers often tried to charge these customer claims back to finishing companies, alleging that the finishers had damaged high-quality goods. According to Kirk, area manufacturers briefly took advantage of young Bob Shaw in this area, at least until Shaw tightened his internal inspection processes. One could witness incredible acts of cooperation within the Dalton industrial district, but sharks inhabited these waters as well. Bob Shaw quickly learned self-defense.[32]

Thanks to the patience of most of Star's early customers and the determination of Sewell, Morrison, Hemphill, and others, Star smoothed out the technical glitches in short order. By the mid-1960s, "we were dyeing for everybody and his brother," according to Walter Hemphill. Bob Shaw made an early key decision that probably helped move Star to the top of the heap among carpet finishers. Star Finishing invested in massive warehouse space, essentially carrying inventory for its customers. "We couldn't keep the buildings built fast enough to store the carpet coming in." Star Finishing effectively served as a warehouse for a host of carpet manufacturers. For example, "We'd wind up with a warehouse full of Coronet, and sometimes I think they'd forget where it was. We kept trying to build enough buildings to hold the incoming goods, knowing that we'd get to dye it sooner or later when the colors were assigned." Star's customers wanted to delay the final color decision as long as possible, of course, and were happy to have Star carry the cost of warehousing greige, or undyed, goods.[33]

Hemphill noted that all manufacturers faced a difficult task in maintaining a labor force in the 1960s. "We were growing so fast that I couldn't hire people fast enough, and the people I hired I couldn't keep on the payroll long enough to get to know them. If they got aggravated at Star Finishing, they could walk across the street and get a job the same day and go to work. We were all guilty of hiring warm bodies that walked through the door. But we had to have numbers. It was very frustrating. We'd hire maybe a dozen and be lucky if two or three of them would stay with us. If you were willing to work in a dye house, you could get a job in Dalton anywhere you wanted to go." The labor shortage continued through the 1970s, and the turnover among the hourly employees "amazed" Elbert Shaw in the mid-1970s. "The reason, I was told, was that there were 1,500 open jobs in Dalton. We had then, and still have, people commuting from Chattanooga, Ellijay, Blue Ridge, Lafayette, etc. If a person decided he wanted to work for another company, maybe where his girlfriend worked, he'd just walk off."[34] The concentration of the carpet industry in the Dalton area created cost advantages for manufacturers but also brought potential problems.

Catherine Evans Whitener with some of her trademark hand-tufted bedspreads, 1950. Courtesy of the Carpet and Rug Institute.

Catherine Evans Whitener inspects a carpet tufting machine, ca. 1958. She helped create the foundation for northwest Georgia's homegrown tufted textile industry. Shaw Industries files.

Tabletop sewing machines were also adapted for use in bedspread tufting.

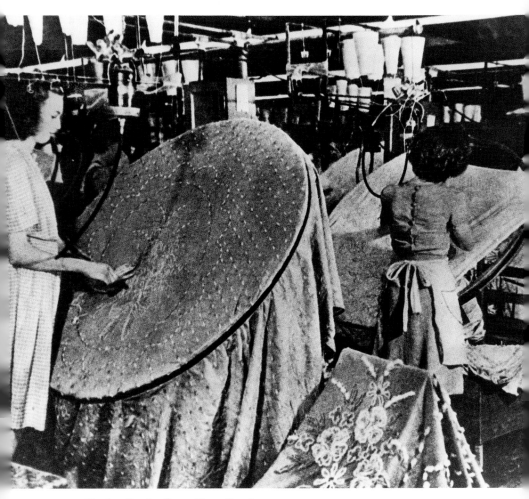

Hand-tufting in a "spread house" setting, 1930s.

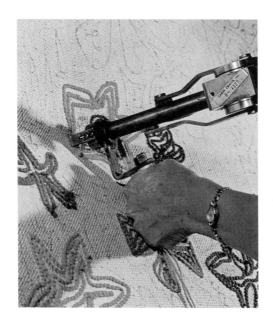

Woman using Cabin Crafts needlepunch gun to create a custom rug, 1964. The method is the same as that for making a pattern on a bedspread. Cabin Crafts developed its own lightweight gun for spreads and this heavier gun for rugs.

Clarence Shaw as a high school senior. Cartersville High School Yearbook, 1913. Courtesy of Etowah Valley Historical Society.

Cabin Crafts machine shop (1959), where Otis Payne and his colleagues built and modified tufting machines and other equipment. Cabin Crafts raced with Chattanooga machine makers to produce the first wide carpet tufting machine around 1950. *The Westpointer,* February 1959.

Cabin Crafts original plant, ca. 1934. Courtesy of WestPoint Stevens and *The Westpointer.*

Cabin Crafts founders: Fred Westcott, Lamar Westcott, and Robert McCamy, 1955.

Opposite: Shown here are examples of all the various tufted textile goods made by Cabin Crafts in the 1950s. Products ranged from chenille bedspreads and small rugs to wall-to-wall carpeting. Courtesy WestPoint Stevens and *The Westpointer,* February 1959.

This Cabin Crafts ad for the "Collector's Group" of rugs illustrates the company's marketing approach for these "high-end" products. To a greater extent than any other tufted carpet manufacturer in the 1950s, Cabin developed brand name recognition. Courtesy WestPoint Stevens and *The Westpointer*, February 1959.

This man inspected carpets for small flaws and fixed those gaps with a handheld needlepunch gun modeled on the guns used by Cabin Crafts years earlier for bedspread and small-rug tufting.

John Kirk provided some insight into the labor problem at Star and at carpet tufting and finishing plants in general. The longtime Star Dye employee moved to Star Finishing shortly after it opened. Kirk recalled that a relatively stable core of "old Star Dye people" gave Star Finishing some advantages. Like Kirk and Buddy Sewell, these workers had developed some sense of loyalty to Clarence Shaw and apparently transferred that to Bob Shaw. Clarence Shaw had used a highly personal style of management, but he had retained some distance—he practiced a limited paternalism. Bob Shaw clearly retained some of his father's practices. The annual Christmas parties, complete with gifts selected for each employee's child and a Santa to pass out the presents, continued until the company became too large in the 1970s. The younger Shaw also exhibited the same kind of loyalty to long-term employees that Clarence had practiced. He knew workers by name, and he made frequent walks through the plant. He would often pitch in and help out with production work.[35]

Yet Bob Shaw did not precisely duplicate his father's style, probably in large part because of his age. Star Dye's employees were generally Bob's age or older. In a pattern reminiscent of many Dalton-area mill owners, Bob seemed to develop a camaraderie with employees. John Kirk recalled numerous incidents from the early days of Star Finishing that illustrated the point. For example, Star and other carpet companies began using lift trucks in the 1950s to move materials around the plants. These were expensive machines in those early days, and Star Finishing had only a handful. One of Star's newest models developed a transmission problem. Shaw called on Kirk and his maintenance crew to fix the problem. Kirk "called the manufacturer several times to get directions and pulled the transmission out, took it apart, and put it back together eleven times. We finally got it fixed." Kirk recalled that during the days he labored over the lift truck, Bob Shaw would often come by, talk over the situation, and offer encouragement by saying, "well, boys, give out but don't give up." He seemed to project an image of being "one of the guys" to veterans like Kirk, even treating workers to occasional parties and barbecues.[36]

Kirk and the rest of Star's employees worked long hours—twelve-hour shifts and six-day (occasionally seven-day) weeks. This was a consequence of the labor shortage. These long hours had both negative and positive aspects. Work could be a grind with little time for leisure, but Kirk expressed appreciation for the extra pay that accompanied large amounts of overtime.

Star Finishing began operations in the early 1960s just as the Textile Workers Union of America (TWUA) began a major organizing campaign among northwest Georgia's tufted textile workers. The Tufted Textile Manufacturers Association (TTMA) took the lead in organizing the mills to resist the campaign. The union hoped to use its local unions at Crown Cotton Mills and the nearby American Thread Company as examples to attract members from the rapidly growing carpet industry. For almost three years, organizers attempted to convince workers to sign union cards in Whitfield, Gordon, and Bartow Counties. The union, unable to penetrate most mills to any great extent, petitioned for few elections. TWUA won only one election during this period—at Dixie Belle Mills in Calhoun—and lost several. By 1964, the union had folded its Dalton area organizing drive.[37]

Workers certainly faced some difficult conditions in the carpet industry, yet most rejected the prospect of organization for a variety of reasons. The rapidly growing number of mills in the area created great competition for labor and apparently drove wages up somewhat. The carpet mills offered other advantages for workers aside from wages, however. Former cotton mill and bedspread mill workers attested to the better working conditions in carpet factories. The noise level in the new mills, while not nonexistent, was below the deafening roar of a cotton mill. In the cotton mills and in the bedspread mills that worked primarily with cotton, lint was a constant companion. It covered workers' clothing and inhibited their breathing, often leading to "brown lung" syndrome. Comparatively speaking, the tufting mills were cleaner and less noxious. In the Dalton area, alternative employment was difficult to find. Carpet mill workers could compare their wages and working conditions with Crown, American Thread, and the bedspread mills, all of which were in decline. In such a comparison, work in a carpet mill came out far ahead of the alternatives.[38]

Carpet mill managers, prodded by the threat of union organization and encouraged by TTMA, also raised wages and increased benefits in the early and mid-1960s. Mill owners apparently followed, to a degree, advice given to them by Frank Constangy, one of the most prominent antilabor attorneys in the post–World War II South. Constangy told mill owners that the best way to avoid union organization was to get their own houses in order by instituting rational personnel procedures, boosting wages and benefits, and guaranteeing a certain minimum of respect and courtesy for workers. Up until the 1960s, a large number of Dalton-area carpet mills—perhaps a majority—offered no paid holidays. If plants were shut down on a holiday, workers simply went without pay. Constangy urged the mills to adopt a policy of at least two paid holidays per year. TTMA followed up on Constangy's 1963 lecture with seminars in personnel practices throughout the 1960s to train managers in preventing union organization, or "personnel preventive maintenance," as the association termed it.[39]

Carpet mills had room to maneuver in the area of wages. Bedspread manufacture in the 1930s and 1940s had been a low value-added activity, even within the labor-intensive textile industry. Carpet manufacture in the 1960s, by contrast, was a high value-added industry in comparison with other segments of the textile business. Production workers in Georgia's tufting mills added nearly twice as much value per hour ($6.94) as workers in the state's overall textile sector ($3.57). Value-added per hour in tufted carpet exceeded the Georgia average for all manufacturing industries in the 1960s ($5.59). Though the Dalton district's carpet mills lagged behind the national average for value-added in manufacturing ($7.84), carpet making was clearly well above average in terms of value-added within the state and the textile industry. In addition, Georgia's carpet mills paid a much smaller percentage of total revenues out as wages than other textile mills. Production workers' wages as a percentage of value-added in Georgia textile mills amounted to 46 percent, while carpet mills paid out only 23 percent in wages in 1963. Labor formed a much smaller portion of total cost in the carpet segment of textile manufacture. Employers had, therefore, some flexibility to boost wages, and they did. By 1967, carpet mills had slightly increased the share of value-added paid out in wages (to 25 percent), while the proportion for all textiles in the state fell (to 42 percent).[40] Though limited, these small wage gains, combined with the freedom to choose an employer, defused unrest, particularly among younger workers, in the Dalton district. Limited paternalism, personal contact, and expanded benefits helped keep older workers in place.

TTMA also publicized the efforts of area carpet mills to improve community life. In one of the best-publicized episodes, the trade association encouraged members to contribute to a fund for building a new recreation center in Dalton. Cabin Crafts ($27,500), Barwick Mills ($15,000), and Coronet Carpets ($10,000), three of the largest Dalton mills, contributed the lion's share of funds, but smaller firms also participated. Star Finishing contributed $1,000 to the building fund in 1962, joining three other smaller firms.[41] Such corporate philanthropy promoted the idea that carpet mills were good corporate citizens.

The larger mills in the Dalton district also began tentative "economic education" efforts. Barwick Mills, the leading firm in the area in the 1960s, established a newsletter in the midst of the union campaign in the early 1960s. The Barwick newsletter promoted the company's scholarship program for employees and their children and published columns extolling the virtues of free enterprise and explaining the concept of risk. The *B-Line News* told workers that the best way to build job security was through individual effort and that management needed maximum freedom in making decisions about work assignments in order to maintain the company's competitive edge.[42] Workers traded the promise of collective security for the reality of being able to choose from a variety of employers.

Star Finishing was a relatively small firm in the early 1960s and remained on the periphery of these developments. John Kirk recalled that TWUA organizers tried to make inroads at Star Finishing, but Kirk and other Star employees were less than receptive. Kirk's father had died at a young age, forcing his mother into the workforce. Kirk's family moved into the Crown Mill village, and his mother went to work in the cotton mill. She joined the union at Crown, "but all she got out of it was the privilege of paying union dues." Kirk remembered that his mother became increasingly disenchanted with the Crown TWUA local. Kirk, then, had little inclination to join a union. Moreover, he had imbibed at least some of the economic education that permeated the air in Dalton during that period. Kirk remembered telling union organizers that "if a man had the know-how and ability to build a business, then he should be able to run it as he saw fit," with no interference from a union. He recalled that this sentiment was common among Star Finishing's stable core of production workers.[43]

Kirk well remembered the labor turnover of the 1960s and 1970s, though. Star's manufacturing superintendent, Walter Hemphill, often used to say, "if they can walk or crawl, drag 'em in here," according to Kirk. But Kirk also observed that while warm bodies were much in demand, not all the transient workers who passed through Star Finishing's doors were worth keeping. The key, he believed, was to maintain a core of good, reliable, and experienced workers as machine operators and in maintenance. In other areas, turnover was less costly, though never free of cost for management, of course. Star (and other companies) instituted profit-sharing plans in the 1960s to encourage workers to remain in place. Workers might now be able to identify a stake in the company's future. Later, Shaw Industries converted the profit-sharing plan into a 401K retirement plan, but the goal was the same.[44] Bob Shaw's management style seemed suited to accomplishing these goals.

Carpet manufacturers slightly increased wages and granted paid holidays, health insurance, profit-sharing plans, and other benefits during the 1960s, in part as a response to urging by the trade association. Workers from the one island of unionism in the Dalton district (Calhoun's Dixie Belle Mills) soon learned that non-union employees gained similar or (occasionally) superior benefits. Raymond Roach, president of the local union in Calhoun, remarked that TWUA tried to expand from its base at Dixie Belle. Workers from other mills would occasionally attend union meetings in the mid-1960s. Management responded to any expression of sympathy for the union by granting a new paid holiday, by making a ten-cent-per-hour wage increase, or by firing a particularly obnoxious supervisor. In fact, some Dixie Belle workers believed that the existence of their local benefited unorganized workers more than union members. Some felt that in order to discourage their workers from joining the union, managers of unorganized mills offered more holidays, wage increases, and benefits than the union won through its contract negotiations. The title of a recent book on southern textile labor aptly summarized the view of many unorganized workers in such a situation—*"What Do We Need a Union For?"*[45] Workers in the Dalton area opted to remain unorganized.

Textile World profiled Star Finishing in October 1962, less than two years after the firm opened. The venerable trade journal encapsulated Star Finishing's credo in a single word: "efficiency." The word summarized the Shaw philosophy as well as any, and it was evident at this early date in the company's history. Efficiency was "the byword" when Bob and Bud Shaw "decided there was room for a $750,000 carpet dyehouse in Dalton, Georgia." Both tufters and finishers faced a boom market in the 1960s, but the capital requirements differed dramatically. Finishers faced greater investments in equipment but also stood to gain greater profit margins from efficient operation. From the beginning, Star Finishing sought economies of scale through constant expansion.[46]

Star opened in 1960 with six Gowin Machinery Company dye becks. By October 1962, the number had grown to eleven. Star's early product mix emphasized the still relatively new BCF nylon products. Inexpensive level-loop BCF nylon carpets accounted for about 85 percent of Star's production, with the remainder divided among cut-pile goods, wool-face rugs, and a scattering of cotton carpets. Star's weekly production amounted to 200,000 pounds in 1962. Rolls handled varied from 100 to 400 feet in length, almost all in either 12-foot or 15-foot widths. The *Textile World* profile offered a glimpse into the process of beck-dyeing carpets in the early 1960s. Star began "with jute-backed tufted carpets right off the tufting machines. Loads are made up to weigh 575 to 600 pounds, where the order permits." Smaller loads could be processed, *Textile World* noted, though "less economically."

The first step in the dyeing process involved "wetting-out" the carpet by bathing it in warm water (110 degrees Fahrenheit) mixed with trisodium phosphate and detergent. This helped get the yarn ready for dyeing and also started the process of shrinking the jute backing. As the jute shrank, it would "close in on the tufts and help lock them in place."[47] Star and other finishing companies had two options in beck dyeing—rope and open-width. In both methods, the ends of the carpet roll are sewn together to form a loop and passed over a reel many times (see figure C). In open-width dyeing, the only difference is the addition of a spreader roll. Without the spreader roll, carpeting, particularly lighter weights, could crease and fold. The spreader roll reduced this problem, but occasionally caused another—poor center-side color matching. Rope dyeing offered more even dye penetration and greater speed. The rope-dyeing method has always been far more popular in the United States because of the speed and superior center-side matching, while most European carpet finishers have preferred the open-width method.[48]

Star Finishing used both methods, occasionally on the same piece of carpeting. Heavier carpets—generally 20 ounces of face yarn per square yard or more—rarely presented a creasing problem in rope dyeing. Carpet constructions with 14 to 16 ounces of face yarn, on the other hand, created a much greater likelihood of creasing and benefited from the spreader roll. Star often combined the two methods on these lighter-weight carpets.[49]

Operators then added dyes and began increasing the temperature inside the beck, 2–4 degrees per minute, until it reached atmospheric boiling, or 212 degrees. Workers checked the carpet after half an hour. Additional dye often had to be added at this point to reach the proper shade, which meant another 10–15 minutes. The carpet then got a 10-minute cold rinse. The entire process of piece-dyeing a 400-foot roll of carpet might take, then, as much as two hours. Star added cationic and antistatic materials at this last stage to reduce the tendency of the carpet to soil. Lighter-weight carpets were then pulled and smoothed out in a brief round of finishing in an open-width beck with a spreader roll. A power-driven reel then hauled the carpet out and piled it onto long trucks or into buggies for transport to the dryer. Star's 70-foot Gowin dryers could process carpet at speeds ranging from 8 to 22 feet per minute, depending on weight and fiber content.[50]

Whirlwind growth characterized Star Finishing's first year of operation. In the early years, Bob Shaw played many roles. Walter Hemphill remembered what struck him most the first time he came to Dalton to interview with Shaw. "I was impressed with his age"—at the time, Shaw was thirty-one—"being as young as he was in the position he was in. Here was a young man who had been thrust into a business that was prosperous, that was busy, that was rushing. Bob was trying to do the managing, the selling—he was our salesman when I came here. He was wearing several hats, and it soon became apparent that he had more than any one man should have on him. So we began to think in terms of building the management team early on."[51]

Carl Pate was a key building block in that early management team. Pate

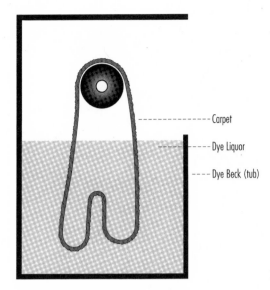

Carpet

Dye Liquor

Dye Beck (tub)

Figure C: Beck dyeing

graduated from Clemson in 1956 with a degree in textile manufacturing. After his graduation, he had worked with American Viscose, a leading supplier of fiber for U.S. textile manufacturers. Early on Pate had focused on the growing number of tufted rug and carpet manufacturers of the Dalton area, developing close contacts with the new industry. By late 1962, Pate was assistant coordinator of acetate sales for American Viscose. Bob Shaw again exhibited an eye for talent when he created a new position to attract Pate in January 1963—sales manager for Star Finishing.[52] Shaw had decided that, as Walter Hemphill observed, he could no longer do it all and needed capable help. Bob Shaw, then, was already beginning the process of creating a team, overcoming one of the weaknesses that often handicaps entrepreneurs—the obsession to handle every detail.

"Carl was the best salesman that any Shaw entity has ever had," according to Warren Sims. "He was one of the reasons that Star Finishing was the largest commercial finisher in the industry." Moreover, Sims remembered, "Carl Pate was among Bob Shaw's best friends." Bill Lusk, who came to Star Finishing in 1967 as company controller, affirmed Pate's sales ability: "He could sell snow cones to the Eskimos. It was just what he loved to do." Pate's energy and ability helped Star increase its account base rapidly in the mid-1960s. Pate was an excellent salesman, but what made him exceptional, Lusk observed, was his ability "to understand what he was doing. He knew when he made pricing decisions, he knew the impact on the profitability of the business." More significantly, "he was also Bob's friend. He could walk into Bob's office and express himself without getting in trouble. Bob at that time was young and volatile and temperamental, but Carl understood him, and they were good partners."[53]

Carl Pate died in 1977 of a heart attack. Pate's death "was a blow to all of us," Lusk recalled. "Over time, the sales area has probably seen more changes than any other management division," the longtime company treasurer observed, as Pate's shoes proved difficult to fill with one person. Pate had helped Bob Shaw "immensely" in the creation of Star Finishing and Shaw Industries.[54]

Star Finishing's expansion plans suffered a serious setback that would test the company's ability to weather hard times just two years after the company went into operation. Two workers were killed and three more injured in a boiler explosion early on the morning of March 11, 1963. Boiler room operator William E. Davis, thirty-seven, and vat operator Herbert Painter, twenty-three, died in an explosion that "ripped the boiler room to pieces." Star management faced two difficult tasks in caring for the families of the deceased and in re-building.[55]

The advantages of industrial concentration were never more apparent than during the ensuing crisis. Star Finishing benefited from the aid of competitors and the understanding of customers, almost all of whom were also neighbors. Bob Shaw initially announced that the company would have to suspend operations for as much as six weeks while repairs were made. By March 25, though, Star was ready to begin limited operations. Rival finishing companies allowed Star to rent their facilities for limited periods to fill backlogged orders, and tufted carpet manufacturers accepted delays in processing orders. In essence, Star's rivals—such as Rollins Jolly's Constellation, for example—did not try to take advantage of the situation but instead helped give Star breathing space to get back on its feet. As Bob Shaw observed when Star Finishing reopened, "No spirit of cooperation can top what our competitors have done to help following the disaster."[56]

Warren Sims was still with the First National Bank of Dalton when the explosion occurred. "The whole community poured out, particularly the suppliers—Lee Office Supply, First National Bank, and others—to be sure that all of Star Finishing's needs were met" and to give "any help they needed to the families who had lost a loved one, any physical help they needed. People were there on the spot," including Sims's boss at the bank, George Rice, who would later serve on the Shaw Industries board of directors. The incident illustrated, Sims pointed out, the close-knit nature of the business community of Dalton.[57]

The precise cause of the explosion was apparently never determined, but authorities assured the community that all equipment and safety procedures had been maintained according to insurance standards. John Kirk recalled that this was not the first boiler explosion in Dalton or at Star. The company did announce that it would move a main gas line "to strike off any remote possibility of it being near any new equipment."[58]

The explosion highlighted the importance of safety considerations in this emerging new industry. By the mid-1970s, the tufted carpet and rug industry boasted a lost workday accident rate well below the national average for all manufacturing, but it was still slightly higher than the average for all textile mills. A decade later, safety conditions had improved, thanks in part to individual mill efforts and workshops offered by the trade association. By the end of the 1980s, a carpet mill worker was slightly less likely to be involved in a lost workday accident than the average textile worker.[59]

Star Finishing seemed to have recovered fully by autumn. The company announced new expansion plans as the Dalton Boosters named Star Finishing the city's "Industry of the Month" in September 1963. The *Daily Citizen-News* paraphrase of Bob Shaw's explanation of the firm's continued expansion simply captured the spirit of the Dalton carpet district in the go-go 1960s: "Company President R. E. Shaw explained that Star Finishing is continually expanding because the entire tufted textile industry is growing." Bob Shaw went on to project that the trend would continue: "The future growth of Star Finishing will be in keeping with the growth of the tufting industry." The latest expansion would more than triple the original 22,000 square feet of space Star had occupied in January 1961. Star would soon have a new central dye department where all dyes and chemicals would be prepared in mixing tanks and piped directly to dye becks. Star's 105 employees earned a payroll of more than $500,000 annually, and the company's assets, including buildings, were valued at more than $1 million.[60]

Star Finishing continued to grow over the next four years. By 1967, the company had become the largest commission finisher in the carpet industry. During the first half of the 1960s, Bob's brother, Bud, had played a large role in Star Finishing's affairs, but Bud clearly had many other irons in the fire during those years. Warren Sims recalled that though Bud was Clarence Shaw's eldest son, "there was no thought of Bud coming back" to run the family business. "Bud was a career person with J. P. Stevens." Sims felt that Bud enjoyed part-ownership of Star Finishing "at a distance."[61]

In spite of that distance, Bud Shaw played a key role in Star Finishing. The elder Shaw brother brought several talented textile men into the Star operation in the early 1960s. Shaw hired George Kirkpatrick away from Cabin Crafts, for example, and brought him into the Rocky Creek Mills operation. Later, Kirkpatrick took Shaw's place at Rocky Creek. Shaw then brought Kirkpatrick back to Dalton to work with Star Finishing. Bud Shaw also brought Doug Squillario into the Star operation. Squillario came from the J. P. Stevens organization; Shaw had come into contact with him through Rocky Creek Mills. Walter Hemphill also came to Star through the Marion Manufacturing/Rocky Creek/Bud Shaw connection.

Marion Manufacturing sold the physical assets of Rocky Creek Mills—the carpet yarn facility—to J. P. Stevens in 1964, against Bud Shaw's wishes. Stevens integrated the yarn operation more fully into the company's growing business in manufacturing automotive floor mats. Stevens asked Bud Shaw to move to Greenville, South Carolina, to run the automotive division. "That was very traumatic on our family," Bud's son Julius recalled. "I remember him announcing it in August of 1964. We loved Statesville; we did not want to move." But the family moved in October 1964.[62]

"I came in to J. P. Stevens as manager of their yarn plant and then became manager of their overall automotive plant, which meant I had the responsibility for the making of the floor mats and the making of the yarns," Bud Shaw recalled. Even though the floor mats were produced just like tufted rugs and carpets, Shaw warned: "Now, don't ever get floor mats for automobiles confused with being in the carpet business. That's an automotive part just like a headlight is. I got a good enough taste of Detroit" during this period. "You know, we had [only] three customers with the specialty product," the major U.S. automakers.[63]

Bud Shaw impressed his employers at Stevens and other textile firms. In July 1965, Dan River Mills offered him a job that would bring the family back to its northwest Georgia roots. Dan River wanted Bud Shaw to run its carpet mill in White, Georgia. White was a small community in northern Bartow County, just a few miles from Cartersville. "Dad liked the fact that this was a carpet mill," Julius observed; "he had worked in yarn mills up to now (Crown, Rocky Creek, and Stevens), and the carpet industry was evolving." Carpet was an exciting new industry, and Bud Shaw was glad to get an opportunity to get into this emerging industry right in his own backyard. So the family moved again, though this move amounted to a homecoming.[64]

"If Jim Daughdrill had not received a call to the ministry," Warren Sims insisted in a 1999 interview, "there never would have been a Shaw Industries as we know it today." Daughdrill was the president of Kingston Mills in White, Georgia. He received a call to the ministry in the Presbyterian Church in 1964, and he and his father decided to sell the company to Dan River Mills. Daughdrill went on to become the highly effective president of the prestigious Presbyterian Rhodes College. It was his career decision that set in motion the chain of events that brought Bud Shaw back to Bartow County and into the north-west Georgia carpet business. Sims explained that Dan River "called Bud down from Greenville to become general manager of what became Dan River Carpets in White, Georgia."[65]

Dan River's purchase of Kingston Mills also brought Warren Sims into the carpet industry. Sims would prove to be an invaluable member of the management team at Shaw Industries over the next three decades, though he seemed an unlikely candidate for such a change in the mid-1960s. By 1964, "I had been the vice president and cashier of the First National Bank in Dalton for eleven years," he stated, so one might have expected him to remain with First National and perhaps serve as its president at some point in the future. Sims went on to explain, however, that he was only a few years younger than his immediate boss at the bank, so his chances of moving up were slim. Moreover, "most of my friends, relatives, and associates were in carpet or carpet-related businesses." Indeed, during the late 1950s, Sims "told the First National Bank that at some point in time I was going into the carpet business. They were very understanding and generous and wanted me to stay. They said, 'You just let us know when you find something.'" Sims even went to work at Cabin Crafts—on the night shift—on a trial basis in the early 1960s to learn something about the business and to try it out. Though he decided not to leave the bank to go to work full-time for an old established firm like Cabin Crafts (owned in part by his uncle, Bob McCamy), Sims remained interested in the carpet business and kept his eyes and ears open for opportunities.[66]

The right opportunity came in 1965. Sims's old high school pal, Bud Shaw, came back to Georgia to run Dan River's newly acquired carpet mill. "Bud came to Dan River, and I came down here and talked to him. I decided that's what I wanted to do, so I went back and told the bank that I'd found what I wanted to do. I became office manager at Dan River Carpets." Sims thus began his carpet career. "That lasted a year or so. We made Dan River Carpets profitable." Bud Shaw's management skills played no small role in helping Dan River turn a profit at the White plant. "Bud Shaw was a manager's manager," Sims recalled. Shaw had graduated from Georgia Tech with a degree in textile engineering, and he seemed to have a knack for the correct application of textbook management techniques. "He did things the way the book said to do them. He taught me a lot. Bud Shaw ran his companies by the book."[67]

Sims cited the Dan River Christmas party as an example of Shaw's management style. "When we had our Christmas party at Dan River, we had it at two o'clock in the morning. Bud said, 'Those third-shift people are just as important as our first-shift people.'" Sims tried "to get a preacher to pray and couldn't get one to come out at that time, so I had to say the blessing." Bud Shaw's second- and third-shift plant visits became a trademark. "Bud visited those plants on the third shift. That was one of his favorite things to do, to go and talk to the machine operators, fixers, creelers at three o'clock in the morning. That got their attention, and he loved that attention. And he has maintained those relationships with those people, even now. And it's because he did it the way the book said you ought to." Shaw was a popular manager among production workers because he made them feel that they were an integral part of the operation.[68] Bud Shaw was not a paternalist, but he did make expressions of concern for the lives of his employees a regular part of his routine. He also made certain that production workers were treated with respect and dignity at a time when management skills in the carpet industry were, to put it charitably, less than adequate. Bud Shaw stood out as a top manager.

Dan River's management was so pleased with the turnaround at the White mill, Sims recounted, that "they wanted us to make Wunda Weve Carpets in Greenville, which they also owned, profitable." Dan River decided to combine the two carpet operations and leave only a yarn manufacturing facility in White, Georgia. They invited everyone to go to Greenville." This put Shaw and Sims in a difficult position. "They wanted Bud to stay and run the yarn mill, but Bud said he had run a yarn mill when he was twenty-three years old, and he could do better than that, so he was going into the carpet business. So he resigned." Bud Shaw, then, made the decision that the time was right to enter the carpet business on his own terms.

Sims hesitated. "I said, 'Well, I'm new in the textile business; I've only been here a year, so I think I'd like to stay. I don't want to move to Greenville, but I'd like to stay with Dan River Carpets' yarn mill." Sims remained with the yarn mill in White, and in the process "we closed down the carpet customer service section. Thirty people who had worked for me ended up either getting new jobs or moving to Greenville. One day Clyde Johnson, their treasurer, flew down to Cartersville from Wunda Weve and very gently told me that I didn't have anybody reporting to me, and they really didn't need me any longer." So Warren Sims, less than two years after leaving a safe, secure job at First National Bank, was unemployed. The Dan River experience, though, "gave me a good education. I had the customer service division, the planning section, the accounting section, and personnel, and all of those divisions were reporting to me." Sims now had extensive experience in managing personnel in the carpet industry.[69]

Bud Shaw had already begun putting together a carpet operation in partnership with George Lane, a former vice president with Barwick Mills. Shaw now invited Sims to join the new firm. "I told him that I wasn't sure whether I wanted to do that or not, and I decided to look around. So I went to a head-hunter down in the Fulton National Bank building in Atlanta to see what was available. I was going up the elevator in Fulton National Bank Building, and I ran into a past paid executive with the Georgia Bankers Association and a vice president of Fulton National Bank. He offered me a job in the elevator." Sims explained that he was on his way to an interview and would think about the offer, but "I had already decided that I was not going to work in Atlanta. Driving from Cartersville to Atlanta to work every morning was not something I wanted to do the rest of my life. So I came back and told Bud that I still wasn't sure, but I'd be glad to help them get started."[70]

Julius Shaw remembered sitting around the family dinner table in 1967 and tossing around names for his father's new company. It was "an exciting experience," starting a new business. Warren Sims recalled coming up with the name that stuck. "My uncle had been shot down over Ploesti in the first Ploesti oil raid" during World War II, he explained. "My grandmother had just died, so I had to go up to Dalton for the funeral. I had admired for years the saber he used when he was at West Point. While nobody was looking, I took that saber off the wall and brought it to Cartersville." When they were trying to come up with a name for Bud and George's carpet mill, Sims saw the saber on the wall and suggested Sabre Carpets, "because the leader always carries a saber. So we named it Sabre Carpet Mills. And then I decided that I might as well go in this thing, I was that deeply involved."[71]

Sabre effectively had a standby workforce "because of the layoffs at Dan River in the carpet operation." The partners hired many of Dan River's old production workers, brought Ken Woodall down as plant manager, and brought in "a couple of the ladies" from the old Dan River operation to run the office. Within six months, Sabre was "selling at the rate of about $4.6 million a year." Bud Shaw, always on the lookout for new ideas and opportunities, soon found one. With the new company barely six months old, Bud announced his intention to buy the Philadelphia Carpet Company, a 120-year-old firm with deep roots in the old woven industry and an established trade name.[72]

Just as Bud Shaw's Rocky Creek Mills had helped in the creation of Star Finishing, Bob Shaw and Star became partners in the Philadelphia venture. The 1967 Philadelphia acquisition created the business organization that would eventually become Shaw Industries at about the same time that Star Finishing began moving into a new and lucrative product line—printed carpets. Bob and Bud Shaw began creating an organization in the 1960s that would help transform the entire carpet industry over the next two decades.

CHAPTER THREE

A Philadelphia Story

About six months after Sabre Carpets went into operation, Bud Shaw walked into the office one day and asked Warren Sims, "What would you think about buying Philadelphia Carpet?" Sims told his friend that he was "crazy as hell." But Bud Shaw had already held preliminary discussions with Philadelphia manager Dick Culbertson. Shaw had little patience for tedium and constantly sought new challenges. He had moved up the ladder quickly at Stevens and Dan River but had always chafed at outside control. Shaw took advantage of the Dan River consolidation to launch his own carpet business. He, Sims, and others made that business successful quickly, but within six months Shaw again was on the lookout for new opportunities. Warren Sims observed that Bud was "never a detail person," that he was always more interested in the big picture. His brother, Bob, saw Bud a little differently: "He is a lot more interested in creating than running. He likes to play in a lot of things." Bob insisted that Bud was great at details as long as he was interested in a project. Bob agreed with the assessment of longtime Shaw associates such as Ken Jackson that Bud could quickly cut to the heart of the matter in any meeting and was excellent at identifying and crystallizing crucial issues.[1] He found this sort of strategic role much more to his liking than managing the day-to-day affairs of a company. Shaw found his next challenge virtually next door in the Philadelphia Carpet Company.

Revonah Spinning Mills, a leading supplier to the carpet trade, published a pamphlet profiling the leading firms in the old woven carpet industry in 1960. According to the Revonah publication, Philadelphia Carpet Company dated its origin back to 1846, "when Philip Doerr set up hand looms to produce ingrain carpets in a house next door to his residence in Philadelphia." Doerr, following the customary procedure, rented the looms to weavers and furnished them with wool yarn and other materials. He also rented a nearby store in which to sell the carpets. Doerr and the hand weavers split the proceeds fifty-fifty. Doerr's sons joined him in the business in the late 1860s. In 1870, the Doerr family shifted some of its production from hand to power looms, closed the store, and built a factory. Naming the reorganized firm Philip Doerr and Sons, the family expanded its ingrain line to include both 27-inch- and 36-inch-wide carpets.[2]

Philip Doerr and sons expanded in 1904, renting another mill across the street for the production of velvet carpets, also in the traditional 27-inch and 36-inch widths. The new mill was called Philadelphia Carpet Company, the first appearance of that name. The company closed its original mill building in 1908 and adopted Philadelphia Carpet Company as the name for the entire firm, not just the velvet mill. In 1918, the company moved to a building at Allegheny Avenue and C Street. It continued to produce narrow-width carpets exclusively until 1929. The firm expanded into broadloom production for the first time in the year of the stock market crash by "purchasing the wide looms of John and James Dobson," another Philadelphia carpet maker. The Doerr family built a "modern new plant" at the same Allegheny Avenue and C Street location in 1937 and consolidated all weaving operations at that location. The company also added its first 15-foot Wilton looms that year. Like most textile firms, Philadelphia converted to military production during World War II. The company wove cotton duck and tarpaulins for U.S. and Allied forces from 1942 through mid-1945.[3]

"The next notable advance" for Philadelphia Carpet Company, according to the 1960 summary, "occurred in 1958, with the acquisition of a tufting mill in Cartersville, Georgia." This acquisition reflected a general trend among the old woven carpet establishment. Most woven mills moved to establish a presence in tufting during the 1950s. Philadelphia Carpet Company was still very much a family-owned and -operated business. Herbert Doerr Sr., grandson of Philip Doerr, was president of the company, and one of his sons, John, served as executive vice president. The move into tufting caused controversy among Doerr family members. According to former Philadelphia employees, it was another of Herbert's sons, Herbert (Bud) Jr., who pushed for the move into tufting. Herbert Sr. opposed the company's foray into the new technology, while son John acquiesced.[4]

The Doerrs technically acquired a tufted carpet mill called Mylu in December 1957, though the new management did not take over the mill until 1958. Mylu owners Stuart Myers and Hans Lutjens (hence the name) sold their firm to John and Bud Doerr, and Lutjens stayed on as plant superintendent. John served as president and general manager, and Bud became vice president, treasurer, and sales manager for Mylu and also continued as sales manager for

Philadelphia. Philadelphia took over all distribution of Mylu products, but the two companies, for the time being, remained separate entities. The Mylu name was dropped, and the company was now dubbed Doerr Carpets.[5]

Philadelphia Carpet Company entered the tufting arena in 1958, but the old firm kept its traditional marketing philosophy intact. Philadelphia had always "pursued a marketing policy of selective distribution that encourage[d] the realization of full mark-ups for its retail accounts."[6] The company's philosophy of limited distribution and slow growth fit the old woven industry. The company tried to bring that philosophy to the new field of tufted carpet but had limited success.

Spright Holland became involved with the Philadelphia Carpet Company in the early 1960s. Holland was born in Blount County, Alabama—Sand Mountain—in 1936 and grew up in the Heart of Dixie. He received an undergraduate degree in industrial engineering from Auburn University and an MBA in accounting from the University of Alabama (and subsequently suffered from a split personality at least one Saturday afternoon each November when the two rivals met on the football field). He went to work for the major accounting firm of Arthur Andersen after graduating from Alabama. One of his first account assignments was the Philadelphia Carpet Company. He observed firsthand the effects of the firm's limited-distribution philosophy: "The philosophy of that company was not to get all that big. They believed in limited distribution, and they restricted distribution. They would only sell maybe one account in a town. They had only about one salesman per state," even in tufting. "They were not really interested in getting real big." The Philadelphia Carpet Company "was a high-end wool company, even in the tufting end of the business." Philadelphia used pre-dyed yarns almost exclusively, even when the firm began using some synthetic fibers, including "Acrilan, which was cheaper, but it was still a pre-dyed yarn." The Philadelphia Carpet Company management simply was not interested in trying to penetrate the emerging low-end mass market by moving toward piece dyeing. Holland noted that the technology of weaving in carpet manufacture did not lend itself as easily to mass production. "You couldn't make that much anyway. You could only get so much off those looms. Some of them were 27-inch looms, which were used" to make carpeting "for corridors and small public spaces. They couldn't afford" to grow much, and "they didn't believe in that philosophy anyway."[7] While the philosophy originated in the realm of woven carpeting, the Doerr family clung to it even in the midst of the tufting revolution. They tried to apply the old strategy—make high-quality products, limit the distribution, keep the prices up, and make good profit margins on low volume—to tufting. The changing nature of the carpet marketplace in the 1950s and 1960s made the Doerrs' strategy obsolete.

There was apparently conflict within the Doerr family, and Herbert Doerr Jr. abruptly resigned from the firm in June 1960. Two years later, the Philadelphia Carpet Company merged the Cartersville operation fully into its old organization and dropped the Doerr Carpets name. The family made an effort to revive the company's sagging fortunes with decisive moves, both geographically and in terms of product mix.

In February 1963, John Doerr announced that the Philadelphia Carpet Company would close its weaving mill. The company would maintain its general offices, customer service and purchasing departments, warehouse space, and cut order department at the old Allegheny Avenue and C Street location. It would drop three of its nine lines of woven carpets, and the remaining six lines would continue in limited production through a contract arrangement with the Hardwick and Magee Company. In making the announcement, John Doerr said that the move was being made to free working capital in order to expand the company's overall operations and make technological improvements—that is, new machines—at the Cartersville plant. "These new arrangements will greatly strengthen Philadelphia's competitive position," Doerr insisted. "As everyone in the industry knows, the phenomenal growth of tufting has made heavy inroads into woven qualities, especially at popular price levels." In making changes at Philadelphia, "we are being realistic," Doerr acknowledged.[8]

A few months later, in June 1963, John Doerr announced that the company would move its headquarters from Philadelphia to Cartersville, thus leaving the city that had given the firm its name. The physical shift of the company's base of operations gave tacit recognition to the dominance of tufting in the carpet industry. It also created an anomalous, and in a sense amusing, situation: a company created in and named for a large, bustling northern city was now based in a small, sleepy southern town.[9] This would not be the last instance of such incongruities in the carpet industry.

At the same time, the Philadelphia Carpet Company quietly dropped the marketing of all its woven running lines, though the firm continued to produce commercial woven goods through its contract relationship with Hardwick and Magee. Philadelphia thus exited the residential market in woven carpeting. Interestingly, John Doerr insisted that Philadelphia had not dropped the woven lines until the company was convinced that it could "successfully produce all its woven lines on tufted machinery." In fact, he announced that his company would introduce the first tufted simulations of old Philadelphia woven products later that year. The decision to try and duplicate existing woven styles with tufting machines clearly revealed the conservatism of Philadelphia's management.[10]

While Philadelphia focused more attention on the tufting operation after 1963, it soon had to reopen a portion of its old manufacturing plant. The building had been sold, but the company leased a portion of it in which to produce specialty carpets. "The reason they opened it back up," Spright Holland recalled, "was that they were able to hire a few agents of another company that had just gone out of business which had been selling to hotels, especially the Las Vegas and New York markets. They were making specialized high-end carpet for the hotel-casino type business." Intricately patterned woven carpets held the hotel market longer than others because of their durability and capacity to hide damage.[11]

Former Philadelphia salesman Bob Foltz commented on the use of wool carpets in the hotel and casino trade. "We made a lot of carpet for Las Vegas and out that way. See, they liked wool carpet as against the early nylons because if you dropped a cigarette on wool, it would burn out without going all the way through to the back. You could go in there with a knife and scoop out the edge of the ashes, and it wasn't too visible. But nylon, or anything synthetic, that cigarette would go right to the back." He remembered a later effort to make a nylon carpet via printing that might hide those ugly burns. "We made a [printed] carpet one time with burnt cigarettes all over it," so that cigarette burns would not be as noticeable.[12]

John Doerr made a valiant effort to succeed in tufting with a woven philosophy. He hired Dick Culberson as the new general manager for the Philadelphia Carpet Company when it moved to Cartersville in 1963. Culberson had an extensive background in textiles. *Home Furnishings Daily* noted that Culberson "had spent 11 years in various posts in the production phases of the textile industry." More recently, Culberson had been a manager in the administrative services division of Arthur Andersen and had worked on the company's transfer to Georgia along with Spright Holland. Holland joined Culberson in leaving Arthur Andersen to embark on a new career in the carpet industry. Holland remained at the Philadelphia Carpet Company through the company's acquisition by the Shaw family, and he remains a valuable figure at Shaw Industries today.[13]

Philadelphia also expanded its operation in Cartersville. The company bought an adjacent plant in September 1963 that brought the firm's total production and warehouse space to more than 100,000 square feet. The company estimated that this expansion would make possible a 25 percent increase in its custom tufting production.[14]

John Doerr reshuffled and expanded his sales staff and hired Travis (Dusty) Rhodes as Philadelphia's new director of product development. Rhodes, a well-known commodity in the northwest Georgia tufting district, had worked as a designer for Cabin Crafts, James Lees, and Coronet. He was one of the leading proponents of high-end, high-style products in the industry. He spent much of his life crusading against the "race to the bottom" mentality in the tufted carpet industry and advocating more emphasis on style and greater value-added in terms of design. This move clearly signaled that Philadelphia intended to retain its position in the medium to high end of the marketplace— with a definite tilt toward the high end. If Philadelphia were going to go with the tufting revolution, it would at least try to go in style.[15]

In spite of all these efforts, the Philadelphia Carpet Company continued to struggle. By the mid-1960s, "we were in a cash bind, we had cash-flow problems," according to Spright Holland. "We didn't have any capital for growth. What really got us was this. They had come up with a site in Cartersville— about 40 acres—to build a new plant, and a bank there had agreed to build us a building out there. Due to some kind of zoning [technicality] it got turned down at the last minute. That was the last straw. We were past due with everybody and couldn't really grow." Several companies had inquired about the availability of Philadelphia Carpet, and the Doerrs began listening more seriously to those offers. They "saw a way to get enough money to retire comfortably, so they decided to sell it. In addition, it had always been a family business, and John Doerr's son was not interested in—or capable of—running the company, so he didn't have anybody to turn it over to. His only choice was to sell out."[16]

Holland remembered the period leading up to the sale. His boss, Dick Culberson, "knew that John Doerr wanted to sell the company, and Dick wanted to sell it to someone" who would allow him to "stay in the company." Culberson essentially took on the responsibility of finding a buyer. "We talked to several companies that were trying to buy us out, and it didn't work. We talked to Armstrong and several others, and, of course, they didn't buy it." Then Culberson ran into Bud Shaw and "got him interested."[17]

Cabin Crafts was among the potential buyers for Philadelphia. Jack Turner, president of the West Point subsidiary, recalled that Cabin Crafts had attempted to buy the Philadelphia Carpet Company before the Shaws made their move. In 1967 Turner "was trying to get our folks to buy Philadelphia, and I kind of put on a full-court press. I had talked to the Philadelphia people, and they wanted to sell. We kind of had first shot at that. But it just so happened that West Point had just completed the merger with Pepperell to form West-Point Pepperell, and they were under investigation by the Justice Department to see whether they were going to have to unwind that merger. They had merged without Justice Department approval." The WestPoint Pepperell lawyers were against further acquisitions at that time. Turner told them, "Well, this is a little peanut acquisition. I know that we already have the Justice Department looking at us, but we wouldn't control enough of the carpet business to amount to anything." Nevertheless, the WestPoint Pepperell lawyers squelched the idea. "Bob and Bud Shaw made their deal with Philadelphia, and that really put Shaw on their way. But if it hadn't been for the WestPoint Pepperell merger, they never would have gotten it."[18] The history of Shaw Industries again intertwined with that of Cabin Crafts.

It was at this point that Bud Shaw had his fateful lunch meeting with Dick Culberson. "Culberson had told him that the Doerrs were either going to have to invest some more money or sell the company because it was too antiquated. Before Sabre got to be six or seven months old, the canary had swallowed the cat," commented Warren Sims. Bud Shaw, "a master at getting financing," obtained a loan from First National Bank of Atlanta. "He also invited his brother Bob in with Star Finishing. In 1967, we formed Philadelphia Holding Company, and the whole purpose was to acquire Philadelphia Carpet," Warren Sims recalled.[19]

Views of the Philadelphia Carpet Company acquisition varied among top Shaw Industries officials. Bob Shaw emphasized the element of chance involved by observing, "So, with all our brilliance, we went into the carpet business." Bill Lusk, who became Star controller in 1967, characterized the acquisition as a "leveraged buyout, though they didn't call it that back then." Bud Shaw described the process similarly. "Essentially what I did was I bought it with [the Doerrs'] own money, and I used Walter E. Heller Company as the factor, as the primary source of money. I collateralized not only the plant and the machinery but the inventory plus signing personally on the note." In essence, Bud Shaw bought the Philadelphia Carpet Company by using Philadelphia as the collateral for loans. At the time Julius Shaw was a fourteen-year-old boarding student at the Darlington School in nearby Rome, Georgia. All he recalled was that his father "hocked everything we had."[20]

Bud Shaw also secured financing from the First National Bank of Atlanta. The bank wrote him to confirm the financing arrangements on December 12,

1967. The bank's letter spelled out in brief the commitments of the various parties to the acquisition, including both Shaw brothers and the Walter Heller factoring firm. "We want to participate in the financing of your acquisition of Philadelphia Carpet Company," the bank wrote, "by providing the following:

1. $150,000, equipment financing through our Leasing Department.
2. $250,000 secured by land and buildings.
3. $250,000 unsecured, guaranteed by Star Finishing Company, Bob Shaw, and yourself.
4. $800,000 as an undivided 50% participation in a $1,600,000 inventory loan made by Walter E. Heller & Company.
5. All of the above to be secured by the stock of Philadelphia Carpet Company.

The bank letter stated, "As you know, our position is contingent upon Walter E. Heller & Company providing a $600,000 over-loan and a $2,000,000 factoring line. Frank Cole has confirmed Walter E. Heller's commitment to provide this financing and has indicated his belief that the inventory loan will be approved."[21] Bob and Bud Shaw, along with their jointly owned company, Star Finishing, were on the hook for a quarter of a million dollars. In addition, Bud Shaw had signed a personal guarantee with Heller to obtain that portion of the financing. The entire arrangement was, of course, "secured by the stock of the Philadelphia Carpet Company," making it something of a leveraged buyout as characterized by Bill Lusk.

At the last minute, however, the First National Bank reneged on the loan agreement. To this day, Bud Shaw has not figured out precisely why. Scrambling to replace this critical financing, Shaw met with legendary Citizens and Southern Bank president Mills Lane. Lane stepped in to fill the gap, saying that "C&S wanted to become more involved with the Shaw brothers." The deal was saved.[22] Bud Shaw had taken a huge risk, though, in signing the Heller guarantee.

Bud and Bob Shaw formed the Philadelphia Holding Company for the purpose of buying the outstanding capital stock of Philadelphia. The holding company "was incorporated in December 1967," according to a Drexel Firestone summary, "and at that time acquired for cash all outstanding stock of Philadelphia Carpet Company." A few months later, in August 1968, "Philadelphia Holding Company acquired Star Finishing Company, Sabre Carpets, Inc., Star Dye Co., and Rocky Creek Mills, Inc., in an exchange of shares" and these entities were "merged into the company."[23] This brought Bob Shaw and Star Finishing more closely into the orbit of the Philadelphia Carpet Company, but the two companies continued to operate almost completely independently. Why create a holding company? Why not simply form a new corporation and merge Star, Philadelphia, Sabre, and the others? Bob Shaw explained that "we had a tax carryover with the holding company; that's the only reason we had Philadelphia Holding Company." The Shaws wanted to reap the maximum benefit from the tax carryforward.[24]

The stockholder list of the Philadelphia Holding Company illustrated the diverse ownership of the new entity. Marion Manufacturing Company held more than 22 percent of the holding company's stock (through the Rocky Creek Mills connection). In addition, a number of individuals associated with Marion held stock, bringing the total share held by "Marion interests" to 36.5 percent. John McCarty, who had been a silent partner in Star Dye, and the McCarty family held another 21.5 percent of Philadelphia stock. Bud Shaw, Bob Shaw, and other Shaw family members held 34 percent. A number of valued employees held small stakes, including Carl Pate, Walter Hemphill, Douglas Squillario, George Kirkpatrick, Warren Sims, Buddy Sewell, Dick Culberson, and Stuart Morrison. This block amounted to just over 7 percent.[25]

The division of responsibilities within the holding company was clear. Bob Shaw would continue to operate Star Finishing Company and focus on supplying other producers in the carpet industry while Bud Shaw managed Philadelphia and Sabre, the carpet-manufacturing segment of the business. There remained the issue of who would be chief executive officer of the holding company. In something of a surprise, according to close observers, stockholders named Bob Shaw CEO in late 1968. Bud Shaw was the elder brother and in many ways the more experienced textile manager. Moreover, he had initiated the deal and taken substantial personal risks that others had not. Apparently, the Marion and McCarty interests (who held a majority of Philadelphia Holding's stock between them) were dissatisfied with the performance of the Philadelphia Carpet Company portion of the business in the first year after the acquisition, while Star Finishing had prospered. Of course, the Philadelphia segment had been a struggling, nearly bankrupt company before the acquisition. While the Philadelphia Carpet Company had some potential long-term strengths and advantages, insiders understood that it would take some time to turn that operation around. According to family members and close associates, this situation caused no dissension between the brothers but actually led them to stick closer together. During the next few years, one of the family's main goals was to reduce the influence of the Marion interests over the new company's direction.[26]

Reversing the fortunes of the Philadelphia Carpet Company presented Bud

Shaw with a daunting challenge. The company "at the time was broke, flat broke," according to Bill Lusk. "They were very late getting out of the woven business." Warren Sims was equally blunt. The Philadelphia firm "had to be remade over and over," he recalled, because "it had antiquated equipment, bad logistics between Philadelphia and Cartersville and Dalton. The physical assets—machinery and plant—were awful." Sims and company found out quickly that Dick Culberson had been right: if the Doerrs had kept the company, they would have faced massive investments in new plants and equipment just to remain competitive. The Doerr family, however, had recruited and attracted some talented managers and workers. The best thing they got out of Philadelphia, according to Warren Sims, was "some wonderful people. Spright Holland, the controller, is one of the most effective and important people we have today at Shaw Industries. Some of the hourly employees have been with the company for a long time now. That asset—the people—was great."[27]

Bud Shaw attacked the Philadelphia Carpet Company's problems with vigor. Among the chief difficulties he faced was Philadelphia's poor credit rating. As Spright Holland had noted, Philadelphia "was past due with everybody." Suppliers were reluctant to extend any further credit. Bud Shaw and Spright Holland met with yarn suppliers to try to work out a deal. Shaw recalled convincing one supplier to "convert a $700,000 receivable into a note with interest." The idea caught on, and Shaw used it successfully with other suppliers. In order to move beyond the immediate crisis, Shaw converted short-term debts in the form of past-due bills into long-term loans from suppliers. It was "a tight situation," but Shaw's efforts began to pay off. While the new company was not yet thriving by any means, Bud Shaw had averted the immediate crisis and began to "turn Philadelphia around."[28]

Star and Philadelphia "were not integrated" for years, Spright Holland remembered. "We [Philadelphia] did some business with them [Star Finishing], but we had always been a big wool house—with pre-dyed yarns. We got into some white nylon, and Star acquired a finishing plant in Cartersville later," but in truth, most employees in Cartersville had little contact with Star's people in Dalton from 1968 through the mid-1970s.[29] Indeed, a majority of Star and Philadelphia employees at any level below top management probably did not know about the companies' connections. Walter Hemphill, who was vice president of manufacturing at Star, recalled that there were some difficult moments in the Philadelphia-Star relationship in those early years because of this lack of integration. "It created a little bit of a problem" for Star Finishing "when you had more than you could do—are you going to dye Philly's goods or somebody else's? We fought those battles as well as we could."[30]

The Philadelphia Carpet Company had a few other assets as well. A report by J. C. Bradford succinctly summarized Philadelphia's strengths and weaknesses and outlined Bud Shaw's new strategies for growth. The report's author, Norris Nielsen, noted:

Philadelphia Carpet had not succeeded as an independent tufted carpet manufacturer because of concentrating its efforts in the higher-priced segment of the market, thereby missing the dynamic growth in popular priced carpets made possible by the efficiencies of the tufting process. The higher-priced carpet market is estimated at about $150 million, or less than 10% of the total market. While Philadelphia has probably one of the four leading names in the higher-priced market, the potential for expanding volume was limited, which is so important to a profitable tufting operation.

The Shaw purchasing group recognized Philadelphia's weaknesses, and within four years after the acquisition in 1967, the Philadelphia brand had more than doubled its sales. Shaw accomplished this by expanding the Philadelphia brand into medium priced carpeting and by adding lower priced lines, sold through distributors under the Sabre name or under the distributors' own private labels.[31]

The carpet industry generally was plagued with very low brand-name identification, and this had been the case since World War II. Philadelphia Carpet had at least a small level of branded identity, and in a market where most goods had none, a little could mean a lot with retailers and distributors. Philadelphia also had good relations with loyal retailers who liked the high markups on quality goods. Shaw did not want to squander that reputation by quickly moving the company into the production of cheap commodity goods. So Bud Shaw moved slowly, taking cautious steps to try to maintain Philadelphia's quality reputation while expanding the label's sales and adding some less expensive tufted goods toward the middle of the industry's price scale. At the same time, he used the Sabre label and private labels to introduce commodity carpets. These strategies worked, as Nielsen observed in his report, and Philadelphia doubled its sales by 1971.

At Philadelphia, Bud Shaw continued the management style that had won the loyalty of workers at each of his earlier stops at Rocky Creek, Stevens, and Dan River. "Bud was a true engineer," according to Spright Holland. Though he had double-majored in organic chemistry and management rather than engineering, the Georgia Tech influence was obvious. "He believed in budgets, costs, contribution margins, gross profit margins, etc." Just as significantly, Bud Shaw "was a good people manager. He believed in going out and talking to the people out in the plants. He would go talk to the people on first shift, second shift, and third shift. He'd call them by their first name, and they would him, too. He really believed in getting out there and finding out what was going on with them. He always asked them 'How's your job?' and 'How's your family?'"[32]

Bud Shaw and Bob Shaw had become significant players within the carpet industry, and nothing signified that more than Bud Shaw's election as the first president of the new Carpet and Rug Institute (CRI) in 1969. The American Carpet Institute, headquartered in New York and representing principally the older woven carpet mills, and the Tufted Textile Manufacturers Association (TTMA), headquartered in Dalton and representing the dynamic new tufting mills, merged in that year. The new association made its home in Dalton, representing the shift of marketplace power from the older to the newer segment of the industry. The merger also marked a change of focus for the makers of tufted products. While much of TTMA's energy had been expended in the area of encouraging members to improve labor-management practices, CRI devoted more attention to government-industry relations. New consumer safety regulations issued by various federal agencies in the 1970s motivated the association to move in this direction. Bud Shaw helped guide CRI in these early critical years, and Bob Shaw later served many years as treasurer of the organization.[33]

While Bud Shaw worked to revive the sagging fortunes of the Philadelphia Carpet Company in the late 1960s, Bob Shaw and Star Finishing Company continued to try to hang onto the carpet industry in its boom period. At the same time that Bud Shaw implemented new strategies at Philadelphia, Bob Shaw introduced new services at his finishing company, new services that would dramatically affect Star's balance sheet.

Clarence Shaw had always been reticent about going into broadloom carpet dyeing, as we have seen. Bob Shaw recalled that his father had always argued that carpet should be dyed continuously rather than in pieces. In the early 1960s, a few manufacturers and machine makers took the first significant steps in this direction. The initial application of continuous dyeing techniques came with the advent of printing. No U.S. carpet maker did more to promote the new process than E. T. Barwick, a flamboyant entrepreneur whose star burned brightly in the 1950s and 1960s. While Barwick's business eventually exploded in supernova fashion in the late 1970s, he played a key role in developing the technology and products that Star Finishing would go on to perfect in the 1970s.

In the early 1960s Barwick cooperated with Austrian textile machine maker

Peter Zimmer to develop a method for creating intricate patterns and designs in tufted carpeting. The new process bypassed the tufting machine and added a design after initial manufacture by printing. A delegation of technicians and executives from the German carpet industry visited the United States in 1963 to investigate the booming American industry and determine whether there were new ideas that might be useful back home. The German delegation was particularly impressed with what it saw at Barwick Mills—a Zimmer flatbed printing machine. Later the same year, a film presentation at the International Textile Machinery Association show in Hanover, Germany, featured the Barwick-Zimmer TDA 62. The new machine could print 5 meters wide with a 1-meter pattern repeat, at a speed of 360 meters per hour.[34]

Barwick later recalled the introduction of printed carpets as one of his company's most significant innovations. The machinery was complex, and it took some time to get the printers into operation, but "we had it going by 1965." Barwick held the first showing of printed carpets in New York the following year. "It was supposed to be a small gathering" of distributors and retailers, "but more than 5,000 people attended. We shipped $43 million the first year while everyone was saying 'it won't sell, it won't sell.' We proved them wrong."[35] Barwick introduced the highly successful Kitchen Classics line of printed carpets in early 1967, shortly after the New York Show.[36] His firm also developed printed products for other applications—bathrooms, playrooms, commercial spaces.

Barwick ran a loose ship and got into deep financial trouble in the 1970s. To Barwick's credit, Bob Shaw observed, he initiated "printing—the Kitchen Classics line was really the only thing he ever made money on."[37] Barwick's company grew so fast that he probably had a hard time determining whether he was making a profit, and how much profit, in various segments of the business. Barwick's sales never quite caught up with his company's capacity. The ever-ambitious Barwick bought new equipment sometimes before he had developed products and markets to keep it occupied. A company official observed in 1976 that "we had the capacity to [manufacture] approximately $300 million [worth of] carpet a year" by the mid 1970s, but "the best year we ever had was $192 million." Barwick purchased two new continuous dye machines in 1967 for about $450,000 each; as of May 1975 "one of them was still in the crate."[38] He had invested heavily in research and development of the printing process and had pioneered in introducing new products, proving that a market existed for such goods. Barwick Mills was not, however, the firm that took the greatest advantage of the new technology.

Bob Shaw took note of Barwick's quick success with Kitchen Classics in late 1967 and early 1968. Star Finishing bought a similar flatbed Zimmer printing machine in October 1968. Shaw wanted to add printing as a service that could be provided by his finishing company. The machine cost in excess of half a million dollars—startup costs were extremely high. As Barwick already knew, just getting the print line set up required time, effort, and patience. Star did not begin printing carpets until June 1969 because "the new machine required eight months of installation and modification," according to a Drexel Firestone analysis. As Star's production guru, Walter Hemphill, wryly observed, a Zimmer printer was "kind of like a freight train. You start it on one end, and it starts up a piece at a time down through the machine until you get it all running, and when you get it all going, you can't stop it. If it's not right, you're in trouble."[39]

Bill Lusk joined Star Finishing just before the Philadelphia acquisition and the foray into printing. Lusk was born in Red Bank, Tennessee, near Chattanooga. When he was two, his father moved the family out into the country "on the back side of Signal Mountain," and he grew up there. Lusk worked with a Chattanooga accounting firm and did the books for Star Dye Company. Lusk did tax work and came down to Dalton once a month to do financial statements. He continued to handle this sort of work for Star Finishing. Star Finishing quickly outgrew the services provided by an outside accounting firm. Bob Shaw had no one in his organization in the mid-1960s with any training in finance. "I think he first offered my boss the job, but he wouldn't take it," Lusk jokingly recalled. Bob Shaw hired Bill Lusk in April 1967 to serve as company controller. "I decided it would be an adventure, at least. He and I were both young and opinionated. I didn't know how long that situation would last, but I thought it would be a good experience."[40]

Lusk joined the management team at Star just in time to be on board for an eventful ride to the top of the carpet industry. Star Finishing sought to catch up with Barwick in the printing arena quickly, but Lusk agreed with Walter Hemphill that "we had a difficult learning curve," and it took eight months to get the first printer into efficient operation. Even though printing was a small piece of the carpet market in the 1960s and 1970s, "the margins were huge," Lusk observed. Barwick helped open a new market for carpeting with the printing process. Star Finishing watched, learned from Barwick's successes and mistakes, and followed. Of the early printed products, Lusk chided, "Oh, there was some hideous stuff." However, "It was a very profitable business for us." Bob Shaw fondly remembered the role printing played in building his business. "Printing was very, very important. It was the old flatbed printer. The technology was pretty good for level-loops, and it created a different situation where you could make some serious money. It was almost like printing money."[41]

The Zimmer machine could print carpet at high speeds in detailed patterns using up to six colors. Through October 1971, production of printed carpets had been "confined to tufted, tightly constructed nylon carpets having high density foam backing." Star "acquired a second Zimmer printer in July 1970 which was capable of using eight colors, though this machine had not yet been installed as of October 1971." Drexel estimated that the decision to install and operate the second machine would require expenditures of approximately $900,000.[42]

Star Finishing and Barwick Mills were not the only firms engaged in printing by the end of the 1960s. A handful of large manufacturers and finishing companies also followed the trend. Armstrong's E&B Carpet Mills, for example, had two printing machines by 1969. Foremost Processing was probably second only to Barwick in getting into the printing business. By November 1966, Foremost was operating a Zimmer printer. The firm's management claimed to be "the first plant to finish carpets in continuous process." Constellation Finishing operated a roller printer (limited to three colors, but much more compact) by October 1968.[43] Yet Star Finishing became perhaps the best and most consistent practitioner of the new continuous process technology in fairly short order.

By the early 1970s, Bob Shaw and Bud Shaw had created the firm that would become Shaw Industries in the early 1970s. The Philadelphia Holding Company was a transitional form, never intended to last forever. The company combined several great strengths, including Star Finishing's production efficiencies and state-of-the-art dyeing equipment. The Philadelphia Carpet Company and Sabre Carpets also brought advantages: the former in high-end retail marketing, the latter in distributor sales through private labels. But the Philadelphia Holding Company also created a loose management structure that allowed the Star and Philadelphia divisions to remain relatively autonomous. This loose system was retained even after the formation of Shaw Industries in 1971. In the early years this arrangement worked fairly well, but by 1976 the company would face a crisis as the two main divisions essentially grew apart. The company would have to confront this challenge from within, along with a significant challenge from without—the end of the tufted carpet industry's boom period—in the 1970s.

CHAPTER FOUR

The Emergence of Shaw Industries

The Philadelphia Holding Company, having outlived its tax advantages, was reorganized into a new corporate form and became Shaw Industries in 1971. The firm also held its initial public stock offering that same year. In early 1972, Shaw Industries announced to its stockholders that the company's stock commenced trading on the American Stock Exchange on March 21, 1972. The new board of directors consisted primarily of men who had held stock in one of the predecessor firms, as well as representatives of the Marion Manufacturing Company and its interests. The board included John McCarty, an early investor in Star Dye; Stuart Morrison, a key figure and stockholder in Star Finishing Company; Richard Culberson, executive vice president of Philadelphia Carpet Company; and William H. Cheney Sr., a local real estate developer. Marion Manufacturing Company's chairman of the board, Samuel Hamill, and board member T. L. Richie joined President Robert W. Twitty and Vice President Woodrow Greene on the Shaw Industries board. The Marion positions on the board later passed to Samuel Lambert and William Hamill. The only director who had not been a stockholder in one of these related firms was Robert R. Harlin, a partner in the Atlanta law firm of Powell, Goldstein, Frazer, & Murphy. With the public offering in 1971, Shaw appointed its first two "outside" directors to the board, John Dent and George Rice.[1]

Warren Sims recalled that John Dent, president of the Georgia Marble Company, "became Bud's good friend and associate." The Cartersville businessman served on the executive committee for many years. George Rice, former president of Dalton's First National Bank, had long served as an example of business ethics to Sims and other businesspeople in the area. Despite many offers, "George Rice never took a directorship outside the First National Bank while he was active in that bank. . . . When George retired, he became one of our first two outside directors."[2] Rice served on the board's audit committee.

Later, a number of talented individuals served on the board, including family members Julian McCamy and S. Tucker Grigg. Other outside directors included Clifford Kirtland, former Cox Communications chairman; J. Hicks Lanier, Oxford Industries CEO; Thomas Cousins, Atlanta real estate developer; Robert J. Lunn, investment banker; Roberto Garza Delgado, president of the Gard Corporacion; Dakin B. Ferris of Merrill Lynch; Albert J. Bows, formerly of Arthur Andersen and dean of the business school at Emory University; and William R. Bowdoin, former chairman of Trust Company of Georgia Associates. These outside directors contributed management experience, expertise in dealing with the investment community, and connections with regional banks. They played an especially significant role in the formative years and helped guide the firm through its entry into public capital markets.

The public offering also helped reduce the influence of Marion Manufacturing Company. Marion and a few related individuals sold a higher proportion of their stock in the old Philadelphia Holding Company than the Shaw interests. The public offering was "a bonanza for Marion Manufacturing," according to longtime Shaw Industries board member Robert Harlin.[3] Aside from the name change and the addition of outsiders to the company's board, there was little organizational change at Shaw Industries. The company's finishing and carpet divisions each continued to operate with near complete autonomy. The decentralized divisional structure continued until 1977. By then, changes within the industry and the company combined to make change necessary.

In anticipation of Shaw Industries' initial public offering, the company asked Drexel Firestone to estimate the fair market value of its common stock in March 1971. Drexel estimated the stock value at $34.89 per share as of February 10, 1971.[4] More importantly, the Drexel report provides a glimpse into the company and the industry just as the boom period was about to end. The report observed that "the carpet industry is . . . highly competitive, and the number of carpet mills in operation has increased with the growth in sales of tufted carpet. However, no single company enjoys a dominant position in the industry." Drexel noted that the industry had seen a wave of consolidation in the years 1968–1970, characterized by the acquisition of independent carpet companies by significantly larger, more diversified companies. Drexel examined the performance of eight other publicly held carpet companies in order to reach a decision on the value of Philadelphia Holding Company stock. All eight experienced a decline in reported net income during the previous three years, and four were operating at a loss, including Barwick.[5]

Drexel concluded that "there is no single publicly owned carpet company whose business is comparable to that of Philadelphia Holding Company," which was shortly to become Shaw Industries. The investment firm cited the

Star Finishing Division—especially its commission printing operation—as evidence of Philadelphia's unique position. "Company officials believed that each of these operations were the largest in the industry. This unique business mix made the Company in part dependent upon the operating performances of a great many other carpet manufacturers."[6]

The "operating performances" of many of those competitors were less than spectacular in the early 1970s. Though total industry sales continued to grow, many manufacturers found profit margins difficult to maintain. Kurt Salmon Associates, an Atlanta management consulting firm, came to a similar conclusion about the industry even earlier and lamented the subpar management performance of most tufting mills in a 1969 *Textile Industries* article.[7]

The postwar economic boom and the development of tufting technology created an environment in which it was difficult to fail. While tufted carpet mills may not have performed up to standards envisioned by management consultants, firms in the industry continued to rake in tremendous amounts of cash. "It was almost impossible not to make money in the carpet industry in that period of time and under those conditions," one executive recalled. The industry's double-digit growth was both "good and bad," according to Bob Shaw. "Double-digit growth in any industry brings in a lot of foolish money."[8]

Some of that foolish money in the late 1960s belonged to business behemoths known as conglomerates—diversified, multidivisional firms that often produced a variety of unrelated items or services. The U.S. economy experienced its third major merger movement in the 1960s. During this wave of corporate consolidation, large firms sought to diversify for at least two reasons. By diversifying into unrelated business areas and product lines, large companies could hedge against slumps in one sector of the economy. In addition, once industries reached maturity—a point where only a handful of firms controlled the vast bulk of the market for a given class of products—it often became difficult to produce growing returns for investors.[9]

Leaders of America's largest firms—which, of course, tended to be those in mature industries—sought profitable new areas in which to invest capital during the booming 1960s. As the home of one of the four fastest-growing industries of the decade, northwest Georgia attracted increasing attention from harried executives in search of new ways to increase shareholder value. Many of the area's top firms became, in essence, cash cows for conglomerates.

Conglomerates often paid too high premiums for entry into the carpet and home furnishings markets. As a J. C. Bradford analyst put it in 1972, "pure plays" in the home furnishings field had become "a rare commodity in today's stock market. Even the best of the publicly owned companies in the field [such as Coronet Carpets] have proven easy prey to the growth 'conglomerates' who have been willing to pay high prices for participation in this field." Why were conglomerates willing to overpay for entry into the market? "The reason is obvious," according to Bradford analyst Norris Nielsen. "Home furnishings, and carpeting in particular, is the fastest growing consumer-oriented industry" in the nation. Shipments of broadloom carpet increased at an annual rate of 13 percent in 1969 and 1970, or about twice the growth rate of the GNP and personal consumption expenditures.[10] Outsiders increasingly joined the prospecting.

The conglomerates' entry into the tufted carpet industry came on the heels of a wave of initial public offerings among these relatively new firms. Coronet Carpets led the way in 1963. E&B followed in 1965, and a number of other mills, including Barwick, joined the move toward the equity markets by the end of the decade. If conglomerates sought entry into the booming carpet industry as a way to improve cash flow and quarterly returns, what motivated firms like Coronet, E&B, and others to join the merger movement?

Merging with a conglomerate or some other large firm offered advantages similar to those associated with public stock offerings. As a Wharton School of Finance and Commerce study observed in 1970, "many of the acquired mills can be classified as tufters who entered the industry with limited capital and were successful in building up a substantial business." The surging demand of the 1960s brought revenues and profits, to be sure, but along with these came "increased needs for new plant and equipment." For most firms, "the internal generation of funds simply has not been adequate to meet increased capital needs." This was especially true given the introduction of printing and experiments with continuous dyeing. Any mill that intended to achieve even a limited amount of vertical integration forward through dyeing and finishing needed capital.[11]

Moreover, the boom times experienced by the industry were destined to run out in the 1970s. Although tufting did not prove to be a fad, as some analysts and critics had predicted (or hoped), the new industry simply could not sustain its double-digit growth rates indefinitely. The entrepreneurs who sought capital stock sales and mergers with conglomerates had three chief motives, though the importance of each varied from case to case. "Going public" offered an opportunity for entrepreneurs to cash themselves out; in other words, the men who had built successful businesses could sell a portion of the company and convert their past efforts into cash and improved personal net worth. The proceeds from such stock sales might also be applied to reducing a company's outstanding debt or investing in new plant and equipment. The same held true when these companies were sold to conglomerates; the largest stockholders had a chance to cash in again.

Bedspreads such as this one helped create the tufted textile industry in the 1930s. TTMA Directory, 1955.

fabulous

Needletuft

NOBILITY

in broadloom and hand-carved rugs!

Only in Needletuft can you find coordinated carpets and hand-carved rugs to carry your decoration scheme from room to room. Deep luxury pile, 16 fashion colors, soil-resistant, mothproof, washable, made with remarkable new, hard-wearing Spunvis rayon carpet yarn. Shown, diamond-carved "Rajah" rug in Rose Beige, accent and room sizes, about $12.95 sq. yd. "Nobility" broadloom, shown in Cocoa, 9', 12', and 15' widths, about $9.95 sq. yd.

Needletuft rugs and carpets

NEEDLETUFT RUG MILLS, DALTON, GA.
FLOOR COVERING DIVISION OF CABIN CRAFTS, INC.

The Cabin Crafts "Nobility" line, one of the company's most popular from the 1950s. The Needletuft brand was Cabin's trade name for its tufted carpets and rugs in the 1950s. Nobility was made with rayon yarn, though rayon ultimately yielded to nylon as the synthetic fiber of choice in carpeting. This ad described the carpet as having a "deep luxury pile"; it was also a solid color product. Both features—deep pile and solid colors—have characterized the most commercially durable tufted carpets. From *The Westpointer*, November 1954.

The above Cabin Crafts ad illustrates the company's efforts to incorporate design and color trends from around the world. This ad features a Spanish collection. Fred Westcott often returned from international trips with new product suggestions. *The Westpointer,* December 1962.

Under Bud Shaw's leadership after 1967, Philadelphia Carpet Company continued to produce intricately patterned woven carpets, especially for commercial applications such as hotels, restaurants, and high-end apartment complexes. This custom Wilton weave was installed in the Watergate South Apartments, Washington, D.C., in the early 1970s. Shaw Industries files.

A custom Wilton in the Fairmont Hotel, Dallas, Texas, early 1970s. Shaw Industries files.

A worker inspects a shag carpet in 1972. Shag constructions and the earth tone colors (particularly in multicolor combinations) represented here both constituted fads in the late 1960s and early 1970s. Shaw Industries files.

The earliest yarn processing plants acquired by Shaw specialized in heat-setting yarns. The heat-setting process produced yarn ideal for "shag" constructions such as these, so popular in the 1970s, and gave Shaw a significant "in-house" capability to supply raw materials for a popular specialty product line. Shaw Industries files.

Shaw Industries and its predecessor companies capitalized on the popularity of printed carpets, especially for the kitchen, in the late 1960s and early 1970s. Printing was introduced by industry pioneer E. T. Barwick, but Shaw's Star Finishing division seemed to reap the lion's share of rewards in this high-margin product area. The kitchen carpet at left is from the early 1970s. Shaw Industries files.

This brick pattern is from 1981. Shaw Industries files.

Printer in operation at Star Finishing, early 1970s. Shaw Industries files.

Cracked Ice, a random multicolor pattern produced with a Kusters TAK continuous dying range. This became a huge seller for Shaw in the late 1970s, reflecting the consumer tastes of the period. Shaw employees modified the dye range to produce this effect, and the company patented the process, a rarity in the carpet industry. Shaw Industries files.

This cover shot from an industry trade journal illustrates the TAK system of random, multicolor dyeing that became so popular in the 1970s. In this shot, the TAK machine is spattering newly dyed carpet with dots of another color. Courtesy *Carpet and Rug Industry,* April 1976.

TAK dyeing machine in operation at a Shaw finishing plant, 1985. Shaw Industries files.

Solid color, deep, cut-pile carpets like this continued to form the foundation of Shaw's, and the carpet industry's, success in the high-volume residential market throughout the 1980s and 1990s. While some consumers would opt for something unique and different, most consistently preferred more conservative choices. The fact that most consumers replaced carpet only once every ten years or so mitigated against a high volume trade in "specialty" products.

This color board (from a new ad campaign begun in 2001) illustrates the dominance of solid colors in the residential arena, the largest single market segment within the floor covering industry. Color has long been the most important factor in the consumer's selection of carpets. Shaw Industries files.

Polypropylene yarn, like that produced at the Amoco facilities acquired by Shaw in 1992, proved especially useful in the new berber styles that became popular in the 1990s. A subsidiary of Salem Carpets, also acquired by Shaw in 1992, specialized in producing berbers. The two acquisitions complemented each other perfectly and positioned Shaw to exploit fully this emerging market. Shaw Industries files.

Longtime Shaw executives clearly saw their own company differently. "It was our philosophy from very early on that we were going to build an institution that would survive us all, and if personal wealth came, that's fine," Bill Lusk insisted. "But it was not centered around, as most of the industry was, building a base of personal wealth, capitalizing on it, and getting out. The whole industry was a conglomeration of entrepreneurial aspirations, but from the very beginning ours was to build something that would last. I think that philosophy perhaps dictated the way we went about things." Bob Shaw put it much the same way: "I've always said that we were about building a business, and I think that's the difference in our company. We didn't want to sell. We had all kinds of opportunities during that period to sell."[12]

Future Shaw Industries vice chairman Norris Little experienced firsthand the impact of conglomerates and outside capital on northwest Georgia's homegrown industry. Little was born in Marshville, North Carolina, a small town near Charlotte. He attended the University of North Carolina for three years and then graduated from Georgia State University in 1955. In 1958, after working for Armco in Atlanta for three years, Little "applied for a job with James Lees and Sons. They had an opening in Dahlonega, so I went to Dahlonega. They then had an opening in Rabun Gap, so I went there. They had three plants in that area" (the other was a woven plant in Robbinsville, North Carolina), "and I was given responsibility for those plants." Little also worked at the Lees facility in Rabun Gap for three years as manufacturing controller, handling cost accounting, logistics, scheduling, and so on.[13]

Lees, of course, was an old and respected name in the woven carpet business. "They had just begun to enter into the tufted carpet business in the mid-50s," Little recalled. "They made excellent products; they enjoyed an excellent reputation." However, Little observed, the Lees "management had a serious flaw. They resisted tufting, and they thought Dalton's tufted industry was a fly-by-night" industry run by "rednecks and hicks, so they refused to become a part of it—at least seriously. They did put a tufting plant in Rabun Gap, but it never really was successful and has since closed." These attitudes characterized much of the leadership of the old woven industry. Lees survived but eventually had to take tufting more seriously.[14]

Lees proved capable of exploiting the new process in spite of a lack of enthusiasm and a half-hearted commitment to tufting. DuPont's new 501 BCF nylon fueled much of the industry's phenomenal growth in the 1960s, and Little recalled that "when I was with Lees in Rabun Gap, that product was developed" there. "Lees had the first 501 filament nylon in the industry," along with Barwick. "The development work was done there. Lees introduced a product called 'Lasting Star,' which was for many years the leading volume product in the industry. It was made from DuPont 501 filament nylon." DuPont's 501 nylon sold for "$1.57 a pound" in 1958 when Lees introduced it to the marketplace, Little remembered. The price was almost the same more than forty years later. "The raw material for the carpet industry—and again, this has contributed to the growth of the carpet industry—has not increased in price for over forty years. Tufted carpet was a tremendous value compared to what the consumer had been offered in the past. The cost of producing a reasonable quality product was much less. As Bob Shaw has often been quoted as saying, and rightfully so, 'Tufting made carpet available to the masses.'"[15]

After Little had been with Lees for five years, Dalton's Coronet Industries re- cruited him. Little accepted Coronet's offer and came to Dalton in 1961. He started as controller and later served as a vice president, executive vice presi- dent, and a member of the board. Coronet was "a totally different company" from Lees, Little recalled. Coronet was "chartered in 1956. At the time I went with them, they were doing less than $10 million in volume." Coronet's man- agement "was set and primed to take advantage of the explosive growth of the carpet industry that was to take place in the 1960s."[16]

New firms such as Coronet, with no investment in looms or outdated pro- duction facilities, were "in a position to take advantage of this development." In its first dozen years or more, Coronet was one of the best-managed firms in the carpet industry. "The company was started by three individuals—Jack Bandy, Bud Seretean, and Guy Henley." Like management teams in many of the new startup firms in the industry, "each of those had different talents that they brought to the business. Jack had finance, Bud had sales and marketing, and Guy had manufacturing. Coronet was the leader in well-managed com- panies. Barwick was certainly the leader in terms of sales volume, but Barwick was not a well-managed company. Barwick has since gone by the boards. Coro- net was well managed, highly profitable, and enjoyed tremendous growth."[17]

In perhaps the most bizarre acquisition in the carpet industry's history, RCA purchased Coronet in a diversification move in the late 1960s. That ac- quisition "destroyed the company," according to Norris Little. "RCA manage- ment didn't know what they were doing. Their management team was inept." Much later RCA was acquired by General Electric. "GE realized that they didn't know anything about the carpet business, and they divested Coronet. In the process, I think it seriously hurt Coronet." Nevertheless, Coronet survived and eventually wound up as a cornerstone of the Beaulieu group in the late 1980s, but the important point was that the company survived rather than thrived. Such stories became all too common in the Dalton district after the takeover mania of the 1960s. This takeover of Coronet "was not too much different from a number of other situations around town, where conglomerates came in and acquired a small carpet company. That happened over and over again. They didn't know what they were doing, didn't know how to manage it, and ended up closing it or selling it off at substantial losses. That happened many, many times. There were lots of fortunes made during that period of time by entrepreneurs who ran successful businesses. But without those entrepreneurs, the businesses often faltered."[18]

In most of these situations, conglomerates retained the original entrepreneurs as managers. That seemed an elegantly simple solution: let the people who know the business keep on running it while the conglomerate adds the industry's tremendous growth rate and cash flow to its balance sheet. It rarely worked as well as the plan sounded. The conglomerates—such as RCA, Armstrong, S&H Greenstamps—all failed in their forays into the carpet business, Little recalled. "Maybe it was because the way the industry was structured at that particular time required an entrepreneurial approach to the business that the conglomerate couldn't offer. Someone made a very astute comment back in the '60s talking about acquiring companies. He said that he learned a very difficult lesson, and that is *how do you motivate millionaires?*" Little believed "that's one of the reasons for the failure, and probably a prime reason." Banker and former Office of Management and Budget director Bert Lance, of Calhoun, Georgia, echoed the critique. He summed up as well as anyone the problems associated with the conglomerates in the carpet industry in 1975, at perhaps the low point of the industry's first serious recession. "Historically, it's been a seat-of-the-pants industry," Lance observed, "with the owners able to make quick on-the-spot decisions, but when you try to run a mill by conglomerate committee decision, you lose some of the flexibility that has enabled them to survive."[19]

As a result of RCA corporate decisions regarding Coronet's subsidiaries, Little found himself "out of a job" in 1975. Bob Shaw offered Little a job as vice president of manufacturing shortly thereafter. The CEO had known Little for years as a fellow church member and in his role as an executive for a major Star Finishing/Shaw Industries customer, Coronet. Little went on to become one of the most important figures in Shaw Industries' dramatic rise to the top of the industry, eventually serving in a variety of roles including company president and vice chairman of the board. Bob Shaw often described his relationship with Little as a partnership. Little insisted that Shaw's characterization was perhaps overly "magnanimous," but other company insiders tended to echo the CEO's view.[20]

Shaw Industries continued, in Bob Shaw's words, to try to "hang onto the carpet industry" as the growth of the 1960s continued through the early 1970s.

During the first three years of Shaw Industries' existence, 1971–73, the company made strategic decisions that shaped future success. While Dalton remained the "carpet capital of the world," tufting mills sprang up in other areas. A secondary concentration of carpet producers emerged in California in the late 1960s and 1970s. High transportation costs encouraged the new concentration on the West Coast, as did the slightly divergent consumer trends in the area. Popular styles and colors varied from region to region, but not so dramatically as on the West Coast. Proximity to customers combined with these distinctive tastes to open a space for new carpet firms—two dozen by 1972—in California. Shaw Industries, ever watchful for growth markets, tried to take advantage of this new opportunity. The company began construction on a new finishing plant in Cucamonga, California, in May 1972. That plant commenced operations in October.[21]

Shaw Industries continued to expand its role as a provider of services to the carpet industry when the company acquired New Found Industries of Weaverville, North Carolina, a processor of synthetic yarns, in June 1972. The acquisition of New Found put Shaw Industries in "the business of heat-setting nylon yarn." The heat-setting process was an important part of yarn processing in certain applications. The shag carpets that became popular in the late 1960s and 1970s, for example, required heat-set yarns. Shaw Industries' carpet division would use some of the yarn processed at the New Found facility, but most of the plant's production would still be sold to other manufacturers. Shaw invested about $2 million in buying and then upgrading the New Found plant. The company expected the heat-setting operation to produce $4–5 million in revenues in the following fiscal year.[22]

Bill Lusk remembered all of Shaw's yarn mill acquisitions. While Shaw later built a couple of yarn heat-setting plants, "we never built a spinning mill; we acquired all of them. We would rehab them and bring them up to date." All these investments in yarn processing, beginning with New Found, were "good decisions, very profitable decisions. It was probably just as important to get into the yarn-spinning and heat-setting business as it was to get into the fiber-producing business at a later time."[23] Though Shaw's divisions were not fully (or even a little) integrated, the company already positioned itself to take advantage of vertical integration and economies of scale in the future. Such moves may have seemed minor to the industry at large in the early 1970s as the boom continued, but they would loom large later.

Drexel Firestone's 1972 progress report on Shaw Industries offers a snapshot of the company at an early stage. In the carpet division, the Philadelphia label led in sales, producing 42 percent of the company's carpet sales. Philadelphia's products remained exclusively in the medium- to high-price ranges. Thirty-six salesmen distributed Philadelphia's thirty styles to about 2,500 retailers throughout the country. The company, following Bud Shaw's strategy, marketed some lower-end products under its Sabre brand and under "private label" arrangements with a number of distributors. Private-label sales accounted for 26 percent of carpet sales, while Sabre brands made up another 20 percent. The carpet division continued to produce custom-made woven products, chiefly for commercial uses in such places as hotels or casinos. These sales accounted for about 10 percent of Shaw's carpet sales. Custom-designed, wide-width (up to 25 feet) tufted carpets made up the remaining 2 percent.[24]

Drexel noted that printing continued to be the financial cornerstone of the company's success. Shaw's printing facility operated "at full capacity with a 2 months' backlog" in the summer of 1972. The second Zimmer printer was slated to begin production in October of that year. Drexel expected the new printer to produce as much as $12 million in annual sales. It was ironic that while printed carpets mimicked, to a degree, high-end, patterned woven carpets, they actually sold in the lower ranges of the quality and price scale. Printing worked best in nylon constructions with very low pile height. These products found their way into new market areas such as kitchens (led by Barwick's campaign) and commercial spaces such as retail store floors. Patterned carpets could hide stains and dirt, and these printed carpets had the advantage of being cheaper than woven wool carpets. In spite of the low prices of printed products, profits remained healthy. As Drexel dryly observed, "Printed carpet provides higher gross profit margins than other carpet products."[25]

Shaw quickly used its initial public offering to improve its financial situation with creditors, and this impressed Drexel's analyst. While some carpet mills squandered proceeds from public offerings without reducing high-cost debt, Shaw followed a different strategy, perhaps reflecting the "long-run" mentality of the company's management team. "Since the public financing," Drexel noted, the company had renegotiated its terms with Walter Heller's factoring house from a position of strength: Shaw no longer needed factoring services quite as much as in the past. As a result, Shaw "substantially reduced costs associated with factoring."[26]

The Zimmer printer played a significant role in the early history of Shaw Industries and also spurred interest among German machinists in the continuous dyeing of carpet. The continuing rapid growth of the tufted carpet industry in the United States heightened interest among carpet manufacturers and fiber and dye suppliers. As textile technology historian Gary Mock has noted, by the early 1960s "synthetic fibers were spun continuously, carpet was . . . tufted continuously, [and] carpet could be printed on a continuous machine; perhaps carpet could be dyed on a continuous machine. The carpet manufacturers, the fiber and colorants industries, and the textile engineers wanted a solution."[27]

Eduard Kusters Maschinenfabrik of Krefeld, Germany, provided the solution. Kusters had founded his firm in Western-occupied Germany in 1949. Like a host of businesses, the Kusters firm prospered in the new Western European economy primed by the Marshall Plan. By the end of the 1950s, Kusters had become a significant player in the manufacture of capital equipment for several industries including paper, woodworking, and textiles. Eduard Kusters "was always looking for opportunities to turn batch processes into continuous processes"; thus his business strategy meshed well with the continued spread of mass production techniques through the post–World War II economic golden age. By the mid-1960s, Kusters had developed a new adjustable deflection padder for textile applications—it became known quickly as the "Swimming Roll" or simply "S-Roll." In 1967, Kusters exhibited his first continuous carpet dye range at the International Textile Manufacturers Association (ITMA) show in Basel, Switzerland.[28]

Roger McNamara, then director of research and development for Barwick Mills, attended the ITMA show and observed Kusters's test runs. McNamara and two other Barwick officials "were so interested," Gary Mock reported, that "they refused to wait before entering into negotiations that night." Discussions between McNamara's Barwick team and Kusters representatives continued into the early morning hours. Characteristically, Barwick Mills became the first company in the industry to buy one of the Kusters machines.[29] Other mills and finishing companies were slower to leap at this very expensive new technology, but by the early 1970s several Dalton area firms had purchased Kusters ranges. The continuous dyeing range was a better fit with the continuous tufting process. Perfect for long production runs, undyed carpet could be fed endlessly into one end of the range (see figure D).

As with the printing process, Shaw Industries may not have been first with the Kusters range, but the company quickly recognized profitable technologies. After allowing Barwick and other firms to begin ironing out problems in the continuous dyeing process, Shaw Industries expanded its commitment to continuous processing and low-cost production in December 1973. Shaw acquired Elite Processing in exchange for 135,000 shares of Shaw Industries stock. Norris Little's first assignment with Shaw Industries was the Elite Processing acquisition. Little "worked with Joe Johnson, Bill McDaniel, and others trying

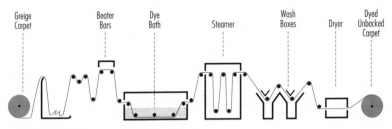

Figure D: Continuous dyeing

to grow the Elite business." This was the first in a series of important assignments for Little.[30] Walter Hemphill was in California when he heard about the Elite acquisition. "I never will forget. . . . I was out in Cucamonga, California, working on some problems out there, and Mr. Shaw called me and said, 'Hurry up and get home, I got you another plant.' It turned out to be Elite Processing. That was our first step into continuous dyeing."

Elite Processing, under president Roy Johnson, pioneered in offering continuous dyeing services on a commission basis. Elite used a Kusters TAK dyeing machine to "produce spots of various colors on a solid shade base." The Kusters TAK dye ranges created the immensely popular random multicolor effects that swept the carpet markets in the 1970s. Johnson claimed that his company's drop-dyeing unit "was the first unit in the United States available on a commission basis." Elite's continuous dye range could process carpet at a rate of 60 feet per minute in solid colors and 32 feet per minute in multicolor styles. Johnson neatly summarized the cost advantages of continuous dyeing: it "eliminates the need of separate yarn inventories in carpet manufacture for each coloration in a style, since we can dye the greige carpet into practically any color combination." In addition to its Kusters ranges, Elite also maintained a full range of dye becks of recent vintage and a new Gowin-Card dryer. The Kusters range ran directly into the 32-foot dryer in a continuous line; the dryer could process up to 90 feet of carpet per minute.[31]

The acquisition of Elite Processing moved Shaw immediately into continuous dyeing with a state-of-the-art, 98,500-square-foot facility. Walter Hemphill recalled the increased efficiency of the Kusters range for long production runs. "In a beck you could get up to 400 feet on most styles, if it wasn't too heavy. When you get into continuous dyeing, if you didn't have 1,000 or 2,000 feet, here again you were in trouble, because you spend all your time changing over. So the industry was educated on the basis that you have to have continuity. . . . We ran thousands of feet instead of hundreds" in the same color. In the early days of continuous dyeing, center-side matching was a problem, but it had become less so over the years. "The real advantage of the becks came early on when a tufting mill could creel up a truckload of yarn, run 25 rolls, and dye all 25 of them a different color. That fit his [the manufacturer's] need at the time," said Hemphill. The becks were great for producing a variety of colors and still presented cost advantages for short production runs. The flexibility of continuous dye ranges had been improved—colors could be changed more quickly by the 1990s—"but it's still a volume dye system."[32]

In the mid-1970s, carpet-finishing managers generally considered 1,500 feet the minimum length that could be profitably dyed using the continuous system. Continuous dye ranges had limited applicability, therefore, for small manufacturers who generally operated with wide color lines but limited orders for each shade within the line. Those finishing companies that invested in continuous dye ranges needed customers with long runs of the same color in order to make effective use of their equipment. If long production runs could be guaranteed, however, the continuous dye processes offered a much lower cost of production than beck dyeing. A dye beck, operating at peak efficiency, could color about 4 feet of carpet per minute in 1974. The continuous ranges could dye carpet at the rate of 45 feet per minute. In that sense, new investments in continuous dyeing represented a step away from flexibility and toward a mass production manufacturing model.[33]

Shaw Industries emerged as the tufted carpet industry's boom period neared its end. During the 1970s, the industry went from explosive growth to near bust. In the 1860s and 1870s, John D. Rockefeller, founder of the giant Standard Oil Company, had faced a similar competitive situation in the oil refining industry. "Every man assumed to struggle hard to get all of the business," Rockefeller ruefully recalled of those days, "even though in so doing he brought himself and the competitors in the business nothing but disaster." Rockefeller's most recent biographer pointed out that in those days of "primitive accounting systems, many refiners had only the haziest notion of their profitability or lack thereof." Rockefeller himself understood full well the difficult position in which many oil producers found themselves. "Often times the most difficult competition comes, not from the strong, conservative competitor," the oil magnate observed, "but from the man who is holding on by the eyelids and is ignorant of his costs, and anyway he's got to keep running or bust!"[34] Rockefeller responded by trying to persuade as many refiners as possible to join with him or get out of the business. While the northwest Georgia carpet district may have resembled the early oil-refining industry in its competitive atmosphere by the 1970s, Shaw Industries' strategy differed significantly from that of Rockefeller and Standard Oil. Shaw Industries initially sought to succeed through effective competition rather than by pooling or merging with competitors.

The carpet industry's recession, of course, coincided with sharp hikes in the costs of raw materials associated with the oil crisis of 1973 and the appearance of the "stagflation," or inflation combined with persistent, rising unemployment. This was a combination that seemed to defy prevailing economic orthodoxies and confounded policymakers and business leaders alike for a decade. The postwar economic golden age began to tarnish as growth slowed in Western Europe and the United States.[35]

The U.S. tufted carpet industry, in many ways a creature of that golden age, began to struggle as well. After an unbroken string of two decades of advances for the industry, carpet yardage shipments fell by more than 6 percent in 1974 while the mill value of those shipments dropped about 1 percent (price hikes made up for some of the decline). Shipments declined by almost 11 percent the following year, with the value of shipments falling about 8 percent.[36] It appeared that the easy money party of the boom years was over.

The recession took a human toll as well. The *Atlanta Constitution* reported extensively on the carpet capital's woes in January 1975. "From November 1973 to November 1974," the newspaper noted, "unemployment in Whitfield County . . . rose from 3.9 to 10.1 percent." As evidence of the persistent rural culture of the Dalton area, "[m]any of the laid-off workers say they are feeding their families from summer garden caches, but county officials say requests for food and money are skyrocketing. The welfare office reported 370 and 399 requests for food stamps in November and December respectively, compared to only 74 for July. But in the first three days of January alone, the office received 103 requests." Calhoun banker Bert Lance said that as bad as unemployment statistics were, they "gloss over the picture" because of widespread underemployment. Many of those accustomed to working six or seven days a week with substantial overtime pay now worked only two to three days a week. Lance's bank had seen a substantial increase in auto loan delinquencies in the previous few months, evidence of the distress felt by mill workers.[37]

Shaw Industries weathered this recession perhaps better than most firms. The company increased its dividend payment three consecutive quarters in 1974 despite the general economic slowdown. Shaw's annual revenues rose to $98.4 million (from $78.2 million, a 25.8 percent increase) in 1974. The company's sales rose in first quarter of fiscal 1975 (ending September 28, 1974), but earnings declined from 37 cents per share to 36 cents. This reflected continued escalation in costs of raw materials and delays in passing along those costs due to price controls. Shaw, like other firms, sought cost-cutting measures. As an example, the company ended its consulting relationship with the McDonald and Little public relations firm.[38]

The nation's economy experienced a measure of recovery by the spring of 1975, though inflation remained a problem. Bob Shaw announced to stockholders that "the downward trend in our industry appears to have abated" in April of that year. The recovery proved painstakingly slow and all too gradual. Shaw Industries' 1975 earnings fell 50 percent from the previous year. The company's overarching strategy, however, showed through as the anemic recovery continued in early 1976. After encouraging trade shows, the company told its stockholders that "we share the optimism and confidence voiced by dealers at the recent winter markets about the improvement of the economy." Traffic at those trade shows was "brisk," according to Bob Shaw. Moreover, in a seemingly innocuous statement, Shaw observed that "economies can be realized in production from higher volumes." That simple statement about the economies to be reaped from high-volume production encapsulated the secret of Shaw's future success. The company's entry into continuous dyeing exemplified the mass production strategy that Bob Shaw used to combat the problems of slow growth.[39]

Shaw Industries and other manufacturers also cooperated to diminish the impact of the energy crisis. Warren Sims recalled the cooperative spirit that blended with competition in the Dalton district. "We almost had to shut down the carpet industry in north Georgia except for cooperation" during the fuel crisis of 1973–74. Dalton's Water, Light & Sinking Fund "set up a schedule—we would run our coater on a certain shift, Queen would run theirs on another shift, etc. If Queen had an emergency, they would send it over to us if we were running the coater when they needed something, and the same thing with the other folks. As an industry, we went to Washington and got permission to buy natural gas at higher [than ceiling] prices—people had it all stored in caves out in Arizona and such. About the time we got that approved, the crisis was over, but we had a plan." Though the plan to purchase additional natural gas at above-ceiling prices proved unnecessary in the long run, it illustrated "the cooperation among the manufacturers." This sort of cooperation characterized Dalton's carpet industry in the 1960s and 1970s. "If somebody had a fire, who was the first to go see them? A competitor, to see if they could run something for them." Such cooperative efforts, according to Sims, helped "make the industry such a success. It's a pretty good deal to have friends at the top—or bottom or middle—of another company."[40]

From one perspective, the recession of the mid-1970s was easily explainable by short-term causes. The Arab oil embargo and resulting energy crisis led to higher prices for virtually everything and had a particularly severe impact on the carpet industry. The oil crisis raised transportation costs by making gasoline more expensive, as it did for all industries. The carpet industry's chief raw materials—synthetic yarns—were also petroleum–based, and costs of raw materials skyrocketed as well. This double cost bind squeezed profit margins and made life difficult for carpet makers.

The cost crisis exacerbated a perennial problem for textile manufacturers—inventory control. Wholesalers long played a significant role in the distribution of tufted carpet products. Many mills had increased sales to retailers and expanded regional warehouse facilities in the late 1960s and early 1970s. Retailers shifted toward stricter inventory controls after 1973 to reduce their own costs. Bob Shaw noted this trend in a February 1976 speech to the Home Products Analysts Group at the New York Chamber of Commerce. Shaw's Philadelphia division was particularly well situated to spot this emerging trend since about 80 percent of Philadelphia's sales went directly to retailers. Shaw observed that retailers had scaled back significantly on orders for roll goods. Retailers now placed an increasing volume of "cut orders" for smaller pieces of particular styles and colors, in spite of paying a 12–15 percent premium to the mill for cut-order service. This trend indicated that retailers were willing to pay more per yard for carpet in order to avoid taking a larger risk on stocking large volumes of color and style lines. Bob Shaw predicted (correctly, as it turned out) a major shift by most mills away from direct sales to retailers and toward wholesalers.[41] Wholesalers already exerted a significant influence over the tufted carpet industry, accounting for perhaps half of the industry's sales. That influence grew during the late 1970s and early 1980s as mills followed the strategy predicted by Shaw management. By the mid-1980s, wholesalers purchased about 80 percent of the tufted carpet industry's volume.

Shaw went on to assess the industry's future in a more general sense. New firm creation in the tufting industry would slow significantly, he believed, as slower growth reduced the attraction for new capital to enter the business. "Capitalization for new mills is down," he observed. The industry's future would depend upon "existing mills." To succeed in the new environment, established mills "will have to be able to afford research and development, and their management must be close enough to the market to spend their capital dollars wisely." Shaw placed existing mills into three categories. There were the "broke" mills, those he argued were being "held up" by banks and factors. These mills would eventually have to close. "Disillusioned" manufacturers made up a second category. These carpet makers were of relatively recent origins, and their operations had failed to produce anticipated quick riches. The remainder—clearly a minority, in Bob Shaw's view—were the mills with strong balance sheets, the mills "who can afford to grow." Shaw also emphasized the importance of the continuing shift toward the increasing use of white yarn combined with continuous dyeing methods as mills moved away from using pre-dyed yarns and piece dyeing methods.[42]

From a slightly longer perspective the recession of the 1970s marked the end of an era, for both the U.S. economy in general and for the carpet industry in particular. U.S. manufacturers encountered increasing international competition and an ever more fragmented home market. The carpet industry faced a maturing marketplace as it entered a new product life-cycle phase. If it had been almost impossible to fail in the 1960s, it became exceedingly difficult to succeed in the carpet business by the end of the 1970s.

In the wake of the energy crisis and the recession of the mid-1970s, Shaw Industries began trying to integrate its disparate operating divisions more tightly. Integration proved more difficult, perhaps, than company officials initially predicted. "The biggest threat that we have had in the history of the company," Warren Sims insisted, "was that transition period" in the mid to late 1970s. Symbolic of this move toward a more vertical management structure with a single line of command was the construction of a new corporate office building in Dalton in 1976.[43] Full integration of the company's operations, however, required more than the bricks and mortar of the new office building.

Shaw Industries faced two serious threats—one external, one internal—in the maturing market of the late 1970s. Perhaps one of the company's greatest strengths in the 1960s and early 1970s had been Star Finishing's prominence in commission finishing. By the mid-1970s, Star's customer base was shrinking. Larger manufacturers—firms such as Coronet—began installing their own continuous dye ranges to reap the advantages of economies of scale. At the same time, the maturing market made life increasingly difficult for smaller manufacturers who tried to compete in the residential market—that is, those smaller firms that would be most likely to use Star Finishing's Kusters ranges. Norris Little observed that in the late 1970s "we were selling to many manufacturers who were underfinanced and, with bankruptcies and nonpayment of bills, it was becoming more and more difficult to be successful in that business [commission finishing]. We continued to lose accounts to business failures, and a lot of entrepreneurs just couldn't make it. We incurred substantial losses in receivables during that time."[44] What had been one of Star's, and Shaw's, greatest strengths in an expanding market—the company's sharing of risks with scores of carpet makers—became a liability as weak management and financial difficulties put those small firms in jeopardy.

With many small manufacturers struggling and larger firms installing their own dyeing and finishing equipment, Shaw's management team changed course. In an initial draft of Shaw Industries' January 1978 Interim Report, the company announced, "[f]or several months, we have been decreasing our sales to other manufacturers, closing out our service business in California, and working very hard to increase our sales base through distributors and retailers." This sentence was deleted from the final report, perhaps because company officials believed that it might be best to downplay these major strategic shifts.[45] Nevertheless, the statement accurately reflected Shaw's new corporate strategy. Shaw Industries would begin exiting the commission finishing business and instead focus on selling the company's own products.

The Philadelphia division had, of course, always produced a total product. By the mid-1970s, the Star Finishing division was making carpet as well. Star encountered quality-control problems in commission printing. In order to solve those problems, Star began producing the total printed carpet product. As Bob Shaw observed, "the reason we did that was you had to have a good base, you had to have a good yarn base, because if you were just taking other peoples' material in and printing it," it was impossible to maintain any quality control. Printing was a delicate process, and slight variations in the quality of the base of tufted carpet could produce a poor print. "So we started selling carpet already printed. It was a 12-ounce, level loop, 5/64 gauge product, and unless you had a good base you couldn't get a good print. We called it broadbased distribution. We were printing carpet for companies like Jorges Carpet and a series of others, and they were selling it under their label. If you didn't control the yarn, the backing, everything, you were constantly fussing with your customers." With Philadelphia producing carpets and now with Star moving into the production of carpet as well as finishing, Shaw officials began to question the wisdom of continuing to finish goods for competitors. By the spring of 1977, the company had decided to get out of the commission finishing business.[46]

Bob Shaw indicated as much to his board of directors in April 1977. In reviewing results for the Star division, Shaw explained that "the nature of the business of the Star division had changed to the extent that this division was substantially out of the commission finishing business and was almost exclusively into the sale of a complete product line. The entire output of the supply operations of Star was now being consumed by the rest of the manufacturing operations of the Company." In large that was due to the success of the Philadelphia division. Bud Shaw had managed to turn what had been a near-bankrupt operation in 1967 into a solid operation by the mid-1970s. Philadelphia's profit margin rivaled that of Star Finishing in 1976.[47]

Internal factors also contributed to the demise of the company's decentralized management structure. "During this period of time," Warren Sims remembered, "we were going two different directions. Star Finishing was going one way—they had carpet-manufacturing customers. Philadelphia was going another way—we were competing with all these people Star Finishing was servicing. In the long term it didn't make a lot sense to continue competing against ourselves." The company was spending money on two different operations, trying to upgrade and keep each competitive, "and we didn't have that much money and credit at that time. Here again is that confidence factor. We decided that we had to get vertical; we were spreading ourselves too thin." Sims switched his base of operations from Cartersville to Dalton in 1976 in anticipation of a move toward greater integration. "We were going to get vertical at some point, and we were building an office building in Dalton. I knew most of the people in Dalton and all of the people in Cartersville, and it was only natural that I be a part of establishing the headquarters in Dalton."[48]

Early efforts to "get vertical" met with limited success. By the late 1970s, Bud Shaw had developed numerous other business connections, including Post Properties and several other firms. He was "trying to manage all these diverse interests and maintain a handle on the Philadelphia carpet division." In addition, he began experiencing health problems, building (in hindsight) toward a major heart attack in 1981. The Star Finishing division sent one of its salesmen to Cartersville to run the Philadelphia marketing operation, Sims recalled, "and he went wild spending money." At one point, Star Finishing's Bill Lusk was locked out of a Philadelphia sales meeting at a Chicago market. This was the final straw. "Shortly thereafter, Bob and Bud got together and decided that they needed to streamline the operation and stop competing with each other for capital."[49]

Bob Shaw similarly recalled the crunch period of 1976–77. "The truth of the matter is that Philadelphia was doing okay. But we really had decided to concentrate on downstream distribution. We had decided that . . . we were going to get out of the commission finishing business and go on and sell our carpet directly to the distributors. And the organization was starting to look like just a carpet mill rather than a finishing mill and a carpet mill." The separate divisions no longer had much purpose. "Bud more or less backed out of the day-to-day operations. I was always the chief executive of the company, but Bud and I were equal partners. A lot of what he began doing at that time had to do with our personal investments. It was kind of a natural thing—you just can't have two CEOs; it just won't work. So when we were bringing the companies together, then Bud began looking more at other things—we had Post Properties and a lot of other things going by that time. Bud remained chairman of the board" and continued to have input on strategic matters, but he "was not active in running the business" on a day-to-day basis.[50]

Bob Shaw presented an extensive management reorganization plan to the board of directors in October 1977. Shaw told the board that "the various divisions of the company and their operations were becoming increasingly more integrated, thereby making it necessary that the management of the various divisions be consolidated for greater efficiency." The proposal, "endorsed by Mr. J. C. Shaw," reiterated Robert E. Shaw's position as CEO of Shaw Industries. In addition, Bob Shaw would "assume authority over and responsibility for the operations of all divisions of the company as well as any operations which related to the ultimate profit and loss of the corporation."[51] In essence, Bob Shaw took over all management responsibilities for the corporation.

Bud Shaw remained as chairman of the board, but the chairman's responsibilities were defined anew. Under the new management structure, the chairman's duties included stockholder relations and responsibility for the "coordination of the Board and the Executive Committee's activities, including the creation of both standing and ad hoc committees." Bud Shaw continued to play a leading role in representing the company in relations with government agencies and industry organizations, such as the Carpet and Rug Institute. The chairman continued to aid in the development and maintenance of "relationships with financial institutions, including commercial banks, institutional lenders, and investment bankers," as well as consultants of various types. Bud Shaw also continued to play an important advisory role in overall strategic planning. But from October 1977, Bob Shaw assumed complete authority over all Shaw Industries operations.[52]

"So Bud agreed to become chairman of the board and Bob became chief executive officer," Warren Sims observed. "We kidded about them being Mr. Inside and Mr. Outside." In essence, Sims's characterization aptly described the new management structure. Bud Shaw continued to handle Shaw Industries' relations with external constituencies such as investors and trade associations, leaving Bob Shaw free to focus on managing the company. "It's been that way ever since," Sims noted, "and it's been a very successful arrangement."[53]

Bud Shaw continued to play a key role in strategic planning as chairman of the board while developing other business interests such as Post Properties. He was an early investor in and counselor to the Atlanta-based real estate firm. By the 1990s, Post had become the leading developer of "upscale" apartment communities in the United States. When Shaw retired from Post's board in 2000 to become a director emeritus, CEO John Williams characterized Bud Shaw's counsel and advice as "essential for the growth and success of our company from its beginnings" in the early 1970s. In addition, Shaw continued to develop new business ideas.[54]

A month later, Bob Shaw updated the executive committee on the progress of the management reorganization. Shaw and marketing executive Doug Squillario were "currently becoming personally acquainted with all of the major accounts of the company." Shaw noted that "serious study was being given to making an effort to acquire at least one national account to replace the former 'broad-based' account structure previously had by the Star Division." By broad-based account structure, Shaw was referring to Star's former policy of selling complete tufted products to various manufacturers and other customers who then sold the goods under their labels. The company "was already doing business with the three largest distributor type accounts," Shaw reported in November 1977, and "business in this area looked quite favorable, especially in view of the recent reorganization" of the rising distributor L. D. Brinkman.[55]

At the same meeting, Bill Lusk noted that the "unsettling effect" of the transition on employees seemed to be fading. For some time, however, the Dalton and Cartersville operations had difficulties and misunderstandings. Philadelphia employees often imagined that "Dalton got all the money" while the Cartersville plants suffered. Such misperceptions faded only with time and the increasing integration of the firm's operations. All accounting functions were consolidated in Dalton, for example, in early 1978. Spright Holland began commuting to the new corporate headquarters building in Dalton with that change, as Warren Sims already had been doing. Gradually, the old Star and Philadelphia divisions blended together into a single corporate entity.[56]

Along with the management changes and the move away from commission sales, Shaw Industries adopted new marketing strategies. The Philadelphia division had expanded the Doerrs' old limited distribution system, but it still focused marketing efforts on retailers and emphasized the Philadelphia brand name. The Sabre lines and the private labels often went straight to wholesale distributors. The company needed rapidly increased sales given Shaw's exit from the commission finishing business. Distributors and large national accounts represented the best chance for quick sales gains. Bob Shaw reported to the executive committee in January 1978 that the company had sacrificed about $40 million in sales "in the move away from broad-based sales," and "the company was still experiencing the cost of replacing these sales through a new and more stable account structure." Shaw emphasized the need to produce larger and broader ranges of samples and to introduce new products more frequently.[57]

At this point, Shaw Industries' history again intersected with that of Barwick Mills. E. T. Barwick's company was in severe financial trouble by early

1978, and this innovative but loosely managed company began losing important accounts. In March 1978, a rising Shaw Industries benefited from Barwick's decline. The Shaw CEO informed the executive committee that Shaw
Industries had "been added to the approved list of suppliers for Sears in place
of Barwick Industries." In addition, Sears had discussed with Shaw the introduction of a number of Shaw's new products. Along with new distributor accounts mentioned above, the new Sears relationship provided important sales
to fill the commission gap.[58]

During the transitional late 1970s, Bud's son, Julius Shaw, came to work at
Shaw Industries. Julius eventually became involved in several aspects of the
company's shift away from commission finishing; indeed, his career with the
company began at about the same time as the management reorganization and
has covered the two and a half decades of dramatic growth in Shaw Industries'
history. Julius attended Georgia Tech and the University of Georgia from 1972
to 1976. He started working at Philadelphia Carpet during summers and school
breaks during college, beginning in 1973.[59]

Julius graduated from the University of Georgia on June 6, 1976. On the
following day, because "Dad wasn't real big on vacations," Julius started work
for Shaw Industries, beginning with an office job in customer service. The
company still had no training program, so customer service clerks had to
"learn styles, production dates, shipping, how to treat customers." It proved
to be valuable experience. In early 1977, Julius started a sample order department. Until then, anybody could take sample orders, and "we got into some
trouble because nobody was specialized" in sample orders. Sampling had always been a cost problem for the industry. Julius was picked to head up a three-
person staff to coordinate sample orders. The company thus moved to begin
upgrading its sampling activities.[60]

"Dad thought it would be a good idea for me to move around," so in the fall
of 1977 Julius was made accounts receivable manager. "Dad said I had worn the
white hat—getting people stock and helping them with their orders—long
enough, and now I was going to wear the black hat." Julius remained as accounts receivable manager for about a year. On February 5, 1978, that division
was transferred to Dalton, and Julius briefly became a credit manager. He
moved around, indeed.[61]

In 1979, Bob Shaw asked Julius to move into the sales division. At that time
Shaw Industries still made or finished some carpet for other manufacturers. "It
was a declining part of our business, but one that at that time was still important to us," said Julius. He was placed in charge of sales to manufacturers as
Shaw Industries exited the commission finishing business. This was the first,
but by no means the last, tough job that Julius tackled. He had to try and main-

tain good relations with the company's dwindling number of commission customers.[62]

In late 1979, Julius "was given the best job I've ever had. I was given the job of running an operation we had called Carpet Values, our off-goods and promotional division. As we were getting into making our own carpet we were making a lot of mistakes, so we had a lot of seconds and a lot of dead inventory. It was a tremendous drain on our company." Bob Shaw asked Julius to run Carpet Values, selling these seconds and cutting down on associated losses. Why Julius? "Number one, you needed somebody honest. . . . in that type of business. It was a very hands-on business; you had to run it, from pricing your own goods to collecting your own receivables to getting as much as you could for those goods." Julius also encountered Norris Little during his time at the Carpet Values division. Concerned about the amount of "off goods" being produced by manufacturing, Julius dashed off an impulsive, complaining letter to the CEO and several others. Julius was then summoned to the office of the vice president for manufacturing, Norris Little. He gave the younger Shaw "the worst chewing out I've ever received." The very next day, Little visited Carpet Values. Julius was "quite scared," but Little "extended his hand and asked if I was okay." The incident typified Little's management style. He was tough and demanding yet compassionate. Little would make great strides in improving Shaw's quality control procedures and manufacturing processes. In the late 1980s, he brought in one of the few outside consultants used by Shaw in those years, quality guru Philip Crosby. Little and Crosby helped introduce a successful quality improvement process.[63]

Julius Shaw, then, had a varied and hectic introduction to the carpet industry. The company survived the internal and external difficulties of the late 1970s, and in the process of surviving, it reinvented itself as a carpet manufacturer. Shaw introduced important new products in this period that boosted sales and helped the company make the transition. None was more important than Cracked Ice.

Most Shaw officials are still quick to mention Cracked Ice as an important product in the company's history. It came at a fortuitous time in 1976, as the industry and the company struggled with a changing environment. Buddy Sewell remembered the product well. By the mid-1970s, he was working in Technical Resources as a special project engineer. His job was to develop new styles in random multicolored carpets, a popular styling innovation of the 1970s. The initial Kusters dye ranges could produce multicolor effects, with differences of shading and blending of different colors to produce what were considered exciting visual effects, much more effectively than they could produce solid color carpets. (Becks were still more effective for that purpose, though not for much longer.) "So I looked at printing and all the multicolors, and I loved it." Sewell had tired of the routine work involved in producing solid-color carpets in the becks or on the new continuous ranges. "It was a joy to go to work in the morning" during the years he worked in Technical Resources, experimenting with new multicolor designs.[64]

This distinctive new look of Cracked Ice resulted from Shaw Industries' experiments with Kusters TAK dyeing, a random multicolor offshoot of the Kusters solid-color dye ranges. The idea for Cracked Ice came from "just playing in the lab. Well, not playing, but searching. That was the first one we did with this gum shield," which produced streaked effects. "I put on too much gum one day onto a little piece, and it so happened that the pattern I had on the machine that day gave that look—it looked like a broken windshield. They used to meet upstairs—Bill Lusk, Bob, and all of them—well, I'd take all these pieces out and throw them down on the floor when they were upstairs. Of course, they had to walk across it when they came back down. They picked up on it."[65]

"That was in February, and we had to wait until July 4 in order to change our steamer so that we could actually run it." Shaw also made adjustments to its machinery to make the Cracked Ice pattern easier to duplicate. "We put a gum shield down, and we ran it through the TAK machine," but then they figured out how to plug up the dye applicator. "We got this guy over here in town at this leather shop to make us some little rubber plugs to slip in these slots, so we diverted the dye from coming down here and made it go around back. So that's the way we made Cracked Ice." Buddy Sewell recalled that "no one was ever able to duplicate Cracked Ice." He and his colleagues also "worked out a way to use four colors on the two-color TAK machine, which was also a homerun" in terms of sales. Many new multicolor looks were developed in the 1970s, but "Cracked Ice was the biggest one." Indeed, the product was featured in Shaw Industries' Annual Report in 1976.[66]

The recession of the mid-1970s abated, and carpet firms developed new products such as Shaw's Cracked Ice that appealed to the tastes of late-1970s consumers. But the industry did not return to its double-digit growth rates of the previous decade. Shaw Industries emerged as a unified corporate entity in an increasingly hostile environment characterized by an overcrowded marketplace. Having barely recovered from the oil shocks of the 1970s, the U.S. economy and the carpet industry entered a deep recession in the early 1980s. The company would have to continue to change and adapt to new conditions.

CHAPTER FIVE

Survival of the Fittest

Shaw Industries became the leading manufacturer of carpet in the U.S. during the 1980s. As the company "got vertical" in the late 1970s, Shaw was not a dominant player. Other firms—World, RCA's Coronet division, WestPoint Pepperell's Cabin Crafts division, Burlington-Lees—dwarfed Shaw in terms of sales volume and market share. Shaw Industries had, however, quietly positioned itself for major expansion. Unlike many firms in the industry, insiders noted, Bob Shaw always kept his eye on the company's balance sheet; Shaw Industries was always well capitalized. Bob Shaw and his management team made decisive moves in the early 1980s to build on this solid base. The company grew in two distinct phases. The first phase, 1980–86, was characterized by internal growth. During these years, Shaw grew to become the nation's top-ranked carpet manufacturer without acquiring any major competitors. Beginning in 1987, Shaw consolidated its top position by acquiring several competitors. The internal growth of the first period laid the foundation for a successful merger movement in the second. In the late 1980s and early 1990s, Shaw Industries took the lead in consolidating the carpet industry.

The Carpet and Rug Institute (CRI) surveyed its membership in 1979 to try to gauge the sense of the industry about its future. Industry executives were asked to identify the "single biggest problem facing the industry." Government regulation had become a significant factor for this industry in the 1970s for the first time, and it might be natural to assume that business leaders in the carpet trade would single out government regulation. Surprisingly, they did not. "Profitability led the problem parade," CRI's president concluded. Overcapacity, bad price structure, and a variety of other terms were used to express this underlying concern. Indeed, several company officials said that the best thing that could happen to the industry in the near future would be "for two-thirds of the companies in the industry to go out of business."[1] In the early 1980s, those executives would come closer to getting their wish than they probably imagined (or wanted).

The recession of 1981–82 was a turning point for the carpet industry. The "gold coast" era, which had tarnished a bit during the 1970s, finally ran out in the 1980s. The number of U.S. carpet-making companies fell by half in the 1980s. Many mills were acquired by larger, stronger firms; many simply went under. This recession formed the backdrop for Shaw's rise to the top—the key decisions were made in the midst of the carpet industry's most serious crisis since the advent of tufting. Coming on the heels of the downturn of the 1970s driven by the energy crisis, the sharp recession of the early 1980s took a heavy toll on an already weakened industry. Shaw Industries had already begun exiting the commission finishing business in 1976 in part because of the poor financial health of many of the firm's customers. The more serious 1981–82 downturn pushed most of those shaky customers over the edge. The 1982 recession hit Shaw Industries hard as well. Shaw's sales fell by $18 million in one year, reaching only $232 million in 1982. Shaw's international sales, a relatively new growth area that accounted for 5.5 percent of company sales, fell by 27 percent.[2]

In the midst of the economic crisis, Shaw Industries' senior vice president, Bill Lusk, joined a Carpet and Rug Institute delegation to testify before the House Banking Committee in December 1981. Lusk and other executives joined CRI president Ron VanGelderen in providing "input on the status of the economy and its impact on our industry." VanGelderen observed the close connection between the health of the housing sector and prospects within the carpet industry. "While our industry has experienced continuous growth throughout the last 20 years," he noted that "carpet growth began to decline" as "interest rates began to climb dramatically in 1980." The carpet industry was now "beset with growing inflation of the costs of raw materials, high interest rates, and low consumer confidence." Carpet shipments fell 10 percent in 1980 and then stabilized in the first half of 1981, but the second half of 1981 was "disastrous." Shipments were down 22 percent in October 1981. The unemployment rate in Whitfield County, Georgia, climbed into double digits in the fall of 1981, as shipments fell and mills cut back on production.[3]

The CRI delegation clearly hoped to spur changes in federal policy to make more financing available for housing. The same CRI Newsletter that reprinted VanGelderen's remarks to Congress also carried a story on the President's Commission on Housing. The commission had recently published its findings on "the pent-up demand for housing." The newsletter story opened with a reference to Franklin Roosevelt's famous assertion in the 1930s that one-third of the nation's citizens lived in substandard housing. The commission, CRI noted, estimated that only 7 percent of the U.S. population now lived in such conditions. That progress was not unalloyed, however, and had been eroded during the 1970s. At the beginning of that decade, the commission estimated that half of American households could afford to buy a new home; by 1980, it declared, less than 7 percent of American families could realistically afford to make such a purchase. CRI noted that although demand for housing continued to grow, new housing starts had not kept pace. CRI agreed with the commission in recommending that "housing would become more available if state and local governments were given unrestricted access to private capital markets" and if "excessive Federal regulations on land development and housing production could be eliminated." The commission asserted that "20 percent of housing costs can be traced to excessive government regulations." As part of the Reagan administration's offensive against the regulatory state, the commission made clear its view that government was not the answer; it was the problem.[4]

President Reagan had already taken some action. In the fall of 1981, the Department of Labor announced revisions to its regulations on pension funds that made it possible for construction-oriented pension plans to invest in residential mortgages. In early 1982, the Reagan administration further relaxed regulations "to allow private pension funds to invest directly in residential mortgages." Pension funds amounted to half a trillion dollars in 1981, and government estimates projected that total to rise to more than $3 trillion by the mid-1990s. Yet government regulations regarding the tax-exempt status of such funds made it difficult or impossible for most pension fund managers to invest in real estate, especially home mortgages. CRI and other construction-related trade groups believed that tapping into this rapidly expanding pool of capital would help reduce mortgage interest rates and spur housing starts. In the deep recession of the early 1980s, the industry sought relief wherever possible.[5]

The Shaw Industries Executive Committee met in May 1981 to approve the company's listing on the New York Stock Exchange. In the course of that meeting, the CEO observed that although the company's current annual revenues amounted to about $250 million, manufacturing capacity probably approached $400 million. The only thing holding Shaw Industries back, Bob Shaw contended, was a bottleneck in distribution.[6]

Characteristically, Bob Shaw forged ahead in spite of the recession. He moved forcefully to break that bottleneck in 1982 by making dramatic changes in the company's sales and marketing programs. Shaw insiders met in 1982 to map out a new company strategy. The firm had already made great strides toward becoming the low-cost producer in the industry. Shaw management would continue to pursue manufacturing efficiencies, but the company also began shifting its distribution strategy. Bob Shaw and his management team confidently set a new goal for the company: $1 billion in annual sales. Word of the goal leaked out within the industry, and many business insiders scoffed at the very notion of a billion-dollar carpet company.[7]

Vance Bell was a key player in these changes. A native of Macon, Georgia, Bell graduated from Georgia Tech in 1973 with a degree in industrial management. He took a job with WestPoint Pepperell's Carpet and Rug Division immediately upon graduation. Based at the Cabin Crafts yarn division in Newnan, Bell worked in a variety of technical and manufacturing jobs for about two years.[8]

The talented young Bell tired of "the same four walls in Newnan, Georgia," however, and in 1975 he discussed his situation with his boss, Inman Shepherd (who, incidentally, later went on to serve as yarn director at Shaw for many years). Bell told his superior that he was a little dissatisfied, and an understanding Shepherd arranged for Bell to interview with the Cabin Crafts divisional sales office in Dalton. Bell's wife had grown up in Dalton, and through that connection as well as his work with WestPoint, he had come to know several carpet manufacturers in northwest Georgia. He arranged initial interviews with several of these contacts as well. At his father-in-law's suggestion, Bell also arranged an interview with Bob Shaw. Two days after that initial contact, Bell recalled, he received a phone call from Bob Shaw. "Get me a few references," Shaw told him. "We'd really like to talk with you." Shortly after, Bell joined Shaw Industries in the Star Finishing division.[9]

Bell worked a little in research and development and then as an account representative for a while. Soon Bell began "calling on some of the local manufacturers" in the northwest Georgia area. "We were primarily in the flatbed printing and beck dyeing business," and Bell sold this service to a variety of firms, including WestPoint Pepperell, Gulistan, and Jorges Carpet. "It was pretty good training because I was able to get into and look at the other manufacturers, and into their R&D and product development process, and even some of their marketing process." This was "pretty much a local job, traveling around north Georgia, calling on manufacturers. At the time there were only three salespeople in the entire group."[10]

In the late 1970s, Shaw management began to get concerned about the financial health of many of the company's customers. "We were concerned about our business because we were selling to manufacturers who weren't tremendously strong or well-capitalized, and we were a little bit worried about our customer base. We decided that we needed to take a step forward and get a distribution vehicle" to go straight to the wholesale distributors. "So we acquired Magee Carpets. At the same time, we started a private-label distributor division." Bell was placed in charge of the private-label division.[11]

The Magee line sold to "one group of distributors that was probably an older line, more mature group." With the private-label division, Bell and David Wilkerson "started something from scratch and started calling on distributors that were probably the up and coming, stronger distributors—L. D. Brinkman, Carson Pirie Scott," among others. The private-label division "hit fairly big. We had a couple of good products, and frankly we probably outsold the whole Magee line. We did that until 1980–81." At that time Bell took over the Magee label as well and became the national sales manager for the distributor division. In 1982, Bell became vice president for sales.[12]

Bell's advance into top management coincided with the deep recession of 1981–82. "That was a tremendous recession. Business went down 20–25 percent. Bob Shaw, with his tremendous vision," suggested doing "something different." Bell had noticed a significant change in the makeup of the retail distribution chain in carpeting and brought this change to the attention of Bob Shaw and other senior managers. "One of the things that I had noticed was the tremendous growth of the small specialty stores in retail. Small, 'mom and pop' retail shops, floor-covering stores" began springing up in large numbers—"where before furniture stores, department stores, etc., were the premiere outlets for carpet."[13]

"At the same time," Bell observed, "we were looking at our distributors and saying, frankly, some of them are not capitalized well, and they were not performing some of the functions that a distributor should do well." In essence, Shaw Industries began to take a hard look at its distributors in the early 1980s as it had done with its manufacturing customers in the late 1970s. "The distributor basically stocks carpet and gives credit. It's a service machine. And some of them weren't stocking the amount of carpet we thought they should, they weren't as aggressive in their credit policies and service policies, and we just saw an opportunity." Bell put together "a white paper saying this is what we ought to do. We all talked about it internally" and decided that they needed to start selling directly to these small stores.[14]

In order to penetrate the growing market in small retail stores, Shaw would have to expand its sales force dramatically. The company "started putting in a field sales force" in 1982. At the same time, Bell and other company officials determined that Shaw's new sales force would differ from others in the industry. The company established a comprehensive training program for its new sales recruits and changed the compensation system for sales representatives. Both these changes represented dramatic departures from industry norms.[15]

First, Shaw Industries had to begin hiring and training salespeople in larger numbers. Bob Shaw's cousin Elbert Shaw helped establish an effective program for training new hires in manufacturing supervisory positions. "Vance Bell . . . called me one day," Elbert recalled. "He said, 'I want you to set up a training program for sales like we have for manufacturing . . . we'd like you to start recruiting for sales.'" Initially, Shaw Industries just added one more school onto the recruiting list—the University of Tennessee. Shaw's campus recruiting list then consisted of Auburn, Georgia Tech, Clemson, and Southern Tech. Until 1982, Shaw's college recruiters focused almost exclusively on the manufacturing and technical side of the business.[16]

"Of course, it takes a while to get name recognition on campus," Elbert Shaw observed regarding the difficulties in college recruiting for a relatively unknown firm like Shaw Industries in an industry with little brand name recognition. "I interviewed a fellow from Clemson, who later came to work with us. He said that he wanted to get some experience interviewing and that he had never heard of our company; he thought it must be some little chicken coop company." On learning Elbert's last name, the young man said, "'they must be sending the president of the company over here trying to impress us.' He said when he got to Dalton he had no idea how big the company was."[17]

Elbert Shaw quickly discovered that Shaw Industries would have to expand recruiting efforts even further. Vance Bell told him that "we are a national company now, and I don't know whether it will work or not, but we'd like for you to start interviewing at some schools outside the southeast." Bell suggested starting with a school in the Midwest and one in the Northeast. Boston College and the University of Nebraska were selected. "So we started going to Boston and to Nebraska, and the thing just kept expanding and expanding. Everything was escalating."[18]

Shaw focused on recruiting "high-quality people." This meant "not just quality from a sales standpoint, but from a moral standpoint." Elbert Shaw illustrated the commitment to quality with an anecdote. His department for years reported to Warren Sims, Shaw Industries' vice president for administration. "I remember one time we brought a fellow here from Georgia Tech, and I was just really impressed with him. Warren interviewed him and immediately sent his evaluation back to me and checked 'do not employ.' I called Warren and set up an appointment to talk about it. He said, 'I knew you were going to get me on that one.' I said, 'This is one of the best people I have come up with, I don't understand.' And Warren said, 'Yeah, but he wasn't as good as the last one you brought. . . . Every one of them has to be better than the last one.' I would go to Georgia Tech and stay three or four days, or to the University of Nebraska, or wherever, and interview maybe forty people at each place. And out of those forty I had to select maybe four to come to Dalton for a second interview." This approach—casting a wider net while maintaining high standards—succeeded as Shaw Industries successfully expanded its sales force.[19]

Elbert Shaw also established an intensive sales training program for the new recruits. "I went to each of the heads of each department that I felt these people should train in—and, of course, the salespeople also trained in manufacturing departments, not just in sales. In fact, they trained more in manufacturing, because it was important for them to know how to make carpet." The initial plan proved to be a bit too intensive. "Our first sales training program actually was set up to be about nine months. That rapidly changed to five months and then down to about three months because of the need out in the field" as sales territories multiplied. Elbert Shaw encouraged the area sales managers "to anticipate their needs well in advance, and then we would try to recruit from those areas. If they anticipated that six months from now they were going to divide a territory in Arizona or Nebraska or wherever, we would try to recruit in those areas." The company "quickly found out that the people from the Southeast wanted to come back to the Southeast. We called it the Georgia Tech syndrome—they wanted to work anywhere within two blocks of North Avenue."[20]

The new strategy probably worked better than even Bell had hoped. *Sales and Marketing Management* reported on Shaw's progress in early 1984. Through "astute restructuring of its sales and marketing," the magazine observed, Shaw Industries achieved remarkable results. Shaw more than doubled the size of its sales force within a year, from 45 to 110. The company recorded a 30 percent increase in sales in fiscal 1983. Moreover, the company's market share jumped from 6 percent to almost 9 percent "in a highly fragmented industry in which a 10% share is unheard of." Shaw's sales rose by $150 million, accounting for 25 percent of all new growth in the carpet industry. "Our timing was excellent," Vance Bell told the marketing journal. The company's new sales structure was in place by the first quarter of fiscal 1983, just in time to take full advantage of the rebound in new-housing starts.[21]

Bob Shaw suggested another key element of the new sales structure. "One of the things we did that came straight from Bob Shaw," Bell recalled, "was that we changed the compensation of the salespeople to something that was very different in the industry." At that time most salespeople throughout the carpet industry were paid primarily on a commission basis. Bell noted that commission salespeople often functioned "like their own company. They tended to look out for what was best for their pocket. It was very difficult to reduce the size of territories, to add somebody in there, because they thought, 'you're affecting my income.'" Of course, Shaw's new direct-to-retailers strategy would involve significant and rapid splitting and creation of new sales territories. "So we put people on a base salary and a growth incentive, tied to sales volume, and we put our district managers on the same arrangement." This was a gamble because Bell and others "were concerned that we would lose a lot of people. And we may have lost a handful of the big producer types who were upset with the new arrangement."[22]

The Shaw sales team, then, contained a heavy concentration of new recruits fresh off college campuses. Julius Shaw recalled that these new employees were often referred to within the company as "the Kiddie Corps." This represented a significant risk, but it "facilitated us adding salespeople and splitting territories," Bell remembered, "because we'd split a territory, and if 75 percent of the compensation were salary, it didn't affect them that much. We would split, and they would grow, and we'd split again, and we just kept adding salespeople and territories. Because of the tremendous fragmentation and this growth of all these small specialty stores, we just kept following that growth."[23]

Bell told *Sales and Marketing Management* in 1984 that the salary-plus-bonus arrangement had three distinct advantages. The change helped make salespeople "feel like true employees" and helped encourage greater loyalty to the company. In conjunction with the training program, the new arrangement helped create an esprit de corps that came to characterize Shaw's salespeople. "We stamped a big red *S* on their chests," as Julius Shaw put it. The change also made it possible to rapidly increase the number of sales territories without creating dissension within the ranks over reduced commissions. Just as important, the new system allowed greater managerial control over sales. The old Shaw system had consisted of a half-dozen sales managers. In late 1982, the company increased the number of managers to twenty, each of whom would be responsible for only four to six salespeople. The goal, Bell maintained, "was actually to be overmanaged," because of the fragmented nature of the market and Shaw's aggressive sales goals.[24]

"Every time we'd split a territory and put a person in there, the service of that person, the quality of our products, and our pricing," Bell noted, led to greater sales. This, of course, made existing relationships with distributors difficult. "We had some longtime distributor arrangements and contracts. One of my jobs, which was not pleasant, was going around and getting out of those arrangements so that we could then go direct within those territories," Bell observed. "We would follow the salespeople with distribution centers. We just had tremendous, explosive growth and totally changed the landscape of the industry. We became a carpet distributor." Shaw Industries integrated forward into distribution at precisely the right time.[25]

The investment community took note of Shaw's new distribution strategy. *Forbes* reported that Merrill Lynch analysts were "high on Shaw Industries" in December 1984. Analysts singled out Shaw's "strong distribution system," highlighted by eleven warehouses and a salaried sales force of 150, as the key to recent growth. *Forbes* noted that Shaw had "aggressively gone after the fastest-growing segment of the market, small carpet retailers that operate one or two stores—people who don't try to squeeze the last dime out of a manufacturer."[26]

In spite of resentment among some distributors, Shaw Industries retained a substantial portion of the wholesaler market. Julius Shaw vividly recalled getting a call from Bob Shaw in early 1983 asking him to take over the distributor division during this transition period. Julius admitted, "it was a difficult job to accept. I didn't sleep that night" after Bob called about the job. The next morning Julius met with Bob to discuss the job and "begged him, 'Please don't make me take this job.' I think I cried," Julius joked. He reported that Bob responded, "Julius, you're going to take this; we need you to do this. I need you to do this job." So Julius "went from a job I loved at Carpet Values to a job that I knew was going to be a tough one." Shaw Industries had to retain as much of a presence as possible within the distributor market, in part as a hedge against potential setbacks in the new retail program. If the move toward direct sales to retailers faltered, Shaw Industries would need the distributors.[27]

Julius Shaw received "tremendous company support" in his new position. "The country was coming out of a recession," so "from a macroeconomic standpoint" the timing, at least, was good. The company used "great products, great service, great pricing to keep as much of the distributor business as we could" during this time when the company was moving into direct sales to retailers. "Between a good economy and great product and service, we actually grew our distributor business the next two years. It didn't go away."[28]

Shaw's products, prices, and service overcame the ill will and hurt feelings of many distributors. "We encountered a lot of negative feelings, a lot of bad press from that segment of the market," Bell recalled. "Those were trying times, and we weren't the favorite of those people, although we still sell to them and still have good relationships with many of them." A wave of consolidation swept through the distributor segment in the 1980s, in part prompted by Shaw's end run around the wholesalers. "It ended up bringing a lot of consolidation to the distribution segment of the business. A lot of people went out of business when consolidation happened. But it was going to happen anyway; somebody was going to do it; it just happened to be us."[29]

The entire industry had become dependent on wholesale distributors for marketing carpet by the early 1980s. Distributors marketed around 80 percent of total carpet production in the United States in 1982. According to some analysts, the power inherent in this dominance led many distributors to try to force mills to sell at lower and lower costs. Industry consultant Reg Burnett contended that "[w]holesalers have been holding the mills' feet to the fire, so to speak, by trying to use their muscle to buy low cost." Because of the Philadelphia division's long-term relationships with the retail marketplace, Shaw was less dependent on distributors than the industry average. Nevertheless, 55 percent of Shaw's 1982 sales were to distributors, national accounts and overseas accounts; only 45 percent of company sales were made directly to retailers. Within three years, the company had dramatically altered the mix. About 80 percent of Shaw's 1985 sales went straight to retailers, so Shaw was able to bypass the 22 percent average distributor markup, sell more cheaply to retailers, and still increase profit margins.[30]

The decision to move away from the distributors, of course, involved much more than a larger sales force. Shaw expanded its regional warehouse facilities from two to ten. In order to bypass the distributors, the company had to have facilities to provide inventory storage and service quickly to customers nationwide. This move nearly doubled overhead costs. Shaw also invested in new telephone and computer systems to keep up with the rapid increase in the number of customer accounts: up from 3,400 to more than 14,000 within two years of the changes.[31]

In another related move, Shaw Industries created a trucking subsidiary in March 1982. Bill Lusk placed particular emphasis on Shaw Trucking in the company's great leap forward in the mid-1980s. "The delivery system was all common carriers at the time," Lusk recalled. Everyone used the same contract trucking services. Trucks "would come over here and pick up 20 rolls, go over to Coronet and pick up 15, and so on. So actually they were delivering for the industry, and everybody's delivery was the same. You just didn't have any control over what your service levels were going to be." By the early 1980s, Shaw's volume had reached a level, Lusk believed, that would justify investment in the company's own transportation system. "If we could fill a truck with Shaw goods," he observed, "then we could deliver on a more timely basis. Strictly from a competitive standpoint, should our delivery get better, then our competitors should get a little worse." This was so because "we found that we were the filler for the entire industry because of our volume." When Shaw's volume was subtracted from the common carriers serving the Dalton area, trucks had to make more stops to fill out a load.[32]

Shaw's "service levels improved, and we branched from there into regional distribution centers," recalled Lusk. Shaw "ran big trucks in" to the distribution centers and "little trucks out" to make direct deliveries to retail outlets. "It was expensive and frustrating, and yet it was very satisfying" as it began to pay off. These distribution centers started out stocking certain popular lines and items, but by the mid-1990s they had evolved into redistribution centers. "The delivery system was so good," Lusk observed, that there was no longer any need for these facilities to carry significant inventories. This move "took an educational process for the retailer out there because he was so used to having the distributor inventory." Retailers initially feared that they "couldn't survive." In fact, Lusk maintained, Shaw Industries kept large inventories in the early years of the distribution centers just to ease the minds of retailers. "A lot of the inventory in these facilities was a facade in an educational period of time for the retailers." Retailers had to be convinced that Shaw could meet their needs without large regional inventories before they were completely comfortable with the new direct relationship.[33]

In the midst of the recession, then, Shaw began forging a new strategy. That strategy was still incomplete in May 1982, when Bob Shaw assessed the state of the industry and his company for Shaw's executive committee. Shaw observed that the industry was "still plagued by severe price competition and overcapacity. A real question for the industry," he maintained, was "the source of new working capital and additional capital for modernization and improvement as business conditions improve." Shaw also told the executive committee that "yarn capacity has exceeded capacity for finished goods and this has been a major factor in adversely affecting operating results for carpet manufacturers in general. At the present time, it is more economical for nonintegrated manufacturers to purchase finished fiber from outside sources than it is for integrated manufacturers to process their own fiber."[34]

This was a potentially serious problem for Shaw's vertical integration strategy. If yarn-processing capacity continued to run ahead of finishing capacity, there would be little economic incentive for Shaw to integrate backward toward yarn mills. If Shaw's new marketing and distribution strategies succeeded, however, the company could generate enough demand to justify expanding finishing facilities. In other words, it was up to the company to generate enough new sales to raise industry volume to a point where backward vertical integration made sense.

By late 1983, Shaw's sales had increased dramatically, and the national economy had entered a strong recovery. Meanwhile, the recession had taken its toll on yarn manufacturers with excess capacity. Shaw took advantage of the recession to buy six yarn-spinning mills at roughly twenty-five cents on the dollar, including a portion of the Comer family's Avondale Mills in Alabama in December 1983. Shaw's goal was to achieve long-term cuts in costs of materials through vertical integration. Yarn production was the most logical place to look for cost savings: face yarn made up about 65 percent of the cost of producing carpet. By 1985, Shaw senior vice president Bill Lusk could boast that "we have control over virtually 100% of our yarn supply in-house. . . . It's very comforting."[35] Shaw had long had yarn production capacity in-house, and other carpet mills also had yarn facilities, including WestPoint Pepperell's Cabin Crafts division. What set Shaw's new moves apart was the scale of the internal yarn production capacity the company now had. In the past, those carpet firms with yarn mills rarely had the capacity to produce more than half of their yarn needs. Shaw now could process virtually all its own yarns, as Lusk noted. In a rapidly growing but uncertain market, it had made little sense for carpet makers to get carried away with building yarn capacity that might not be needed tomorrow. The maturing of the carpet market seemed to indicate to Shaw management that the time had come to intensify its backward vertical integration.

After the acquisition of the yarn mills, Shaw implemented a new production strategy. Shaw Industries began to produce yarn and carpet regardless of economic conditions. In a recession, Shaw cut prices to maintain sales and increase market share. When the economy picked up again, Shaw maintained a portion of the market share gained by price cuts, and bumped prices up a bit. In either case, production continued apace. The consistent market Shaw provided for the chemical companies helped cut the company's raw materials costs. Shaw's acquisition of the yarn mills was an example of the company's continuing commitment to capital expenditures for expanding and improving plant and equipment. Since the mid-1970s, Shaw typically spent about twice the industry average on capital improvements, measured as a percentage of total sales.[36] Bill Lusk recalled the early 1980s and the acquisitions of the yarn mills. All the yarn-spinning mills "were Heller's boys," he insisted. The Heller company kept struggling yarn and carpet mills afloat, factoring receivables for both sides of the supply equation in the late 1970s and early 1980s. The recession of 1981–82 finally brought down that house of cards, and Shaw was able to acquire yarn mills for a fraction of book value. Shaw's massive investments in yarn processing in the 1980s "enhanced the profit base." While Shaw built a couple of yarn heat-setting mills, "we never built a spinning mill," Lusk remembered with pride, "we acquired all of them. We would rehab them and bring them up-to-date." All the investments in yarn processing were "good decisions, very profitable decisions."[37]

Walter Hemphill played a major role in the "rehabbing" and improvement of these yarns mills. Hemphill was deeply involved in the company's backward vertical integration, including the Avondale acquisition in 1982. "We were buying some of Avondale's yarn, but their business was not good. They were running two to three days a week. We bought the mill, and I went over there and called all the employees together with the plant manager in the warehouse. We cleared out the warehouse and put circles of bales of fiber for people to sit on. I stood up in front of them and told them we needed more 250s than they could produce, and they grinned from ear to ear. But we turned them from a three-day a week operation to a seven-day a week operation in about thirty days. And they have been a good volume acquisition. The Decatur [Tennessee] plant was small when we bought it, but we developed it into one of the leading filament heat-set plants in the industry. The idea carried forward—we bought one small and made it big as soon as we could. One of the things Mr. Shaw would do, he'd look at me and grin and say, 'How are we going to get another million pounds a week?' Then he got to where he would tell me, 'Walt, you need to add three zeroes to your thinking.' We were producing between eight and nine million pounds [of yarn] a week when I retired [in 1990]. We had fourteen yarn mills and got four more from E&B the day I retired."[38]

Shaw Industries moved to make maximum use of its decreasing costs in April 1985. Bob Shaw had long been angered by what he perceived as a "sloppy market with prices" nationwide in the carpet industry, as well as the numerous "special deals" cut by many competitors with distributors. Shaw began cutting prices on broad lines of carpeting, undercutting many of those "special deals." Rather than negotiating individual deals, Shaw offered lower prices with no strings attached for dealers.[39]

Julius Shaw had managed the company's distributor accounts during the transitional period while these new strategies were being implemented. In early 1985, Julius was able to leave that thankless but successful task for what he considered a more attractive position: he became a regional sales vice president (RVP) and in that position was able to observe the impact of Shaw's new strategies in the field. After a brief stint as RVP for the Midwest, Julius received the "best news of my business life." He became RVP for Shaw's southeast region, the company's largest in terms of sales volume. He remained in that position for ten years and recalled many memorable moments from that busy decade at Shaw. Julius's recollections of a 1986 sales meeting perhaps encapsulate the buoyant, can-do atmosphere of the mid to late 1980s at Shaw. "We were having a sales meeting, and Mr. Shaw came down to speak to us. He said that we were going to grow, as a company, 30 percent that year. We all looked at each other—we thought 10–12 percent was pretty good. He said, 'No, we're going to grow 30 percent, internal growth [not counting any acquisitions].' I'll be darned, but at the end of 1986, we as a region grew 30 percent, and the company grew 30 percent. It was probably the most exciting time I can remember in the carpet industry because we had made such strides in our trucking, our service, our quality, and we were very aggressive in our pricing. It was so exciting because all the changes we had made in the early 1980s were now in place. We were so far ahead of our competition in the number of salesmen we had. We opened up a tremendous number of accounts. Most of all, we were hungry, and we were the price king. It was like taking candy from a baby. We would target other manufacturers' big accounts, and between the service, the quality, and the price, it was easy pickings."[40]

Shaw Industries' success far exceeded that of the carpet industry generally. Broadloom carpet shipments surpassed 1.2 billion square yards in 1979; industry shipments declined during the recession of the early 1980s to about 885 million square yards in 1982. The industry's yardage shipments jumped by 23 percent in 1983 as the general economy began to recover, but growth flattened quickly to an average growth rate of about 3 percent for 1984 and 1985. The dollar value of mill shipments mirrored the decline of the early 1980s, falling from a high of almost $5.1 billion in 1979 to $4.9 billion in 1980. Dollar sales recovered more quickly than yardage sales due to substantial price increases (almost 10 percent in 1980, followed by a hike of more than 14 percent in 1981), and carpet makers' total sales of $5.2 billion in 1981 barely exceeded the 1979 level. Sales dipped again in 1982, though, falling back to $4.9 billion, before jumping almost 22 percent in 1983. The roller coaster ride slowed through the mid-1980s as sales gains matched yardage gains at about 3 percent in 1984 and 1985.[41]

Shaw Industries never flinched from making large capital investments. More importantly, the company's management ably anticipated emerging trends. The strategic shifts of the early 1980s catapulted Shaw Industries from obscurity to the top of the nation's floor-covering industry. Other large firms from the 1960s either merged with conglomerates or disappeared altogether in the 1970s and 1980s. Why had Shaw survived and thrived while others had struggled or disappeared? For many of the mills that originated in the 1950s and 1960s, building an organization for the long term may not have been a high priority. "I don't think there was an unwillingness" to build an organization, Bob Shaw reluctantly observed, "but things were so easy. During the go-go '50s, right on up to 1980 or so, with one minor recession, it was hell-bent-for-election, and you didn't need any controls." Many companies probably "never really figured out where their profit was." Sales grew so fast that it was difficult to fail until the 1970s. Even then, the market grew enough to sustain a large number of small firms and to allow a certain laxity with regard to efficiency. At least, Bob Shaw observed, "until the recession came, and you had to figure out who you were and why."[42]

Shaw's characterization of the industry reflected his confidence in his own abilities and those of his management team. Warren Sims, who worked closely with both Bob and Bud Shaw for a quarter-century, identified that confidence as a key ingredient in the success of Shaw Industries. "Now, they were very confident—both Bob and Bud. One of their greatest assets is their confidence. A lot of people would call it ego. But that's one of the things that made Shaw Industries successful." Echoing a familiar Bob Shaw saying, Sims recalled, "Bob always got after me, he would say, 'You just need to add another zero to your thinking.'" That confidence and the desire to create "something that would last" drove the growth of Shaw Industries in the 1980s. "Particularly at that time," Vance Bell recalled, in the late 1970s and 1980s, Bob Shaw "was a tremendous driver. He was a visionary. He wanted this company to be a large, well-managed, profitable company that would transcend his ownership and his lifetime."[43]

By 1986, Shaw had built just that—a large, profitable, well-managed company. In the mid-1980s Shaw Industries dueled with Burlington-Lees for the top spot among U.S. carpet manufacturers on the basis of internal growth alone. Bob Shaw's emphasis on the mantra "low-cost production" had laid the groundwork for the firm's meteoric rise from relative obscurity to the pinnacle of the industry. Shaw Industries then entered a new phase in the maturation of the company and the industry. In 1987 Shaw took the initial step toward the consolidation of the U.S. carpet industry with the first in a series of major acquisitions. By the mid-1990s, Shaw would solidify its position as the leading U.S. carpet manufacturer.

CHAPTER SIX

Leadership in a Maturing Industry

Shaw Industries' southeast regional sales vice president Julius Shaw was summoned to a meeting in the spring of 1986. "We were told we were going to go up to Chattanooga, and there was going to be a big announcement. So all the salespeople, the vice presidents, and the district managers flew in here." At this Shaw sales meeting, DuPont launched "its new Stainmaster concept." DuPont chemists performed "the Kool-Aid trick," where they spilled Kool-Aid on the carpet and "just wiped it right up." Shaw's salespeople were properly impressed. Following "the biggest advertising campaign ever in the carpet industry," sales skyrocketed. Julius Shaw acknowledged that "DuPont did it right. They got the salespeople and the manufacturers excited; they got the consumers excited."[1]

The Stainmaster craze burst onto the carpet market in late 1986 just as Shaw Industries was solidifying its top position among U.S. carpet manufacturers. The Stainmaster mini-boom boosted carpet sales but proved a mixed blessing for the industry. It highlighted carpet manufacturers' continuing dependence on fiber suppliers such as DuPont and spurred Shaw and other firms to reexamine management strategies.

The carpet industry's severe recession of the early 1980s, followed by slow growth in the middle years of the decade, affected a major profit center for DuPont. The chemical giant had stagnated in the 1970s, as the firm fell from sixth to thirteenth place on the Fortune 500 rankings of the nation's largest companies. Many observers claimed that the old giant had become complacent. In early 1985, DuPont's traditional emphasis on research and development produced a breakthrough that promised to rescue at least the flooring systems section of the textile fiber department. DuPont chemist Armand Zinnato discovered a process that "would impart stain resistance" in carpet fibers. Zinnato conducted experiments that confirmed his preliminary finding: the introduction of certain chemicals (dye-resist agents) could make carpeting "nearly impossible to stain."[2]

A DuPont strategist within the flooring systems division advocated an aggressive marketing strategy for the new process as a way to boost carpet fiber sales. Bruce Koepcke convinced upper management to fund a $50 million promotional campaign for the new process, quickly dubbed "Stainmaster." DuPont's allocation for this campaign constituted "the largest consumer product marketing effort ever staged" by the company.[3]

DuPont had scheduled Stainmaster for introduction at the January 1987 carpet trade shows. Information on the new process leaked to the trade press in the spring of 1986, however, and DuPont also learned that rival Monsanto was developing its own stain-resist process, so DuPont management decided to speed up the introduction of Stainmaster. The company began presentations to carpet mill management teams in May 1986, and the first carpets made with the DuPont Stainmaster chemicals were certified in September 1986. The consumer advertising campaign began in October 1986.[4]

American consumers quickly came to recognize red-haired "little Ricky," the protagonist in Stainmaster commercials. Ricky spilled all manner of messy foods and beverages on white carpet touted as stain-proof. The ads ranked as among the most effective in recent marketing history. The Stainmaster ads ranked in the top ten in effectiveness for 1987 according to surveys conducted by Campaign Monitor, an independent organization. The ads also won a prestigious Clio award.[5]

Consumers eagerly accepted the new Stainmaster product lines. Stainmaster boosted carpet sales dramatically. Mill shipments increased an average of 9 percent per year during the first three years of Stainmaster. Longtime industry observer Frank O'Neill believed that the Stainmaster campaign represented "an important turning point for the modern carpet industry."[6]

Carpet manufacturers were less than ecstatic about the new product. The rapid transition to Stainmaster involved tremendous costs. The chemicals were applied during the manufacturing process, so production machinery had to be modified. The chemicals themselves added cost to carpet making. Just as significantly, the advertising campaign made existing inventories of non-Stainmaster products difficult to move. The "little Ricky" commercials forced mills to produce new stain-resistant lines more quickly than they had planned. Most firms had anticipated being able to convert slowly to stain-resistant carpets, spreading the cost out over a year or two. Intense consumer demand, spurred by advertising, made that impossible. And carpet mills had to produce samples of the new stain-resistant lines. The still intense competition within the industry only compounded these cost problems. An industry observer estimated that the new process had added about 15 cents per pound to the cost of carpet production, but "the volume-oriented mills have not increased prices to compensate for the higher costs." Total sales volume did increase, as O'Neill noted, but already slim profit margins almost disappeared. Shaw Industries' sales were up 23 percent in the second quarter of 1987 as compared to the same quarter in 1986, but net income barely moved.[7]

Bob Shaw expressed what many executives in the industry probably thought about Stainmaster after the whirlwind introduction. He concluded in 1989 that if Shaw was selling more carpet at lower margins, then the new process detracted from the industry. "We can talk about how it cost us a lot of money as an industry. We had to resample. We had manufacturing learning curves to go through. But I'd be the last to tell you what would have happened if stain-resistant hadn't come along."[8] Later, as DuPont's Stainmaster program evolved (or devolved, from Shaw's perspective), his doubts about the long-term benefits of the process mounted.

After getting through the initial startup costs involved with Stainmaster, both DuPont and the carpet manufacturers made money, at least for a while. "What was really funny was that their business was so good, there was only a limited amount of nylon we were able to get."[9] Most manufacturers used filament nylon for their Stainmaster line. Filament nylon typically found its chief application in the low to medium segments of the marketplace. Shaw Industries chose a different product route. "Interestingly enough," Julius Shaw recalled, "the main horse, product-wise, that we put on [Stainmaster] was a spun, not a filament, textured, low-luster product called the Masters Series—Masters Choice, Masters Touch, etc. They were 35-, 45-, and 55-ounce textured, spun, low-luster products. I thought to myself at the time, Why in the world would we bring out a spun product, and a low-luster spun product at that?"[10]

There was method to the apparent madness. Shaw Industries' increased yarn-spinning capacity, acquired during the early and mid-1980s, made spun nylon yarn a logical option if a successful product line could be developed. Shaw had also modernized those plants and increased their efficiency, reducing (though not eliminating) the cost advantages of filament nylon. No carpet mills, including Shaw, had yet entered the field of extruding nylon filament, so reliance on filament products increased dependence on outside sources of raw materials. Spun yarns also were typically used in medium-range and higher-end products. Shaw focused on a slightly higher market segment with its Stainmaster carpets. "We placed thousands of samples. When those samples hit, we had all the yarn mills that could process this spun yarn. This was a product that was selling for about $9–19 a yard, and it was our biggest product in dollars that year. We were making big margins on it."[11]

Dupont perhaps got greedy after the initial success of Stainmaster. At the outset, DuPont had set relatively high standards. Manufacturers had to meet DuPont's specifications for yarn face weight in order to qualify for a Stainmaster label. Stainmaster carpets had to have at least 35–36 ounces of spun yarn or 30 ounces of filament yarn per square yard. "That lasted for about a year," Julius Shaw remembered, "and then I think DuPont made some strategic mistakes or miscalculations. It was going so good for both the mills and DuPont that they decided they would lower the standards. This relatively high standard "was a great idea," Julius observed, because "it kept the price up, it was a good carpet, it guaranteed that the manufacturers would make good carpet."[12]

Julius joked that "it was like the old saying that goes, 'pigs get fat and hogs get slaughtered.'" DuPont apparently decided to start lowering the required minimum face weights. By bringing down the minimum standards, cheaper and cheaper Stainmaster products appeared, and volume increased. "Within a year, the filament weight minimum went down to 25 ounces; within two years, it went down to 18 ounces. I don't recall where spun went. Within three years, you could buy a Stainmaster carpet that had 18 ounces" of face yarn per square yard. It became difficult for the mills to maintain any profit margin at all on such high-volume, low-priced goods. "All of a sudden, it became unprofitable for the mills. That was really interesting because DuPont had a great concept—everybody was making money on it, including the retailers—then they started dropping the weights. You could go into a retail store in 1991 and say, 'I want to see a Stainmaster,' and they would show you an 18-ounce piece of carpet. Then retailers weren't making money on it, manufacturers weren't making money on it, but they had to have it. What was a great deal in '87 and '88 turned out to be a really bad deal three years later."[13]

As a result of the Stainmaster disaster, Shaw Industries and other manufacturers as well as retailers "started moving away from Stainmaster and into products that could be more profitable." Julius Shaw observed with a sense of irony that "what was once the most powerful carpet brand—it was a fiber, but most people thought it was a carpet—by the early '90s had all but disappeared. It was a beautiful deal for everybody concerned for about two years, and then it just absolutely disintegrated."[14]

Bill Lusk concurred with Julius Shaw's assessment, though he had fewer kind words for the initial phase of Stainmaster. Lusk observed that "it was an old technology that they dragged out of the trash can. It wasn't really ready to go to the market" in the fall of 1986. DuPont's marketing blitz, however, made it impossible for carpet makers to wait on putting the carpet on the market. "The costs were horrible, and the claims were horrible." Moreover, Lusk noted, the marketing blitz "raised consumer expectations to a very unrealistic point that the technology didn't catch up with for many years." And there was the copycat syndrome as other fiber producers rushed to catch up with DuPont. "Of course, Allied had to come out with a 'me, too'—Anso IV—and, of course, it wasn't ready" for release. In the end, Lusk insisted, "nobody made any money out of it. DuPont certainly didn't because they blew it all on advertising on the other side trying to prop up an idea whose time was dead. And we didn't because they charged us so much" for the chemical applications.[15]

Bob Shaw identified the Stainmaster affair as "the last straw" in an escalation of tensions between fiber producers and carpet manufacturers. Since the 1950s, Shaw observed, DuPont and other fiber companies "had the big investment in carpet. That changed as we started backward integrating, extruding our own yarn. During that period of time, we were adding more value and by the '80s and '90s we had the bigger investment in carpet, not the fiber producers." While DuPont still controlled the production of the nylon chips, carpet manufacturers—led, far and away, by Shaw Industries—had moved back along the supply chain, taking out several of the links between the chemical firms and the carpet manufacturer. "The passing of the baton—that was a hard, very difficult period of time. DuPont didn't want to give up their position of dictating downstream, and we wanted to make sure we [manufacturers] were controlling our own destinies. That was the battleground, and it's been fought over the last 12–15 years, really between DuPont and Shaw." Bill Lusk wholeheartedly agreed: "No question about it. That pushed us to get more vertical and get control over our destiny."[16]

Shaw Industries faced some cost problems associated with the introduction of Stainmaster but was better equipped to handle the temporary crunch than most companies. WestPoint Pepperell, parent company of Cabin Crafts, struggled mightily with the new process, suffering a 70 percent decline in earnings for its carpet and rug division in 1986, mainly attributed to the Stratton acquisition and the start-up costs for Stainmaster.[17] That poor performance set the stage for the first major movement toward consolidation within the tufted carpet industry. While many smaller firms had gone under or been acquired during and after the recession of the early 1980s, the top firms in the industry had as yet not begun to merge.

WestPoint's difficulties with the Stainmaster process only highlighted long-term problems within the U.S. textile industry. While carpet manufacture had prospered in the 1960s and 1970s, the broader textile sector struggled. During the 1960s, one scholar noted, "the textile and apparel industries in most industrialized countries felt the impact of increased imports from the low-wage developing countries." From the end of World War II to the mid-1970s, global textile production expanded sevenfold. Demand managed to keep pace during the golden age, but the global downturn after 1973 led to more intense competition. Though U.S. textile firms had complained about competition from cheap imports throughout the 1960s, the situation became acute in the 1970s. Textile firms responded to this new and more competitive atmosphere by downsizing, restructuring, and consolidating. Like other American industrial sectors in the late 1970s and 1980s, textiles tried to adapt to new global competitive pressures.[18]

Textile firms restructured in an effort to cut costs and adapt to consumer demand. The U.S. automobile and steel industries' massive difficulties in the late 1970s and 1980s received more press attention, but textiles faced a similar crisis. The rising tide of international competition coincided with (or caused, or exacerbated, according to a variety of analysts) the end of the golden age, stagflation, and a slowing of real income growth. American business had dominated the global economy in the generation after World War II. The mass-production orientation (called "Fordism" by some), based on a few large units producing ever-increasing amounts of slightly differentiated goods, broke down in the face of renewed competition and the increasing segmentation of the U.S. market.

Like the carpet industry in the 1960s, American textile firms generally had been "production-driven" throughout the twentieth century. During the 1980s, more firms adopted "just-in-time" manufacturing practices, trying to avoid building up large inventories. Companies also invested in new equipment and increased productivity. Textile employment fell precipitously as a result, from 885,000 workers in 1979 to 671,000 in 1992. The number of textile plants fell accordingly, from 7,200 in 1977 to 6,400 just ten years later. In 1978, 75 publicly traded textile manufacturers competed with a host of private firms; by 1989, the number of publicly traded companies had fallen to 28.[19]

The 1980s was the decade characterized by the hostile takeover and the leveraged buyout, and the textile sector followed the national trend. The best known of these takeovers at the national level was the bidding war that developed over RJR-Nabisco, made infamous by the bestseller *Barbarians at the Gate*. *Wall Street Journal* reporters Bryan Burrough and John Helyar detailed the RJR free-for-all that came to define the junk bond–driven merger mania of the 1980s. R. J. Reynolds, like many large American firms, had diversified in the 1960s and 1970s. Its many subsidiaries offered a great opportunity for a buyer to sell off unrelated enterprises for cash. Many of the conglomerates created in the 1960s were broken up in the 1980s. Wall Street investment firms such as Kohlberg, Kravis and Roberts and Drexel, Burnham, Lambert (employer of the most recognizable figure in the financial community in the decade, Michael Milken) used high-interest "junk bonds" to finance many of these mergers and acquisitions.[20]

Many of these takeovers and buyouts proved beneficial to the target companies, leading to a renewed focus on core business activities (after unrelated business segments were spun off). Often, however, they deteriorated into frenzied bidding wars. While stockholders were enriched in the short run by outrageous premiums paid for their stock, the target firms were essentially used as collateral to secure the high-interest, high-risk junk bond financing. Justified as a way to force these flabby companies to "make their assets sweat" (by forcing firms to increase profitability in order to meet debt payments), junk bond financing could as easily saddle companies with unmanageable debt that could inhibit attempts to restore competitiveness. The term "corporate raider" entered the everyday lexicon in U.S. newspapers by the mid-1980s. Raiders such as Carl Icahn and others used junk bond financing to acquire lucrative targets. A leveraged buyout, or LBO, is essentially a method of financing in which a purchaser uses a target company as collateral for credit to accomplish the acquisition. Management groups often used the leveraged buyout to convert a publicly traded company into a private company, essentially pledging to pay the high interest costs of such credit out of the target company's revenues. Management groups would then sell shares to the public again within a few years, thus reaping large rewards in the process. As Burrough and Helyar observed, stockholders, the LBO firm, and the raider generally profited. "The only ones hurt were the company's bondholders, whose holdings were devalued in the face of new debt, and employees, who often lost their jobs" in cost-cutting moves.[21]

Drexel played a key role in perhaps the textile sector's most infamous hostile takeover attempt of the 1980s. WestPoint Pepperell restructured itself during the early 1980s under the leadership of Joseph Lanier Jr., the fourth generation of Laniers to run the company. Lanier tried to make WestPoint "an internationally-oriented marketer of brand-name consumer goods, including imports," *Business Week* noted in 1985. *Business Week* praised Lanier's leadership, noting that he "was ahead of the industry in de-emphasizing high-volume but import-sensitive products like cheap towels and apparel fabrics." Lanier focused his company on "brand-name lines" such as "Lady Pepperell sheets and towels and Cabin Crafts carpets." Lanier also rescued Cluett, Peabody, the maker of Arrow shirts, from a hostile takeover with a friendly buyout in 1985. Though WestPoint's earnings suffered in 1984, the company appeared to have a bright future, and analysts generally applauded the Cluett acquisition.[22]

WestPoint was a large, diversified textile company. Its many divisions and product lines made it a likely target for hostile takeover attempts. Joe Lanier and his firm fought off one such attempt in 1986 but understood that others were in the making. In an effort to strengthen his company for the coming battle, Lanier elected to sell off one of those product divisions in 1987. West-Point had never been as successful in managing the carpet segment of the textile industry. The heavy losses associated with Stainmaster helped convince Lanier it was time to unload the Carpet and Rug division, which consisted primarily of the venerable old Cabin Crafts plants and brand name. This would allow WestPoint to focus more attention on its core business activities such as sheets and towels.

Lanier sought out Shaw Industries. Bill Lusk had a subdued attitude toward the Cabin Crafts acquisition. He insisted that by the 1980s, the Carpet and Rug division of WestPoint-Pepperell, unlike other divisions of the company, was "not run very well." Cabin Crafts was "an old-line company, good reputation, probably should have been the dominant leader in the industry." In Lusk's view, however, the Cabin Crafts division had "philosophically fizzled over a period of time."[23]

The Westcotts and Bob McCamy had continued to run Cabin Crafts as an independent subsidiary until the early 1960s. Even then, old Cabin Crafts hands such as Virgil Hampton and Jack Turner ran the company for years after the founders retired. In the mid-1970s, WestPoint ended the Cabin Crafts run as an almost autonomous subsidiary and brought the new Carpet and Rug division under direct WestPoint management. The home office appointed managers who often had little experience in the carpet industry. Some of these managers did a fine job (Joe Maffett was a prime example), but "WestPoint was primarily an apparel company," Lusk recalled, and WestPoint spent most of its corporate energy focusing on trying to rescue its "core business" during the recession of the 1980s. The Carpet and Rug division languished. Bill Lusk was surprised that CEO Joseph Lanier and his top aids knew so little about the Carpet and Rug division. "I was amazed when we started negotiations. Bob and I went down there to talk to Joe Lanier and learned that the chief financial officer of WestPoint had never visited Dalton. He didn't even know what was up there."[24]

Shaw and WestPoint reached a tentative agreement in late September 1987, but the initial deal fell through in early November. Shaw had planned to issue new stock to help pay for the purchase. The stock market crash in October seemingly torpedoed that plan. A few weeks later, according to *Forbes,* Bob Shaw decided to go "full speed ahead and damn the stock market." Shaw went ahead with the deal, purchasing WestPoint's carpet division for an estimated $140 million.[25]

As far as the general public was concerned, the stock market crash had killed the first attempt to close the Cabin Crafts deal. The real story was more complex, according to Bill Lusk. After making an initial offer, Shaw's financial people began investigating under due diligence. "There was a major inventory valuation problem," and WestPoint management "just couldn't believe it." Shaw made a counteroffer, but WestPoint refused, and the first deal collapsed. Within a few weeks, "Mr. Lanier dispatched his chief financial officer to Dalton. I got a call. He had been up there for three or four days, and he wanted to come by and see me. He said that if we were still interested, he was going back to WestPoint and recommend to Mr. Lanier that he accept our offer, that it was very fair." WestPoint had acquired another carpet maker, Stratton, a few years earlier, and "they never had gotten into it, straightened it out, and valued it properly." The valuation problems Shaw encountered had to do with the blending of Cabin Crafts and Stratton assets. In the end, WestPoint found that Shaw's estimate was much nearer the mark than its own internal calculations. "Mr. Lanier called Mr. Shaw, and we got back together"; the acquisition went forward.[26]

Bill Lusk recalled that there were some problems associated with the Cabin Crafts acquisition. The purchase "got us our first entrée into the rug business," Lusk admitted, though he was no fan of the custom rug portion of the Cabin Crafts business. "It was not very profitable, but it made some good pictures." Cabin Crafts had always been famous for their custom rugs, though "they didn't sell many," Lusk joked. Lusk credited the acquisition with adding to Shaw's reputation for high-quality manufacturing. "We got some [product] lines, and it also added to our account structure, even though we had already established a large account base." Shaw also acquired some good people. The accounting and other management systems, however, "were not compatible" with the systems used by Shaw Industries. "We had to toss all those out. It took us about three months to convert the systems. A lot of people quit," and a few were "let go in the interest of efficiency." Overall, though, Lusk insisted that the acquisition "was a good one" and became increasingly valuable after the initial short-term transition problems were worked out.[27]

For Warren Sims, the significance of the Cabin Crafts acquisition transcended business concerns. "We had Cabin Crafts so deep in our blood," Sims observed. "Cabin Crafts was by far the best business in Dalton, Georgia," for years. The Cabin Crafts name was one of only a very small handful in the carpet industry that carried any weight at all. "I think the name really got them [Bob and Bud] excited. They probably thought 'here is a company that we have patterned our whole operation after.'" Sims, from the perspective of vice president for administration, recalled a somewhat smoother transition than Bill Lusk described. Even though the acquisition "was so huge, it was not that difficult because we knew so many people. There was a mutual respect between people."[28] Bob McCamy's son, Julian, became Bob and Bud Shaw's brother-in-law when he married their sister Eleanor. By 1987, Julian McCamy sat on the Shaw Industries board of directors. He took a special pleasure in reclaiming what he considered the family business.[29]

Yet Bob and Bud Shaw both insisted that too much should not be made of the significance of this particular acquisition. Shaw Industries acquired Cabin Crafts not for any sentimental reasons, they insisted, but because this West-Point division offered tangible advantages and a chance for Shaw to begin the process of consolidation within the carpet industry. The recession of the early 1980s had claimed a large number of small firms. Even so, the industry remained, from Bob Shaw's perspective, too fragmented and inefficient. With the end of the "gold coast" era, the market for carpet had apparently matured, signaling that the time was right for someone to take the lead in consolidating the industry. Differing views on this acquisition within Shaw management reflect the tension between competition and cooperation, or between sentiment and business strategy, that existed within this industrial district.

The acquisition of Cabin Crafts and the rest of WestPoint's carpet division boosted Shaw's annual revenues to $1.2 billion, solidifying Shaw's position as the world's largest carpet manufacturer, a ranking Shaw would continue to hold as it entered the twenty-first century.[30] Shaw had indeed become a billion-dollar company, making good on Bob Shaw's prediction from the early 1980s. Bob wanted to make it clear, however, that he was no corporate raider. As he recalled, all of the competitor acquisitions of the late 1980s and 1990s were friendly buyouts or mergers. In the first two instances (the purchase of the WestPoint and Armstrong carpet divisions), Shaw Industries simply bought divisions from diversified companies struggling to get back to their core businesses. Shaw did not engage in bidding wars to purchase rivals. In fact, Shaw instituted a few new technical procedures to discourage hostile takeover attempts against itself in the mid-1980s.[31]

WestPoint management had little time to celebrate their well-made deal. The Georgia-based textile giant became a target in the summer of 1988 for

William Farley, who had acquired the Fruit of the Loom company in 1985. Joe Lanier Jr. fought to retain control over the company his family had created in the nineteenth century. Farley and angry stockholders eager to sell to him eventually gained enough leverage to oust Lanier, ending the family's control over WestPoint. Farley operated with assurances of junk bond financing from Drexel, Burnham, Lambert, but the company overextended itself in the take-over mania of the 1980s and went bankrupt in 1989, in the midst of a bitter war between Lanier's forces and Farley. In the end, Drexel's bankruptcy destroyed Farley's bid to acquire WestPoint.

Shaw's acquisition of Cabin Crafts not only established the company as the top volume producer in the U.S. carpet industry, but it also gave Shaw Industries a market share unmatched by a single carpet company since the pre-tufting era. Shaw's billion-dollar sales almost doubled those of the company's closest rival, Burlington/Lees (Shaw had 14.3 percent of the market, compared to 7.5 percent for Burlington). Moreover, when automotive, area rug, and other miscellaneous sales were factored out, Shaw's market dominance was even more pronounced. Shaw Industries' broadloom carpet sales accounted for 16.6 percent of the U.S. market, while Burlington's sales amounted to only 5.7 percent. From the late 1950s through the mid-1980s, no single carpet company had managed to acquire as much as a 10 percent market share; the sales volume spread between the top company and the tenth-place company was rarely much greater than about two to one. Shaw's 1987 market share was more than four times greater than that of the tenth largest firm in the industry (Galaxy Mills, with a 3.2 percent share).[32]

Less than a year after Shaw's acquisition of Cabin Crafts and Stratton, industry insiders were mulling over "the Shaw factor." In two thoughtful articles in 1988 and 1989, Michael Berns, a California carpet manufacturer and former business professor, considered the current state of the carpet industry. Berns characterized the problems facing the carpet industry in the 1980s as "carpet mill anemia." The industry suffered from three key weaknesses that kept profits low even in times of strong sales growth. One weakness was the lack of a consumer franchise. Carpet companies all used the same fibers, made by others, and produced very similar products. There was no brand loyalty. Berns argued that lack of brand-name loyalty eliminated a major opportunity to add value to a product. Second, the carpet industry had excess capacity and high barriers to exit. There was a glut of excess equipment, as "the tufting machine is virtually indestructible," and "the great majority of tufting machines ever manufactured are still operable." Individuals wishing to switch resources or get out of the business faced great difficulty getting anything like a reasonable return if they tried to sell. "The tired, marginal producers are unable" to get out, and their mere existence "intensifies price competition," keeping profit margins razor thin. Third, carpet manufacturers were in a weak bargaining position for raw materials in relation to fiber producers, as the "Stainmaster affair" of 1986–87 clearly illustrated. For all these reasons, many carpet companies, large, medium, and small, became "zombie mills," lurching along, unable to merge or get out, forced to struggle with low or non-existent profit margins, and therefore unable to invest adequately in new technology. Shaw Industries had "dramatically altered the carpet industry's way of doing business," making "carpet mill anemia" potentially terminal for many companies. Shaw had forced a greater consciousness of cost to the forefront in the industry. With Shaw's commitment to new technology, other companies were forced to follow suit.[33] Shaw had also forced the industry to reconsider its definition of competitive pricing. Shaw's pricing, "more than any other activity," struck "fear into the hearts of carpet mill executives." Shaw's position as the industry's low-cost producer allowed the company to cut prices on many items "without damaging its bottom line results."[34]

Randy Merritt, director of Shaw's Philadelphia sales force, distributed Berns's article "The Shaw Factor" to his entire sales team. He told his team that "the majority of facts in this article are 100 percent right on, and the philosophy is totally correct." The strategies that Berns described reflected "the way our management team has viewed things for a long time, and this article just substantiates what we've been saying for a long time." While Merritt urged his sales team not to flaunt the article, he made it clear that such evidence should be made available to retailers. Berns's article "supports what we've been saying . . . if you are serious about the carpet business as a dealer, you better be buying from #1."[35] The memo reflected the aggressive, confident, yet team-oriented style cultivated by Shaw management. Randy Merritt rose steadily within the ranks at Shaw, proving to be both a successful salesman and an effective motivator.

Shaw Industries' purchase of WestPoint Pepperell's Carpet and Rug division signaled the beginning of a wave of consolidation within the carpet industry, and the pace quickened over the next decade. Shaw moved to enhance its position as the top carpet producer in the world in December 1989 by acquiring the carpet division of Armstrong World Industries, which included the assets of E&B Carpets, one of the industry leaders of the 1960s.[36]

Evans-Black, or E&B, Carpet Company had exemplified the fluidity of the Dalton district in the 1960s. Eddie Evans and Art Black met in Dallas, Texas, in 1950. Black was in Dallas as a sales representative for a home furnishings distributor. Evans, a Fort Worth native, was the southwestern sales representative for Barwick Mills. The two became friends, and soon Black went to work for Barwick Mills as a sales manager in Atlanta. Black recalled that "we both had this burning desire to be in the carpet business for ourselves, so we left Barwick in 1957 and opened Evans-Black Carpet Company, a wholesale distributor," in Dallas. Evans and Black used the contacts and connections, especially in the Southwest, that they had developed in their years with Barwick to start their own firm. Initially, Evans-Black was a sales-only company, buying carpet from Dalton-area manufacturers and selling to home furnishings retailers. Within two years, the new company was facing stiff competition from manufacturers who had decided to begin selling directly to retailers. "Competition got so rough," Black recalled, "that we formed E&B Carpet Mills in 1959" as a commission seller for direct mill shipments. By the end of 1959, Evans and Black had decided that the company must begin manufacturing its own products. They convinced their silent third partner—Frank McCarty, a former vice president for manufacturing at Barwick Mills and one of the most capable manufacturing managers in the tufting industry—to become an active participant in the business. McCarty came on board to oversee manufacturing operations in Dalton, while Evans and Black remained in the Southwest to manage the firm's sales.[37]

E&B had a family connection to Shaw Industries just as Cabin Crafts had, though it was perhaps not so deep. Frank McCarty's brother, John, had been a partner in Star Dye, an investor in Star Finishing, and a Shaw Industries board member. Frank had shared his expertise in the carpet industry with Bob Shaw in the late 1950s, at John's request.[38]

E&B enjoyed immediate success, due in large part to the contacts of Evans and Black and the manufacturing expertise of Frank McCarty. E&B began with one tufting machine in 1960; by 1966 the company operated twelve tufting machines, and its mill covered more than 140,000 square feet in Dalton. E&B turned out over 650,000 square yards of carpet per month in 1966. Unusual for a medium-sized carpet mill, E&B was fully integrated from yarn spinning through dyeing and finishing. The company focused on selling groups of similar carpet fabrics (exclusively synthetic) rather than individual products. E&B achieved great success with American Cyanamid's acrylic fiber, Creslan. E&B successfully marketed to retailers a Creslan "collection" called "Governor's Row," which included five quality grades and a wide selection of colors. By 1966, E&B employed more than 650 people, with 450 working in manufacturing in Dalton and the rest engaging in sales and administrative work.[39]

Art Black emphasized training for his sales force to a greater degree than most other mill owners. "Art Black . . . was the innovator in sales training programs" in the carpet industry's early days, Bill Lusk remembered. "Everybody wanted to hire his salesmen. So Art got the reputation of being the trainer for the industry." Black's extensive training program paid dividends for his company, though turnover was a nagging problem.[40]

Armstrong World Industries acquired E&B in 1967 in a diversification move. Armstrong was the nation's leading producer of ceramic tiles and other resilient floor coverings. Unlike RCA's purchase of Coronet, the Armstrong move at least made some business sense. Indeed, Armstrong's carpet division, led by E&B, hovered near the top of the carpet industry's list of largest firms by the early 1980s. The E&B division benefited from its association with Armstrong's floor covering distributors.

E&B's training program meshed well with Armstrong's historic commitment to sales training. In 1987, Armstrong's carpet division ranked first among sales forces in the entire textile industry, according to a *Sales and Marketing Management* survey. The E&B division met stiff competition in sales from a well-trained Shaw sales force in the mid-1980s, however. And by 1989, Armstrong had become a target for the kind of hostile takeover attempts that characterized the 1980s. The company's several divisions signaled a high "breakup value" for a potential buyer interested in divesting portions of the company.[41]

Julius Shaw observed closely the difficulties that plagued Armstrong's carpet division in the 1980s from his position as Shaw Industries' southeast regional sales vice president. He was taken aback when he learned that his firm intended to acquire Armstrong's carpet division. "My dad called me up to his house one day in 1989 and said, 'I've got some big news. We're going to buy Armstrong's carpet division.'" Julius's initial reaction was, "Why? What do they have? In the Southeast at least, Evans and Black was almost non-existent." Between the economic downturn of the early 1980s and "the siege that we had in our distribution, quality, and pricing, we had just almost wiped them out, at least in my region." E&B remained strong in other sections, but Shaw's main goal was not the acquisition of E&B's retail market share. The major benefit Shaw Industries received from the acquisition was "the Armstrong distributor business. That was a good business because the Armstrong distributors were the strongest and best-financed in the country. So as far as distributors went, we had the cream of the crop selling only Shaw carpet—or, at the time, Armstrong carpet. The distributor division was probably the best part of that deal." Although Shaw Industries had dramatically decreased the relative share of its sales through distributors, Armstrong had strong relationships with the strongest distributors. This enhanced Shaw's strength on the distributor flank.[42]

Bill Lusk agreed. "It was a good piece of the business when you added the market they had with the wholesale division, called the E&B direct division. We kept that wholesale division as a separate unit of Shaw." It later became the Shawmark division. "It was the network of distributors that Armstrong had a long relationship with. That piece of business was still cranking out $100 million a year when I retired a couple of years ago."[43]

Shaw emerged from the 1980s as the carpet industry's top company. The *Wall Street Journal* reported that Shaw Industries "snared nearly *all* the industry's growth during the latter half of the decade, ending up with almost 20% of the U.S. carpet market, up from 14% in 1985." Shaw had grown "by embracing what many companies shunned or mishandled in the 1980s: debt, and lots of it." Shaw spent over $600 million on capital improvements and acquisitions in that same period. That capital spending, however, helped to establish Shaw as the industry's low-cost producer. And as the company's market share increased, Shaw's sales and cash flow easily kept pace with the debt structure. Shaw's "ability to pay down debt is unmatched in the industry," according to an industry analyst.[44]

The recessions of the early 1980s and early 1990s eliminated many of Shaw's weaker rivals. "It's the natural order of things, isn't it," Bob Shaw observed in a 1991 interview, "the survival of the fittest." The *Wall Street Journal* described Bob Shaw as "all Southern charm on the outside and all George Patton on the inside." The struggle for existence that Shaw alluded to had already claimed over half of the carpet manufacturers in operation in 1980.[45]

Bob Shaw recalled that there were some difficulties involved in all of the mergers and acquisitions of the late 1980s and early 1990s. "Always when you put companies together, you have to merge cultures. We probably got better as we went along, took a little more time to see if we could save as many good people as we could." The carpet industry provided "fertile ground" for a consolidator at that time, however. Shaw's competitors "were not low-cost producers, and we were. We could go in and revamp what they were doing. And we could offer them trucking and warehousing that they didn't have at that time." With most of the acquisitions of the late 1980s and early 1990s, except for Salem, the multiproduct companies such as Armstrong and WestPoint were "spinning off divisions, so we didn't have to deal with personalities." Shaw hinted that Salem presented perhaps a more difficult situation. "Even with Salem, Mr. Foster was already out of it. He owned the company, his son was running it, and he wasn't very happy with what was going on." Nevertheless, the Salem acquisition brought substantial benefits to the company.[46]

W. Douglas Foster had worked backward in creating Salem Carpet Mills. Foster began in the retail carpet business and integrated back to manufacturing. In 1989, Salem acquired Howard Stein's Howard Carpet Mills. Stein's company marketed products under both the Howard and Sutton labels. Howard's Sutton division focused on an emerging new style—berbers—and used primarily polypropylene yarn (discussed further below). The Howard line concentrated primarily on the contract commercial market, the fastest-growing segment of the industry in the late 1980s. Stein remained with Salem to manage the Howard and Sutton divisions.[47]

Foster and Stein built Salem into the nation's fourth largest carpet manufacturer by the early 1990s. Foster's emphasis on and contacts in retail combined with Howard Stein's presence in the commercial market to make a formidable combination. Salem became known as an "aggressive pricer" in the late 1980s and early 1990s. Salem's pricing even undercut Shaw's on occasion.[48]

Shaw completed the acquisition of Salem in May 1992 for an estimated $65 million in cash and Shaw stock. Julius Shaw recalled Salem as "probably the most difficult acquisition we had up to that time. The reason is that we kept very little of its management, stripped many of its products." Shaw Industries dropped many of Salem's "high-end products because we thought they were carrying too much inventory, too many SKUs [stock-keeping units], had slow-moving inventory. But, looking back on it, we hurt ourselves badly by dropping too many products out of Salem. When you looked at the Salem division the next year, what we had when we bought it and what we had the next year was probably down 20–25 percent. We hurt ourselves by dropping all their high-end products."[49]

Julius Shaw remembered two distinct benefits from the Salem acquisition. One was the Sutton division. "What a beautiful thing. Berbers were just getting big—Sutton, with Allen Stein [Howard's son] and his team over there, was totally a berber-producing mill." Berber styles used yarns in natural colors, often with flecks of contrasting colors, with a rough or rugged surface that could create the impression of handcrafting. Such styles, using thick yarns in very tight constructions, were well suited for hiding footprints and vacuum marks. According to Julius, "The Sutton part of the Salem acquisition alone would have been worth it. At the time, I don't think it was more than $80–90 million out of $300–400 million. But it was a great thing because polypropylene and berbers exploded over the next few years, and Sutton was the leading berber supplier."[50]

The second major benefit from the acquisition was Salem's close relationship with Sherwin Williams. "Sherwin Williams was a $40–50 million customer.

Salem was their number one supplier, Shaw was number two. This really provided us a very solid position with Sherwin Williams that we enjoy to this day. Sherwin Williams is still one of our top four or five corporate accounts."[51]

The Salem acquisition left some scars, however. Though no one on the Shaw side was even implicated, a Salem vice president was later convicted of insider trading in the deal. Much more directly damaging to Shaw was the accusation of age and sex discrimination made by several former Salem officers against Shaw Industries. Shaw kept far fewer of Salem's management personnel than had been the case with earlier acquisitions. Several Salem officials who lost their jobs won judgments against Shaw Industries in subsequent years.[52]

Howard Stein remained with Shaw after the merger. He retired in 1993, receiving high praise from CEO Bob Shaw. "Howard Stein has been an influential part of the carpet industry for over forty years. His division has been an important contributor to our company. Howard's skills covered every part of the industry from product design and styling to manufacturing and marketing. He has earned my personal respect. We will all continue to benefit from the good job Howard has done."[53]

Just a few months after the Salem acquisition, Shaw Industries completed what proved to be perhaps the single most profitable acquisition in the company's history. Nylon, in both its staple and filament forms, had dominated the carpet market since the 1960s. Cheaper olefin yarns, such as polyester and polypropylene, had limited applications. During the 1980s, as Shaw and other carpet makers integrated backward toward yarn spinning, smaller manufacturers turned to polypropylene as a way to cut the costs of raw materials and compete with integrated firms. In 1981, U.S. carpet makers used 90 million pounds of polypropylene as face yarn; by 1988, carpet mills used more than 300 million pounds. Smaller mills pushed much of this expansion by focusing on low-end products.[54]

In terms of Shaw Industries' response to polypropylene, Vance Bell admitted, "I remember that for a long time around here we didn't want anything to do with it because we considered it too complex, and it required too much inventory to service." Polypropylene required large inventories because it had to be dyed in the extrusion phase; piece dyeing was not an option. Bell remembered a meeting, probably in 1988 or 1989, in which Bob Shaw made clear his views on polypropylene. Bell brought out some competitor samples and said, "We should be in this business. This is a growth business." He vividly recalled Bob Shaw's reaction: "We cannot be in that business. It doesn't make any sense at all." Bell added that Bob Shaw "said this primarily because at that time we did not have a competitive advantage, and he was right." In addition to the problems with inventory, the products generally were of poor quality. "The reputation of polypropylene was horrible," according to Bill Lusk. "The mills hadn't treated it very well." With many of the polypropylene products that came out in the 1980s, "you could run your shoe sole down over it, and you could burn it." But "the technology in polypropylene, unlike nylon, kept improving."[55]

In spite of these drawbacks, polypropylene kept growing and taking market share. Amoco's Fibers and Fabrics division became a leading producer of polypropylene yarn by the end of the 1980s. Amoco also worked hard, as other firms did, to improve this cheap but troublesome fiber's performance in a variety of applications. Amoco refitted two production facilities in 1989 in Bainbridge, Georgia, and Andalusia, Alabama, to produce improved polypropylene carpet fibers.[56]

Amoco did a superb job in developing new techniques for producing the yarn, but at great cost. Moreover, Amoco sold its polypropylene yarn to many manufacturers, each with slightly different requirements. "It was not a well-run operation by any means," Vance Bell insisted. "Part of that was they were supplying so many different customers who had so many different products and colors and yarn systems. Everybody had their own product lines," and Amoco had difficulty generating significant volume in any single color or product line.[57]

By 1992, Bob Shaw had changed his mind. Given Amoco's improvements in quality and the still-growing market share of polypropylene, he gave the green light to pursue Amoco's facilities in Bainbridge and Andalusia. The memory brought a smile to Bill Lusk's face even after his retirement. "They were old mills, but they were good mills. They had new equipment; they just didn't know how to run it." The facility suffered from poor management, but "they had done some magnificent technical improvements" in the polypropylene production process. "We got it for a very, very good price"—about $90 million. "We caught them at the right time. They were not happy with a lot of things. They were looking to escape, so we helped them to escape." Shaw transformed the old Amoco plant, virtually doubling the facility's output with "the same people and the same equipment."[58]

Vance Bell characterized the Amoco acquisition as "probably . . . the most profitable, the best return on investment, of anything we have ever done. The price we paid for it versus what it's worth today is just unbelievable." Shaw positioned itself perfectly to take advantage of a growing segment of the market. "It got us into extrusion and into a growth part of the market. And we probably helped it gain market share, because polypropylene now had a much stronger distribution vehicle to take it to market." Polypropylene represented 10 percent of the carpet yarn market in 1990; by the end of the decade it had increased its share to 30 percent.[59]

Bob Shaw's reversal on polypropylene symbolized his famous flexibility, often cited by associates as one of his greatest strengths. Bell remembered that "we've always said to our people, 'you've got to be flexible, you had better be willing to change on a dime.'" Bell considered Bob Shaw "open enough that he will look at something one day and say, 'It's not right,' but the next day variables may have changed, and it is right. He is willing to take a risk, and if it doesn't work out, we'll change that, throw it away, sell it, go another direction."[60]

The strong foundation built during the 1970s and 1980s helped the company weather some difficult times. Shaw Industries' noted flexibility would be sorely tested in the mid- and late 1990s. Bob Shaw and his management team had always been willing to take risks in the search for greater control over their firm's destiny. Up to 1992, almost all of those risks had paid off.

In the midst of Shaw's acquisition campaign, Warren Sims summarized the company's management philosophy in a January 1990 internal memorandum. The basic propositions outlined by Sims had been practiced for years, in many cases since the company's inception. Coming from Sims—a twenty-two-year Shaw veteran, senior vice president, and lifelong acquaintance of Bob and Bud Shaw—the statement encapsulated a sincerely held belief about the company's purposes and strategies. Sims began with a simple, modest, and direct mission statement: "to produce a satisfactory return on investment to our shareholders." Sims clearly saw increasing shareholder value as the chief goal of his company. He then listed in outline form a number of strategies employed to achieve that goal. Two of the first three items listed related to employees. Shaw would "compensate our people fairly" and would "always be in the top 10% of our industry" in terms of salaries, wages, and benefits. The company would also "employ good people" who were "loyal, competitive, flexible, able, and ethically superior." "We believe that people are our greatest asset," Sims observed, "and therefore we will treat them as such."[61]

Shaw Industries, like all manufacturers in the Dalton district, faced a continuing labor shortage in the 1980s and early 1990s, making it imperative that the company follow Sims's policy on wages and benefits just to retain good workers. Shaw also maintained an emphasis on safety, partly to retain workers and partly to enhance efficiency and cut costs. In 1990, Sims reported that at least seven of Shaw's plant facilities had completed four years with no lost-time accidents. Norris Little played a key role in implementing Shaw's safety program, which raised the bar for the entire industry. He was also constantly searching for new methods of improving efficiency and quality control in manufacturing processes, moves that often had a safety-related component.[62]

The *Atlanta Constitution* reported on Dalton's labor shortage in 1987 in the midst of the Stainmaster boom: "It is terrible here," Queen Carpet's Julian Saul told the *Constitution*'s Chris Burritt. "There is almost always a labor shortage here when business is not so good. But the problem is amplified when business is as good as it is now." Industry consultant Frank Wilson agreed and elaborated. "Up until about five years ago, Dalton carpet manufacturers had an advantage," he argued. By 1987 he feared that "firms operating outside of the Dalton area now have a competitive edge" in terms of labor. Many feared that the acute shortage might mean that mills would expand in other areas simply to find sufficient workers.[63]

Labor supply had historically just barely equaled demand in northwest Georgia's carpet industry, and often the balance tilted in favor of labor shortage. The tendency of workers in the area to trade higher benefits and wages for flexibility in employment—choosing to leave one employer and to work for another for what many would term non-economic reasons—had in a sense helped relieve some of the upward pressure on wages inherent in such a situation. The recession of the early 1980s had dramatically altered that dynamic as unemployment in Whitfield County exceeded 17 percent in 1982. The Stainmaster mini-boom of the late 1980s created enough demand to push Whitfield's unemployment rate down to about 4 percent. The layoffs of the early 1980s probably led some workers to seek alternative employment. "To get skilled labor, you have to steal it from your competitors," one Dalton area employer quipped.[64]

Anecdotal evidence suggested that Shaw had become one of the most attractive places to work within the Dalton area and the carpet industry. Anne Gentry of Calhoun, Georgia, had spent eighteen years in a variety of carpet- and non-carpet-related textile enterprises by the mid-1990s. She observed in a 1996 interview that she liked her job at Shaw "better than anywhere else." Referring to the frequent turnover that occurred in management in the textile and carpet trades, she observed that "at every other place I worked management changed at least once, sometimes two or three times, in just a few years." The stability of Shaw's management, from the top down to the level of plant supervisory personnel, made it a "good place to work."[65]

Pat Brock began her working life in a small carpet mill just after graduating from high school in the early 1970s. After being laid off from a secretarial position in 1980, Brock began "bothering" the people in the personnel office for Shaw's Calhoun spinning mill. "I was single with two little girls, newly divorced," and "needed a job." Initially Shaw's personnel department wanted to place Brock in a secretarial position like the one she had just left, but she wanted to be out in the plant "where I could make more to raise the kids." Why did she focus her energies on Shaw? "They were the highest-paying mill in this area." Brock got a job in the mill starting at about $7 per hour and immediately began making herself indispensable. Sometimes when her spinning machine broke down, the fixer was busy so she "went to his tool box, got what I needed, and fixed it myself." She moved all over the plant, learning to drive lift trucks and operate virtually all the machinery. After nearly twelve years with Shaw, Brock was promoted to shift supervisor in 1992. The only female supervisor among a dozen at her plant, Brock achieved her position through hard work and determination. She summarized the work environment at Shaw simply. Problems were rare, and when they occurred, they were "easily resolved." Shaw management placed great emphasis, she observed, on maintaining a safe and welcoming work environment.[66]

Shaw Industries dealt with the labor shortage as best it could by rewarding and trying to retain good workers. The philosophy had changed little from Bob Shaw's days at Star Finishing in the early 1960s, except that he could no longer offer the personal involvement that he had earlier. Shaw's workforce grew to more than 30,000 by 2000. But the philosophy outlined by Sims had permeated the organization. The company kept its wages and benefits at or near the top of the industry. By the 1990s, it was commonplace for workers at other companies in northwest Georgia to mention their goal of getting on the payroll at Shaw.

Sims also highlighted Shaw Industries' commitment to "a strong balance sheet" that would "allow us to continuously update buildings and equipment to keep us a *low cost producer*" (emphasis in the original). The single-minded focus on the balance sheet would also permit "market share growth internally and through acquisition" and "sustain us in a slow economy." Growth in market share was a critical component in company success as well. Shaw made it a policy to "maintain sufficient market share to allow full utilization of our production facilities."[67]

Warren Sims encapsulated Shaw Industries guiding strategies in this brief statement. In a sense, Sims merely codified the firm's experience. These strategies had guided the company through its first two decades with spectacular results. While the results were impressive, other aspects of Shaw's philosophy called for keeping the company's light under a bushel, so to speak. Sims asserted that "low visibility" was "a virtue in both public relations and investor relations." Sims also observed that Shaw had enjoyed enviable growth by using the talents of people who had lengthy experience in the carpet industry, the economy of northwest Georgia, or both. This success, achieved by focusing on local resources, bred "independence," according to Sims. That independence, he argued, "has made our company stronger." Shaw had cultivated a rich crop of experienced and talented managers, hence the company would "employ few outside advisors or consultants." As Sims recalled in a later interview, the typical response of Shaw top management to entreaties from consultants eager to advise the company was simply "Where were you when we needed you?"— a pointed reference to the ability of the company's long-serving management to identify emerging patterns and forge effective strategies. "Shaw personnel could do it better, faster, and cheaper, so why do we need you?" Sims would ask prospective consultants. For most of the company's history, this policy worked well.[68]

Warren Sims composed his brief on Shaw's philosophy just as the company opened its new design center in January 1990. By adding the design center to its corporate campus in Dalton, Shaw took another step toward gaining control of as much of its destiny as possible. For decades, carpet mills had traveled to four major trade shows every year. This schedule put pressure on mills to proliferate new styles and samples. Shaw's very size made the trade shows a problem in the late 1980s. Shaw built a design center in 1989 as a showplace for the company's products. The 55,000-square-foot facility included numerous showrooms for the company's myriad product lines.

Bob Shaw held his first press conference to announce the new center. "Since this is my first press conference in my 30 years in business," Shaw joked to reporters from local newspapers and the trade press, "we'll have to have another one in another 30 years when I'm 88 years old." On a more serious note, Shaw described the design center as "a new way of showing carpet." Shaw was "excited to be able to offer our customers a facility which is beautiful, spacious, and not crowded like the market centers," such as the Atlanta Merchandise Mart, traditional home of a major carpet trade show then in progress. The CEO pointed out the growing problem his company had in adequately showing its wares at a trade show. Even if the company rented "the whole fifth floor of the Atlanta Merchandise Mart, which we couldn't afford, we still wouldn't be able to show all of our products."[69]

Bob Shaw insisted that "we're not opposed to markets," but he did believe that it was time for a new approach to marketing carpet to retailers and distributors, the primary customers at the trade shows. Shaw went on to describe an emerging new strategy. "We want to bring people to the mills where we can sell carpet based on quality, instead of selling it by the ounce or by the square yard." Shaw probably referred to the recent Stainmaster craze when he predicted that the 1990s would be the decade when carpet mills took control of the design and marketing of their products. "We must design and style our own products," he declared. "The fiber producers can't do it for us." Shaw believed that it was time for his company to "start advertising our company's name," but he conceded that "we can't compete with the fiber producers." DuPont, for example, had more than ten times the revenues of Shaw Industries. Shaw simply could not mount a consumer advertising campaign that could compete with DuPont's. Shaw would begin working with retailers to promote Shaw Industries' brand name.[70]

Just a few weeks later, Shaw Industries announced plans for another extensive expansion of its corporate headquarters complex. Eventually, the site would include a research and development facility as well as corporate offices and the design center. Bill Lusk announced that the expansion "gives us even deeper roots in our company's home town, and shows our continuing commitment to Dalton." Shaw remained committed to the northwest Georgia region.[71]

The new strategies that Bob Shaw hinted at in his first-ever press conference proved difficult to put into operation effectively. But in the early 1990s, such looming dark clouds were nearly invisible. Shaw Industries placed first within the textile industry in *Fortune*'s 1991 "corporate reputations" study. *Fortune* did not publish most of the individual scores earned by firms in that study. The corporate communications firm of Saatchi and Saatchi sent Warren Sims a copy of the unpublished attribute scores in February 1992. Executives and analysts within the textile industry ranked Shaw number one in seven of eight categories and second in the remaining one. Shaw's overall composite score was a 7.40 out of a possible 10. Only one other textile firm (Springs Industries at 6.99) had a composite score of 6 or better.[72]

In the summer of 1992, Shaw Industries basked in the glow of its successful decade-long climb to unprecedented market dominance in the American carpet industry. During the election campaign of that year, Bob Shaw made no secret of his support for incumbent president George Bush. The president visited Shaw Industries on August 3 and spoke to company employees as well as Dalton-area civic leaders. Bush praised Shaw Industries and the carpet industry for its remarkable flexibility. Dalton's carpet industry, led now by Shaw Industries, symbolized the American dream, the president insisted. "In [the] history of your industry," he told Shaw workers and executives, "you find a parable of American progress. It starts simply—families selling hand-tufted bedspreads that they made themselves out on Highway 41, Peacock Alley, and it continues with these sprawling factories that sprung up after the war, rolling their carpets into homes and offices in every corner of America." Bush's visit focused the nation's attention, at least briefly, on its carpet capital and Shaw Industries.[73]

CHAPTER SEVEN

Difficult Times

"Nothing, it seems, can stop Shaw Industries these days," observed veteran industry watchers Frank O'Neill and Bobbie Carmical in October 1993. Shaw Industries had emerged as the clear leader in the American carpet industry with a market share exceeding 25 percent. Shaw's management, particularly CEO Bob Shaw, had demonstrated an uncanny knack for "seeing around corners," as industry consultant Reg Burnett put it. Bob Shaw phrased it a little differently. "It's like stepping up on a block and seeing a little more of the horizon, then putting another block higher and seeing a little more, and so on." Shaw Industries anticipated and reacted to new trends better and faster than any other firm in the carpet industry throughout the 1970s and 1980s.[1]

Shaw management overreached itself in the mid-1990s. Had the string of earlier successes bred overconfidence? Or did the law of averages simply catch up with a team that had made so few mistakes for two decades? In any case, the company moved deeply into the international marketplace in the 1990s with little success. Shaw also appeared to press vertical integration too far forward with dramatic, ambitious, and expensive changes in its marketing strategies. While Shaw continued to do many things well in the 1990s, these two miscalculations would cost the company dearly.

The October 1993 issue of *Floor Focus* centered on "the relentless rise of Shaw Industries." The magazine's profile included an extended interview with Bob Shaw. From Shaw Industries' unprecedented position of dominance within the American carpet industry, the CEO reflected on his company's ascent and its future prospects. He also mused about the virtues of capitalism and the future of democracy and business enterprise in the former Soviet bloc and China. "China's saying let's make sure our economy's strong and then we'll slowly give the power to the people," Shaw noted, while Russia's leaders "said here's the power to the people, but they have no economy to go with it." Acknowledging that China's approach was the more successful in the short run, Shaw expressed confidence in the power of entrepreneurial capitalism to regenerate all the former Communist states: "They'll work it out. We don't have any license on ingenuity. The trouble with the Russians is they've never been given an opportunity. When people are given the right chance, you find ingenuity all over the world."[2]

The "end of socialism" in Europe and Asia, combined with the increasing economic integration of Western Europe through the European Community, opened new opportunities, along with great risks, for American businesses. Bob Shaw clearly saw expanded international opportunities for his company in the emerging European and Asian marketplaces. Shaw had begun seriously eyeing the international markets in the late 1970s. The company created a sales division entirely for exports, primarily focusing on the United Kingdom and the Middle East. Nevertheless, carpet exports remained marginal to the company's, and the industry's, success. Shaw Industries made its first significant venture into international markets by entering into a joint venture with Capital Carpet Industries Proprietary Limited of Melbourne, Victoria, Australia, in late 1992. Australia offered several advantages: the Australian carpet market itself was among the largest in the Pacific Rim, Shaw faced no language barriers in this English-speaking market, and Australia also offered a base of operations from which to expand sales in Hong Kong, Singapore, and Japan. Those three countries imported more than $100 million in American-made carpet in 1992. The purpose of the venture, according to a company press release, was "to participate in a government-sponsored rationalization of the Australian carpet industry." In British and Australian parlance, "rationalization" implied promoting efficiency through consolidation. The joint venture would hold the current assets of Capital Carpet Industries (CCI) and had already signed letters of intent to acquire two other Australian carpet manufacturers.[3]

Australia and Great Britain seemed likely targets for Shaw's international ambitions. While U.S. carpet makers had long faced cultural barriers in trying to expand into foreign markets, Australians and Britons displayed an encouraging affinity for soft floor coverings. Carpet accounted for about three-quarters of consumer spending for floor covering "down under." The Australian carpet firm was the largest in the region, with total annual mill value of shipments exceeding a half-billion dollars. In the late 1990s, the Carpet Institute of Australia described its industry in terms reminiscent of the Dalton district, noting that the industry had "extensive upstream and downstream linkages" with the Australian economy and observing that it was "a major consumer of locally made intermediate products." Carpet manufacture played "a big part in Australia's regional economies," just as the U.S. carpet industry did in northwest Georgia.[4]

Shaw raised the stakes in its Pacific adventure by acquiring the remaining interest in Capital Carpet Industries in August 1993. Bob Shaw announced that this action would enable Shaw Industries to put all its financial strength behind the venture. Ownership of CCI would establish the company as "a major supplier of carpet products to markets in Australia and throughout the entire Pacific region."[5]

At about the same time, Shaw Industries began moving forcefully into the United Kingdom. The British industry had followed a pattern similar to that of the American carpet trade in the post–World War II years. The historian of Britain's carpet industry, J. Neville Bartlett, titled his 1974 study "Carpeting the Millions." Ironically, the title referred to the nineteenth and early twentieth centuries, when power loom technology reduced costs and made carpets available to more Britons. He covered the years 1918 to 1970 in an epilogue. Bartlett admitted that demand expanded more after World War II than before. As in the United States, British demand for carpets expanded in part due to "forces external to the carpet industry—to a low level of unemployment, rising real incomes, and a substantial volume of residential building." A "considerable part" of the boom in carpet consumption after the war, Bartlett acknowledged, came from new technology, especially "the introduction of tufted carpets." The "growing popularity of tufted carpets" on both sides of the Atlantic "was principally due to their cheapness." Tufting reduced costs even more dramatically than the power looms of the nineteenth century.[6]

British manufacturers were quick to adopt the new American technology of tufting. British firms began producing "significant quantities" of tufted carpets in 1956 when Homfray and Company Limited became the first British firm to install wide carpet tufting machines. Later that year five firms formed a consortium to make tufted carpets under the name Kosset. Other firms followed, but in the 1970s Kosset remained the largest producer of tufted goods in the United Kingdom.[7]

In spite of similarities, the British carpet market remained distinctive in some ways. In the U.S. market, woven goods had largely been driven from the residential sector by the 1970s. Tufted goods had outpaced woven carpets by the late 1950s in America. By the 1970s, tufted goods represented more than 90 percent of total U.S. carpet output. In Britain, consumer demand sustained "a relatively large sector of the carpet industry producing woven carpets and rugs" into the 1970s. As late as 1968, in fact, woven carpets still constituted a slim majority of British sales. Tufting "established a lead" by 1970, but wovens remained a huge market segment. Bartlett concluded that "the difference may reflect a greater insistence on variety and quality by the British consumer." Loom technology still afforded manufacturers much greater flexibility in the production of patterned goods, and British consumers tended to believe that woven carpets were of greater quality than tufted. The demand for tufted carpets grew, but large numbers of British consumers continued to prefer highly styled woven carpets in spite of their price; Britons often simply carpeted fewer rooms with more expensive carpets. In contrast, Americans "were generally content with plain carpets, which tufted manufacturers were well equipped to provide."[8]

British carpet manufacturers also followed the American pattern in the 1970s and 1980s. A boom in the 1960s ran dry in 1973. The English industry, like its American cousin, had experienced "rapid growth, over-borrowing, over-capacity (especially in tufteds), and sudden contraction," according to the *Economist*. Observers expected a turnaround for the industry in the late 1970s and 1980s.[9]

The expected rebound proved less than spectacular. Foreign producers, principally from the United States and Belgium, began penetrating the British market in the early 1970s. In addition, the emergence of "giant multiple groups" (similar to the buying groups that sprang up in the United States in the 1980s) increased the bargaining power of buyers at the expense of manufacturers. This "concentration of buying power . . . also made domestic manufacturers vulnerable to the price pressure imposed by the 'pile it high, sell it cheap' multiples." The growing power of the multiples only added to a difficult situation. The British industry was also highly fragmented; three hundred producers still made carpets in 1988. Management skills within the industry had not kept pace with the times. *Financial Times* correspondent Alice Rawsthorn aptly summarized the state of the industry in 1988: "Threatened by imports, cursed with poor management, bullied by retailers, and awash with surplus capacity, the carpet industry has for years been dismissed as one of the gloomiest areas of the textile sector."[10]

British carpet makers began a process of "rationalization"—consolidation, heavy investment in new equipment, and the trimming of the workforce—in the mid-1980s. A modest recovery in the middle years of that decade ran out in 1988. For the next seven years, Britain's carpet industry slowly declined; through 1995, sales fell by about 25 percent from the illusory peak in 1988. Throughout the early 1990s, analysts predicted an eventual turnaround.[11]

The British carpet industry appeared poised to rebound in the mid-1990s. *Carpet and Rug Industry* reported that many U.K. mills recorded increased sales in the first half of 1993. Moreover, the long-term prospects for carpet in the British Isles appeared bright, with "the U.K. set to become the fastest growing economy in Europe."[12]

It was in this atmosphere that Shaw Industries began acquiring carpet manufacturers in the United Kingdom, perhaps sensing that this market was primed for the sort of rationalization that Shaw had wrought in the American carpet industry. First, Shaw increased its U.K. market presence in 1992 by establishing a distribution center in Preston, England, to boost the company's exports to the United Kingdom. Shaw moved directly into manufacturing in March 1993 by acquiring the venerable Kosset Carpets, Limited, "the largest single-site manufacturer of carpeting in the United Kingdom" and a pioneer in British tufting. Kosset's holdings soon became the basis of Carpets International, a wholly owned Shaw subsidiary. Later in 1993, Shaw's Carpets International purchased Abingdon Carpets of Gwent, England. Shaw added the carpet and rug division of English textile giant Coats Viyella to its U.K. operations in December 1994.[13]

Over the next four years, Shaw Industries invested heavily in reshaping these U.K. operations. The British market proved to be a difficult arena for Shaw management. Shaw faced stiff competition from imports into the British market, especially from Belgian manufacturers across the Channel who were long accustomed to the tastes and business practices of Britons. Industry consultant Reg Burnett, a native of Great Britain, contended that Shaw management, like other U.S. carpet makers, had difficulty in understanding and accommodating the highly segmented U.K. market.[14]

Shaw Industries also found that in spite of rumors of "rationalization" over the preceding decade, the British industry still had a long way to go before becoming as efficient as its American counterpart. The persistent weakness of British textile management, alluded to by British business pundits, probably reinforced Shaw in its traditional determination to rely on its own resources. When Shaw initiated its U.K. effort, "there were no fewer than 16 American executives in the British operation," according to *Textile World*.[15]

Shaw had probably expected some government aid in Britain as well. Indeed, Abingdon Carpets had applied for government aid in 1988 to help the company finance a new polypropylene bulked continuous filament yarn plant in Gwent. The British government approved the request and eventually budgeted 750,000 pounds (more than $1 million U.S.) from a regional grant program for the new plant in 1993. The European Commission (EC), however, overseeing the transition to a more integrated European economy, blocked the grant in December 1994. The EC expressed deep concern over the increased capacity represented by the new facility, coming at a time when the entire European textile sector struggled with excess capacity and dwindling job prospects. "The sectoral effects of aid to the synthetic fibres industry have to be controlled even for the most underdeveloped areas of the Community," the commission decided.[16] Shaw officials certainly had little sympathy in principle with the distribution of such government subsidies to private industry. However, the abrupt cancellation of expected aid by a supra-national body probably caused more than a few second thoughts among company insiders about getting deeply involved in a struggling sector of the rapidly changing European Community.

Shaw managers found an industry in disarray and immediately acted to slash capacity and improve efficiency. In these efforts, Carpets International encountered difficulties that were new to Shaw Industries management. Such cuts were not unique to the carpet trade; total employment in Britain's textile sector had declined from over one million in the late 1960s to just over three hundred thousand by the end of the century. Such job losses necessarily implied significant pain for individuals, families, and communities. Shaw Industries had never faced the difficulty of drastic work force reductions in its U.S. operations. Throughout the numerous competitor and supplier acquisitions of the 1980s and early 1990s, Shaw had been able to retain the vast majority of production workers. In addition, Shaw faced a complicating factor in the existence of strong trade unions in Britain. Shaw's American workers were completely unorganized, leaving management free to rearrange work processes with few impediments.

Bob Shaw and his management team surely knew that entry into manufacturing in the British textile sector would involve dealing with unionized workers, but they almost certainly misjudged the company's ability to adapt to complex labor negotiations and the difficulties—both tangible and in terms of public relations—inherent in dramatically cutting an organized labor force. The controversy over 450 layoffs (or "redundancies," to use the British term) in Gwent and Bradford illustrated the problem. Carpets International decided to get out of the business of producing woven Axminster carpets altogether and to reduce overcapacity in tufting. The Transport and General Workers Union responded bitterly to these proposed employment cuts in December 1996. The decision came "as a complete surprise to the workforce," union national secretary Peter Booth complained, and flew in the face of "numerous assurances" from management about job security. "Firm commitments have been given throughout this period for long-term manufacturing in both of these areas," Booth charged. Union officials believed that the Shaw subsidiary had "reached

These two men are working with a dye beck at Star Finishing, ca. 1967. The work was hot and wet; the turnover rate among "beck pullers" was particularly high. Shaw Industries Files.

THE PHILADELPHIA CARPET COMPANY BROADLOOM PLANT
Is One of the Most Modern in the Industry
Buyers, Retail Salesmen and Anyone interested in the Sale of Floor Coverings, when they may have occasion to visit Phila. are welcome.
It will be our pleasure to show you how the fabrics on which we specialize are manufactured.

Philadelphia Carpet Company's Allegheny Street plant, Philadelphia, Pennsylvania, ca. 1950. This image appeared in the company's pricing guide for salesmen in the late 1950s and early 1960s. Shaw Industries files.

Carpet and Rug Institute Chairman J. C. "Bud" Shaw breaks ground for the organization's new Dalton headquarters, 1969. Shaw served as the first chairman of the new trade association, formed from a merger of the Georgia-dominated Tufted Textile Manufacturers Association and the older, New York–based American Carpet Institute. Courtesy of Carpet and Rug Institute.

This woman is "creeling." The creel racks fed yarn into the tufting machines; creelers were responsible for keeping the racks filled with cones of yarn. By gluing or tying together yarn ends from matched pairs, the tufting process could continue indefinitely on a single piece of carpeting.

Opposite: Shaw's corporate headquarters, completed in 1976. In 1977, Shaw "got vertical" by integrating the management of the Philadelphia and Star divisions and centralizing company management in this facility in Dalton.

Shaw industries top management, 1978. Seated, left to right, W. Norris Little, Robert E. Shaw, J. C. Shaw; standing, left to right, William C. Lusk Jr., Warren W. Sims Jr., C. Douglas Squillario. Under the new management arrangement, Bob Shaw became president and CEO, and J. C. remained chairman of the board as well as chairman of the executive committee.

Bob Shaw presented George Bush with a personalized custom rug.

Robert E. Shaw (left)
and J. C. Shaw, 1978. Shaw
Industries files.

Shaw management in the mid-1990s. Seated, left to right, Vance Bell, Bill Lusk, Bob Shaw, Norris Little. Standing, left to right, Bennie Laughter, Carl Rollins, Ken Jackson, Julius Shaw, Dave Cicchinelli, and Doug Hoskins.

Carpet & Rug Industry magazine profiled Queen Carpet in 1980, just as the company emerged as a major player. This cover photo includes, left to right, Al Hart of C & S Financial Corporation, Queen's VP Julian Saul, marketing director Joel Cohen, company founder Harry Saul, and Sam Gunn, VP of C & S.

Three generations of Shaws joined Warren Buffett at a Shaw dealers' convention. Buffett's Berkshire Hathaway firm acquired Shaw Industries in 2001. Standing from left to right are J. C. "Bud" Shaw, Chairman Bob Shaw, sales rep Jason Shaw (Julius's son), Warren Buffett, and Executive Vice President Julius Shaw. Shaw Industries files.

Shortly after Shaw merged with Queen Carpets in 1998, Julian Saul (left) became president of the company, joining Bob Shaw's management team. Shaw Industries files.

Shaw's original corporate logo symbolized the marriage of Star Finishing and Philadelphia Carpet Company. Star Finishing had used a simple star as its trademark while Philadelphia used the Liberty Bell. This logo was used until 2001.

Shaw's new corporate logo, adopted in 2001.

a unique agreement recognising the primary importance of long-term secure employment for all its employees."[17]

Federal Reserve chairman Alan Greenspan has observed that one of the chief differences between the U.S. economy and the economies of Europe and Japan is labor market flexibility. Simply put, it is, and has long been, easier to fire workers and eliminate jobs in the United States than in most other developed industrial nations. Although British carpet manufacturers faced organized workforces, like those at Gwent and Bradford, Shaw had seldom faced such limitations in labor policy. The company had largely avoided involvement with U.S. unions. In fact, Shaw sold its Cucamonga, California, finishing facility in the late 1970s at least in part because the plant's workers voted to join a union, and Bob Shaw made no secret of his dislike for organized labor.

After Shaw sold its British and Australian subsidiaries, new management continued to have a difficult time reorganizing workforces and modernizing operations in these countries with strong trade unions. Mike Nahan, executive director of Australia's Institute of Public Affairs, referred to Shaw's "outback" adventure in an op-ed piece in the *Victoria Herald Sun* in November 2001. Nahan observed that it appeared that Feltex, the New Zealand firm that bought Shaw's Australian plants, was on the verge of closing its Australian operation and "reverting to importing product" from New Zealand into the Australian market. Nahan argued that in this case, Australians had "once again shot ourselves in the foot." He noted that Shaw had seen the potential of Australia's carpet manufacturing plants. The American firm had sought to realize that potential "through a program of workplace reform, investment and innovation. It failed, and sold the complex less than two years later to Feltex." Lingering disputes over a hotly debated trust fund to guard workers against long-term unemployment led to bitterly contested strikes under Feltex's ownership. Like Shaw before them, Feltex managers seemed anxious to find more flexible labor arrangements. In the mid-twentieth century, Joseph Schumpeter described the importance of "gales of creative destruction" that blew through a capitalist economy. The phrase captured perfectly the nature of modern economic life—competition led to innovation, which in turn led to the destruction of many businesses and turmoil for workers, even as opportunities were created for different businesses and workers. Powerful trade unions helped workers avoid some of the hazards associated with the "destruction," the instability of capitalism, but, observers such as Nahan argued, sometimes at the cost of hindering the "creative" side of Schumpeter's famous conceptual pairing.[18]

In addition to the much less flexible labor market, Shaw Industries faced greater than expected difficulties in a variety of areas in penetrating European markets. The British carpet market never fully recovered from its 1970s swoon. "Mini-booms" in the 1980s and the 1990s led Shaw and others to believe that the British market would offer an attractive entrepôt into other European markets. The British market, and other international markets, "went very sour," according to Bill Lusk. U.K. carpet sales fell 25 percent from 1988 through 1996. Shaw entered the British market on the basis of what turned out to be misplaced optimism. Asian markets also collapsed in the mid- and late 1990s, leaving Shaw with no lucrative beachheads to assault from its base in Australia. Lusk also recalled that Shaw found it very difficult to get "established in the marketplace" in the United Kingdom. Perhaps the reliance on American management made those market relationships harder to establish.[19]

Fluctuating exchange rates also confounded Shaw in the European market. "We found we were competing in a common market without a common currency," Bob Shaw recalled. In a single year, Shaw saw the Belgian franc devalued against the British pound by 23 percent. "We saw our biggest competitor [Belgium-based Beaulieu] using the Belgian franc and we were using the British pound." Admitting that the risks involved in the U.K. operation probably outweighed the potential gains, Shaw ruefully concluded, "you can certainly judge your risk factors better than betting on uncommon currencies in a common market."[20] By the end of 1996, the U.K. operation was in serious trouble.

In December 1996, Bob Shaw sent Ralph Boe to the United Kingdom to try to salvage the situation. Boe was a seasoned veteran of the U.S. industry. He had helped Peter Spirer build Horizon Carpets into a highly respected producer. After Mohawk acquired Horizon in 1993, Boe moved to Diamond Carpet Mills, managing that mill through a difficult period. Boe provided steady leadership, and the fortunes of Carpets International improved, but the return on investment disappointed Shaw management.[21] By late 1997, Shaw executives pondered the long-term viability of the company's U.K. venture.

At about the same time that Shaw Industries began its ill-fated attempt to enter European markets, the company also initiated a new program to try to establish brand-name recognition for its products. Shaw followed this move closely with an even more ambitious venture directly into the retail market. These two related strategies involved considerably greater risks than the European diversion.

Carpet had long been marketed as a commodity; few consumers knew anything about the manufacturers of the materials that covered their floors. In fact, a large number of consumers believed that DuPont manufactured most of the nation's carpet, while most others tended to associate their carpet with the retail establishment from which it had been purchased. Shaw's acceptance of this hard truth had helped pave the way for the company's phenomenal rise in the 1980s. Shaw focused on cutting manufacturing costs through vertical integration and building market share among retailers on the basis of price and service.

Twice before in the company's history, Shaw had gone into direct competition with its largest customers. Shaw Industries' ancestor, Star Finishing, had moved into competition with its manufacturer customers in several steps between 1967 and 1977. Shaw approached retailers directly in the early 1980s, becoming in effect the nation's largest distributor of carpet—directly competing with the wholesalers who had been the company's largest customers. In both cases, Shaw had been both pushed and pulled, in a sense. The financial weakness and potential insolvency of many manufacturers in the 1970s and of a large number of distributors in the 1980s functioned as a push factor, while the potential gains in margins and cost savings acted as a powerful pull factor. Both moves had worked almost perfectly.

While many analysts were stunned by Shaw's retail adventure, the decision was, in broad terms, consistent with the company's established strategy. Bob Shaw put it succinctly: in as many aspects of the business as possible, "we wanted to make sure we were controlling our own destinies."[22] Shaw also sought to bring order to an extremely chaotic segment of the carpet industry's supply chain. Shaw's quest for order and control over his firm's destiny almost inevitably led to the front line of consumption—the carpet retail store. The move would be ambitious and expensive and the risks great. The potential rewards, both in earnings and in autonomy, promised to be substantial as well.

Shaw Industries pressed ahead with its Trustmark program in 1994, an extensive effort aimed at building brand recognition. True to the company's strategic roots, Shaw did not attempt to build brand recognition with a glamorous advertising campaign but instead attempted to build on established company strengths. Trustmark displays and samples (provided by Shaw to participating retailers) attempted to inform consumers about the product they were about to purchase. Shaw inundated consumers with information about fibers, yarn face weights, stain resistance, yarn twist levels, wearability, and a host of other characteristics of tufted carpeting. The Trustmark displays offered pragmatic advice on the best kinds of carpeting for various distinct applications and settings. In addition, the Trustmark program included a training program for retailers. Bob Shaw described Trustmark as "an effort to give the public enough information about a piece of goods to let them make an intelligent choice." Of course, Shaw products met all the suggested specifications.

The company also offered five- and ten-year warranties on products bearing the Trustmark label. Those warranties represented realistic appraisals of the potential performance of Shaw's best products. Shaw Industries sought to build a consumer franchise through the dissemination of information and product guarantees. Shaw emphasized the company's strength—the ability to produce quality carpets at the lowest price in the industry.[23]

On the surface, Trustmark appeared to be a winning strategy. Yet the program failed for several reasons. Bob Shaw blamed Trustmark's poor results on the willingness of other manufacturers and retailers to make exaggerated claims about their alternative products. Trustmark "was not ill-conceived; it was a good program," the CEO insisted in 1999, "but the truth of the matter was that we couldn't make it big enough quick enough. The difference between truth and falsehood on the back of a carpet, you couldn't fight." Shaw's competitors "started warranting carpet no matter what it was. We were making a five-year and a ten-year warranty based on tests, and somebody else would come out with a twenty-year warranty without a test."[24] Most consumers replaced carpets only once in a decade or so, in spite of warranties and recommendations, and had done so since the 1950s. While Bob Shaw argued that the longer warranties offered by other companies were grossly inflated, such paper claims carried inordinate weight in an environment marked by slow turnover among consumers. A warranty on a piece of carpeting could only truly be evaluated over a long period of time, and the mere existence of a promise of quality sufficed for most consumers. The more ambitious effort to educate consumers about the technical specifications of carpeting likewise met little enthusiasm.

Retailers agreed that Shaw's program failed to make a significant impact on consumers. Some described the effort as "ham-handed"; most retailers viewed carpet manufacturers generally, including Shaw, as "inept marketers." Jonathan Trivers, a former president of flooring store franchiser Abbey Carpet Company, aptly summarized the difficulties inherent in Shaw's educational approach to marketing carpet. "You all know the name of the toilet paper and the dork that sells it," Trivers quipped, "but Mr. Whipple doesn't talk about the tensile strength of the product." At the consumer level, Shaw's Trustmark program sank in a sea of technical details.[25]

While the Trustmark program made little headway among consumers, it also proved harmful to Shaw's relationship with the retail community. Julius Shaw characterized Trustmark as "a fiasco for our company" and outlined two reasons for this judgment. "First of all, we disrupted our sample department for an entire year—not introducing new products, just taking existing products and putting different labels on them." This relabeling of products with a Trustmark label created two problems. "Number one, it was very expensive, and number two, if you weren't getting a Trustmark label, your sample service was awful." Non-Trustmark retailers "could wait six months, sometimes, to get a Philadelphia or Salem or E&B sample." In addition to disrupting the sample department, the existence of the Trustmark program "created what a lot of people called the haves and have nots." Retailers had to pay a hefty price for participation in Trustmark, something akin to a franchise fee ranging from $20,000 to $35,000. "A lot of the customers who didn't have Trustmark, either because they weren't offered it or because they couldn't afford [it], felt neglected or discriminated against. It really created a problem with our customers"—the retailers. Julius Shaw suspected that many of those retailers "wouldn't have been so upset" had they "known how ultimately ineffective Trustmark would be. Between the expense, the sample disruption, the PR problems it caused with other accounts that weren't Trustmark, it was not a very successful program."[26]

Shaw's attempt to build brand-name recognition intersected with an even riskier, more ambitious effort in late 1995 and early 1996. Julius Shaw vividly recalled getting the news. "On December 12, 1995, we announced that we were going to move downstream in both the commercial and residential retail arenas. That hit the industry like a sledgehammer," Shaw insisted. Julius was still a regional sales vice president and was "not in the inner circle" at that time. He "had heard that we were thinking about it," but he "never thought we'd do it—ever. So it came as a very big surprise to me. I thought we were going into the commercial end of it, but I never dreamed we were going into the residential arena." Julius "got the announcement, just like our employees and a lot of our customers." Julius remembered calling the biggest dealer in his region, using his car phone during his drive home from Dalton to Cartersville on the night of the big announcement. "I said, 'So that you don't read it in the paper tomorrow—and I'm going to try to call as many people as I can—I want to tell you what we've done.'" Then Julius informed the largest retailer of Shaw carpet in the southeast that Shaw Industries was moving into the retail sales arena. "'I don't know why, but I want you to hear it from me.' He was silent for about thirty seconds. I still remember his comments—he said, 'Well, I guess things will never be the same again in the carpet industry.' That was right."[27]

The next day, Julius Shaw was scheduled to take a group of district sales managers from Dalton to Orlando for a "sales blitz." A company plane carried the sales managers from Dalton and stopped in Cartersville to pick up Julius at 7:30 A.M. on December 13. Julius climbed aboard, looked at the half-dozen people on board, and said, "Anybody who doesn't want to go, I don't blame you, you can get out now." Julius remembered the difficult day with appropriate good humor. "The account that I went to see knew it, at 9 o'clock that morning, but he didn't mention it for an hour—nor did I," he observed with a laugh. More seriously, he remembered the succeeding months as "a tough time for us in sales. From that point on, for the next three years, it was an uphill battle to try to keep what we had while we were trying to build something new."[28]

Shaw's decision to "move downstream" into direct retailing caught the carpet industry by surprise, but it seemed to fit into the company's strategy. The move into retail sales must be understood within this broader context. Though the connection may not appear obvious, Shaw insiders believed that the company's longstanding rivalry with DuPont played a role in provoking this strategic maneuver. The Stainmaster affair of the late 1980s and early 1990s soured the relationship between the carpet industry's principal fiber supplier and its largest manufacturer.

From the late 1950s through the early 1980s, Bob Shaw argued, fiber producers such as DuPont added a greater portion of value to carpet than did manufacturers, yarn spinners and processors, or finishers. If taken together, however, all these later phases of manufacture represented a larger portion of value-added in carpet. Since the introduction of BCF nylon in 1958, DuPont had exerted a great deal of influence over manufacturers. As Shaw Industries began its relentless backward vertical integration in the 1980s, the landscape changed, Bob Shaw recalled, and Shaw Industries and DuPont began a rivalry over leadership within the carpet industry. "During that period of time, we were adding more value and had the bigger investment—in the '80s and '90s—the carpet industry had the investment, not the fiber producers. The passing of the baton—that was a hard, very difficult period of time. DuPont didn't want to give up their position of dictating downstream, and we wanted to make sure we were controlling our own destinies. That was the battleground, and it has been fought over the last 12–15 years, really, between DuPont and Shaw."[29]

The Stainmaster affair in the late 1980s "was the last straw," Shaw insisted. DuPont "started calling it Stainmaster carpet, and also . . . tried to control who we'd sell it to and how you'd sell it." Bob Shaw spent much of the 1980s and 1990s trying to reduce DuPont's—and other fiber producers'—power over the industry. "We had to break that," Shaw maintained. "That's the reason we went into the retail business." Shaw's downstream move into retail, then, can be seen as a product of Shaw's history. Every bold move in the company's past had led, almost inevitably, toward greater rationalization and consolidation within the carpet industry. Shaw had led in the vertical integration of the industry and in the consolidation of manufacturing and wholesale distribution. These moves had eventually put Shaw in a position to challenge DuPont and other fiber producers for final control over carpet marketing.[30]

Shaw's retail venture was also a response to the first tentative signs of consolidation in the carpet retail sector. Shaw Industries bypassed carpet distributors in the early 1980s by going directly to the rapidly growing number of carpet and floor covering specialty stores. In the mid-1980s, buying groups and franchisers emerged. The Maxim Group (owners of the CarpetMax franchise), Carpet One, Abbey Carpet, and others became major factors in carpet retailing by the mid-1990s, threatening to bring small retailers together to enhance the bargaining power of this segment of the industry vis-à-vis manufacturers. In addition to the rise of the buying groups, home centers such as Home Depot and Lowe's also began to enter the business of selling carpeting. Shaw's entry into retailing may be seen in part as a response to the potential threat of a consolidated retail segment.

Related to the desire to short-circuit these emerging centers of market power was a traditional Shaw concern with bringing order and efficiency to a chaotic segment of the carpet trade. Bill Lusk and other Shaw managers complained in the mid-1990s about "a retail structure that was not functioning well." There had to be a better and more efficient way of distributing carpet than through thousands of small, independent retailers, Bob Shaw and others began to believe. Independent retailers, trying to cover all their bases, felt compelled to stock products from all major manufacturers. Shaw produced goods to meet every need a retailer might be asked to fill; Shaw management figured that if they owned the retail stores, duplication of products among several manufacturers could be reduced.[31]

Shaw Industries announced its intent to acquire the Maxim Group in December 1995—the announcement that Julius Shaw referred to above. That deal fell through, but Shaw quickly followed it with two other major acquisitions early in 1996—the New York Carpet World and Carpetland USA chains. In addition, Shaw bought hundreds of small retail establishments. The *Atlanta Journal-Constitution* captured the reaction of industry observers to Shaw's new direction in a business section headline—"Carpet industry stunned by Shaw's decision to enter the retail sector." Bob Shaw insisted that the move would benefit the entire industry in the long run. *Floor Focus* publisher Frank O'Neill offered a less optimistic, if vague, prediction. "I think any time any business disrupts the normal cycle of activity for its industry, you're going to get a reaction," O'Neill observed. "Everyone in the supply chain will feel threatened."[32]

Shaw faced nearly universal criticism over the next few months. Peter Spirer, former CEO of Horizon Carpets and a major figure in the carpet industry since the 1950s, described the retail adventure as "ill-conceived." Spirer observed that "retailers, en masse, are the contact with the consumer in any industry. Traditionally, they have an adversarial relationship with their suppliers. That's the way it should be." Shaw's venture might be a bad thing for the industry, Spirer implied, even if it succeeded. Gary Lester of the Pearl Carpet Company of Cleveland, Ohio, typified the reaction of independent retailers. "One of the first laws of business is you don't buy from your competitors." Lester told the trade publication *HFN* that he was shifting his purchasing toward Shaw's competitors such as Mohawk and Beaulieu. Tom Morris of Boston's Able Rug chain announced that he would no longer carry any Shaw products. "Long-term, Shaw's move is not healthy for the independent retailers," and Morris was "committed to staying independent." Ike Timianko, head of a twenty-seven-store chain based in New York, also announced that his stores would stop buying Shaw's products. "Either you are a wholesaler or a retailer. You can't be both," Timianko argued. "Shaw is a great supplier, one of the best in the business, but he's made the wrong move."[33]

The firestorm of criticism and the exodus of retailers from the list of Shaw customers continued as Shaw added retailers to its list of acquisitions. In 1996, it appeared that a race was on—would Shaw be able to acquire market share through buying retailers as fast as the company was losing sales to former customers? Bob Shaw clearly hoped that the move to bypass independent retailers would work out in much the same way as the move around distributors in the 1980s. That earlier move had also generated intense criticism, but the company had managed to maintain (indeed, to increase) its distributor business in the midst of building direct sales to retailers.

Home Depot, the giant home center innovator, announced in late January 1996 that its 423 stores would no longer carry Shaw products. Instead, Home Depot would shift its business toward Mohawk and Queen Carpet. Bob Shaw acknowledged the loss of this major account with "regret" in a press release. Shaw observed that Home Depot accounted for "less than ½ of a percent of our sales" (or about $15 million annually). That much was true, but Shaw and others clearly understood that carpet sales at Home Depot and other home centers represented the fastest-growing segment of the retail market. Privately, Bob Shaw was considerably less sanguine about this particular loss. A Robinson-Humphrey's analyst insisted in a 1998 interview that "Bob Shaw said you weren't allowed to use the 'H' word [referring to Home Depot] inside the company."[34]

The Home Depot announcement sent Shaw's stock tumbling 9 percent over the succeeding few days. Shaw's direct sales to retailers fell precipitously in 1996 by more than $165 million. The company added $575 million in sales volume through the acquisition of more than four hundred retail stores by the end of 1996, but the costs associated with the acquisitions eliminated any potential profit. In fact, Shaw resold one hundred stores at the end of 1997, according to the *Wall Street Journal*, "because they weren't generating enough profit." Early in 1998, Shaw announced that the retailing division probably would not break even until the end of the year. Industry observers believed that even that estimate was too optimistic.[35]

Shaw also encountered great difficulties in managing the retail sector. Bill Lusk, who presided over most of the retail acquisitions in 1996, described the retail venture as "the most disappointing" setback suffered by the company during his tenure. While "it was fun doing the acquisitions," Lusk recalled that in the long run "the outlook for profitability—return on investment—didn't pan out the way we had understood it would." A move that had seemed eminently logical on paper proved a great deal more difficult than expected to execute.[36]

Reg Burnett offered an assessment of the difficulties Shaw encountered as the company entered the chaotic world of the small, independent retailer. "The big problem," Burnett argued, was "that if you're a small carpet retailer, you're an entrepreneur. If you've got customers who want their carpet installed on Christmas Eve, you get out there and you install it on Christmas Eve. I'm sure that some of those retailers also maybe work 20 days for Uncle Sam and another 8–10 days where what goes on in their store is their own business." Both those elements—the commitment of an entrepreneur and the quality of management—"were misjudged by the Shaw management, who thought that everybody was a good, sound, solid businessperson." The venerable industry consultant described a hypothetical small retailer in tones that echo the views of Shaw managers such as Bill Lusk. Shaw typically retained the former owners of its newly acquired stores as managers. "A man's worked pretty hard, and he's now sold his retail company to Shaw for $2 million worth of Shaw stock. He doesn't want to work on Saturday afternoon; he wants to play golf. And his wife wants him to go on vacation for a week, and she now says, 'you're a millionaire, and we're going to do it.' So you end up with someone else working in the store who doesn't have that entrepreneurial vision. That's one area, and with those who maybe aren't as honest as the majority of retailers, the tendency is now instead of working five days without telling Uncle Sam, I'll work seven days because it's maybe a little easier to do it." Certainly Shaw Industries was motivated to rationalize the business practices of the retail sector, but doing so turned out to be a task of Herculean proportions. Shaw had great difficulty monitoring the business practices of hundreds of small retail outlets and motivating their managers.[37]

There were other problems in moving into the retail sector. The sheer magnitude of the venture—the number of stores to be acquired, the diversity of markets to be served—was daunting. Many of the retail stores proved to be much less profitable than Shaw had imagined. Abnormally high real estate prices in California made it difficult for Shaw stores there to cover operating costs, for example. And Shaw Industries, like other carpet makers before, simply proved to be much more adept at manufacturing low-cost, high-quality products than at marketing those products, as the Trustmark fiasco had shown.[38]

Shaw also encountered problems aside from those associated with its strategic decisions of the mid-1990s. These difficulties, though probably less threatening to the company's long-term future, nonetheless occupied the time and energy of Shaw management during the retail and foreign adventures. In the early 1990s, Diamond Carpet Mills filed an antitrust lawsuit against DuPont and Shaw Industries, charging that Shaw and DuPont conspired to set a minimum price for Stainmaster carpets. Diamond also alleged that Shaw Industries sent a representative to Diamond owner Ed Weaver to explore the possibility of setting prices on polypropylene carpet. Shaw countersued, alleging that Diamond had brought the entire industry into disrepute by selling shoddy goods and misleading consumers and retailers about the contents of its carpeting. The two manufacturers settled their differences out of court in 1995, but by that time the Justice Department had begun its own antitrust investigation into the industry.[39]

The federal antitrust probe focused on alleged attempts by Shaw, Mohawk, and other manufacturers to fix the price of polypropylene carpet, and it brought attention to the concentrated nature of Dalton's carpet industry. The Justice Department succeeded in securing one guilty plea from the owner of a medium-sized firm. Sunrise Carpet's Johnny West pleaded guilty to one count of price-fixing in the spring of 1995 and agreed to cooperate with the government's investigation. A federal district judge served notice to the rest of the industry at West's sentencing hearing, announcing that he had directed prosecutors to pursue other firms vigorously. "I don't know another industry where the competitors are so physically close together. I see a need to create a legend in Dalton that will last."[40]

The Justice Department probe ended with a whimper rather than the bang hoped for by Judge Owen Forrester. In October 1997, Shaw Industries announced that the company had received formal notification from the Atlanta office of the Antitrust Division of the Department of Justice that the carpet industry investigation had been closed.[41] Perhaps prosecutors had come to understand that the dynamics of an industrial district included cooperation among competitors but did not necessarily include conspiracies to fix prices. Or perhaps prosecutors simply believed that they would have a difficult time obtaining convictions. At any rate, the threat of federal intervention subsided, though a civil class-action suit based on the polypropylene matter continued. The federal investigation and civil suit forced Shaw management to produce mountains of internal documents and no doubt took a psychic toll on company officials. Added to the retail and international difficulties, these legal problems underlined the mid-1990s as a period of struggle for Shaw Industries.

The concentration of the carpet industry in the Dalton area made carpet manufacturers particularly vulnerable to charges of antitrust violations. Shaw Industries had realized that possibility long before the federal investigation and began preparing its employees accordingly. The company composed an antitrust policy statement in 1979. This eight-page document was intended to familiarize company personnel with antitrust laws and the consequences of violations. The statement particularly warned against pricing agreements. "Selling below cost or selling at unreasonably low prices are generally construed to be illegal activities," the document noted. Shaw officials took note of the special character of the localized nature of the carpet industry. "Contacts with competitors can be suspect. In our particular industry, especially since so much of it is concentrated in Dalton, contact cannot be avoided. Nevertheless, you should be alert to problems that can arise from contact with competitors not only on a business basis, but also on a social level." Shaw warned personnel to be careful in correspondence and to choose words carefully. Perhaps Shaw's attention to the potential antitrust problems of the industry helped prepare the company to navigate a legal minefield in the 1990s.[42]

The company's legal problems faded, but the drain on financial resources continued as the retail and foreign operations struggled. By the end of 1997, Shaw Industries had reached a crossroads. The company's international operations continued to struggle, and the retail venture was losing money. Julius Shaw watched the events of 1996 and 1997 from a particularly sensitive vantage point. "In January 1996," Julius recalled, "I was asked to leave my sales position and take a position which eventually came to be vice president of investor relations." Though Shaw Industries was a $3 billion company and had been a Fortune 500 corporation for a decade, the company "did not have anybody talking to Wall Street on a regular basis" and did not have an investor relations department. Julius remarked that Bob Shaw felt "we would need somebody to talk with these investors as we were trying to establish ourselves in retail, and I was the person." Over the next "very, very difficult two years," Julius "had a lot of sleepless nights."

After a decade and a half of constant growth, Shaw's stock values fell throughout the retail and international debacles. It was, to say the least, a difficult time to be dealing with the investment community. "In 1994, our stock was at $24 or $25 a share. Between the international moves and now with this move into retail, our stock had dropped to about $14 a share," Julius recalled. "During the next two years while we were in retail, it hovered between as low as $11 and as high as $14 or $15. Quite frankly, we were lucky to trade as high as we did. I think a lot of people had faith that we would either get retail going or get out of it, and I think that is the only reason our stock didn't go down further. It was a difficult two years."[43]

As Shaw entered 1998, Bob Shaw and his management team "made the decision that the climb wasn't worth the view" and began taking action to stop the financial bleeding. Julius Shaw explained a series of January 1998 decisions to Wall Street analysts. "The first thing we did, not knowing yet that we were going to get out of retail, was that we decided to close the least profitable stores—about one hundred of them. We closed them up in January '98." Shaw also elected to sell the U.K. operation and announced that decision in January, "taking a big write-off." Shaw sold Carpets International to a management group led by Ralph Boe, a hint that the decision to sell had been in the making for some time.[44]

In addition to indicating these changes, the company announced fourth-quarter earnings for 1997. The investment community had expected Shaw to earn about 15 cents per share, but "we performed at less than half that," Julius recalled. "That wasn't real pleasant." Shaw's earnings recovered somewhat in the first two quarters of 1998, exceeding analysts' expectations. The company discontinued its dividend and announced plans for a Dutch auction, a scheme that Julius had never heard of before. "That is a method to go in and buy a large block of your stock. We announced that in January and completed the Dutch auction on March 6, 1998, and bought back 10.6 million shares at $12.50" per share. Julius characterized the Dutch auction as a "bold move. That was telling the investment community, 'We know we've had a bad couple of years, we've had a lot of tough announcements this year. Instead of cutting the puppy's tail off an inch at a time, we're going to go ahead and make some moves. We're so confident that we are going to make the right moves that we're going to put up

$120 million and buy our own stock back, so either bet with us or bet against us. If you bet with us, keep your stock. If you bet against us, offer it up and we'll give you $12.50.' That's what the Dutch auction did." Julius recalled January 1998 as "an eventful month—a month in which I might have gotten ten hours sleep" for the whole month.[45]

Shaw's stock responded to the Dutch auction and the efforts to trim non-performing retail operations, boosting shareholder value. The tough medicine of exiting the U.K. market and closing a hundred retail stores also helped boost first-quarter earnings (15 cents per share), which exceeded Wall Street expectations of 10 cents per share by 50 percent. The combination of improved earnings and the Dutch auction reversed the downward trend in the company's stock price. Shaw's stock rose about 12 percent in value from the earnings announcement in April to late June.[46]

Shaw had begun a strategic withdrawal from two problem areas. In doing so, company management implicitly (though never explicitly) acknowledged that they had made mistakes. Reg Burnett believed that these were the only two serious strategic missteps in the company's history. In the summer of 1998, Bob Shaw moved decisively to return his company to what he called its "core competencies."

CHAPTER EIGHT

A Return to Core Competencies

After that tumultuous January, Julius Shaw remarked that "things rocked along pretty quietly" until June 1998. Shaw's point man for investor relations described June 23, 1998, as "the happiest day of my business life," aside from his transfer to the Philadelphia sales division in 1985. That was the day that "we announced that we were exiting retail and that we were returning to our core competency of manufacturing."[1] Julius's characterization of the event spoke volumes about the company's strategic vision. Shaw Industries reached a deal with, ironically, the Maxim Group. The owners of the CarpetMax franchise agreed to purchase 275 of Shaw's 300 retail stores. Shaw closed the remaining 25 stores and took a one-time charge of $141 million ($98 million after taxes), or 79 cents per share against second-quarter earnings.[2]

Julius and others within the company seemed to feel that an albatross had been lifted from around their necks. "Within thirty days, virtually every retailer that had decided to discontinue doing business with us announced that they would return," he recalled with relief. "Carpet One, which had seven hundred members, and Abbey, which had seven hundred members, announced that they were coming back. And thousands of independent retailers that didn't have a voice announced it with their sample purchases. We would hear from our salespeople that 'Joe's Carpet Mart is returning,' etc. It was wonderful to be back doing what we knew how to do." Carpet One (which had $2 billion in 1997 total sales) and Abbey ($700 million) were the two biggest fish to return to the Shaw fold.[3]

Shaw had a more difficult time with Home Depot, however. By 1998, Home Depot had become the nation's second largest retailer of carpet, with more than $1.3 billion in 1997 sales. An industry consultant described Home Depot and other similar "home center" chains, such as Lowe's, as "the driving force in the industry right now." Despite the company's attempt to minimize the impact of losing the Home Depot account, Shaw simply could no longer afford to have its products absent from the pioneer home center's stores. As a consequence of selling off its retail stores to the Maxim Group, Shaw acquired a 16 percent stake in Maxim's stock. Home Depot spokespeople believed that stake in the CarpetMax franchise gave Shaw too large an interest in carpet retailing.[4]

Shaw short-circuited Home Depot by making a dramatic move on another front. Less than two months after announcing an end to the retail experiment, Shaw Industries merged with Queen Carpet, the number four American carpet manufacturer and one of Home Depot's leading suppliers. In the fall of 1998, Home Depot grudgingly agreed to continue stocking carpets with the Queen label, but no other Shaw Industries products. Among Shaw's competitors, none had benefited more from Shaw's abortive retail venture than Julian and Harry Saul's Queen Carpet. The Queen merger signaled Bob Shaw's determination to bring his company back to its strategic roots, according to virtually all company insiders.

The Shaw-Queen merger represented the consummation of a strategic alliance between two of the founding families of Dalton's tufted textile industry. Harry Saul, Julian Saul, and Queen Carpet played important roles in the evolution of the carpet industry in northwest Georgia. In an extended 1993 interview, Julian Saul reflected on his family's business life in the Dalton area.[5]

Harry Saul, one of a group of talented Jewish entrepreneurs who helped to create the tufted textile industry, moved to Dalton and opened a department store in 1939. Julian Saul recalled that his grandfather set Harry and his two sisters up in businesses of their own in Georgia—one in Gainesville, one in Griffin, and one in Dalton. Harry Saul managed a successful department store through World War II. Bob Shaw remembered Harry Saul from the department store days of the 1940s. "He was in the dry goods business, and he had the local Boy Scouts department. You know how much money he made off merit badges," Shaw remarked in jest. "If we couldn't pay for the merit badges, Harry would give them to us and tell us to bring a quarter later on."[6]

Harry Saul rented his store space, and when his landlord's son returned from military service in 1945, the landlord did not renew their lease, Julian Saul remembered, because the son wanted to go into business in the building. The son's name was Paul, so Harry Saul's former landlord "just changed the name of the store from 'S' to 'P.' She didn't even change the sign," just the first letter. "So it went from Saul's to Paul's." Harry moved up the street to a new location.

Harry Saul had taken notice of Dalton's booming tufted textile industry—bedspreads, robes, rugs, and other chenille products. World War II had interrupted most tufted textile manufacture for the consumer market, but in 1946 Harry Saul "decided he would try the chenille business." Saul bought a small chenille company from the Reverend C. T. Pratt, who "had the best business in the world," Julian Saul caustically remarked. "He was ahead of communism. We had our own commune here in Dalton. He had his own drycleaners, car dealership, grocery stores. All his employees turned all their money over to him every week; and he in turn would provide them with food, houses, and everything. It was unbelievable." Pratt's radical sect has been the subject of scholarly research. Pratt campaigned for Henry Wallace, the Progressive Party candidate for president in 1948, and for a time cooperated with a Textile Workers Union of America organizing drive in Dalton's bedspread mills in the mid-1950s.[7] Julian Saul vividly remembered the details of the sale. Pratt "could not read or write. Daddy had to write the bill of sale out for him, and he signed it."

Harry turned most of his attention to the new chenille business while Julian's mother, Helen, ran the department store. In 1947, the Sauls' new landlord also refused to renew their lease—yet another case of a son returning home from the army to take over a location with an established trade. Harry Saul then turned the family's full efforts to the new business. He named the new company Queen Chenille and initially specialized in producing tufted chenille bathrobes. Queen was especially successful with a line of children's robes designed for young girls.[8] "The name of the company, Queen, supposedly came from the fact that the robes were fit for a queen," Julian recalled.

Harry Saul also exploited new markets for tufted products. Queen became the original producer of "tank sets . . . the chenille covers that go over commodes that keep them from sweating." Queen also was awarded a contract from Johnson's Wax to produce cloth-covered application pads, Chenille Glo-Coats. Julian commented that they "graduated" from these assorted products into "scatter rugs." Queen also became the first manufacturer to produce tufted automotive carpeting. Harry Saul took his samples to Detroit but lost the big contract to another manufacturer. "We got the replacement business, though," selling chiefly to auto parts chains. Walter Guinan, former CEO of Karastan and a longtime consultant to the industry, affirmed Queen's accomplishments. Queen was "the first company to make auto replacement carpet." Guinan noted that "the company's early established accounts with Montgomery Ward and J. C. Penney . . . kept the manufacturing focused primarily on rugs." By the early 1960s, Queen had established a solid business in making and marketing small tufted products.[9]

Julian Saul graduated from Georgia Tech in 1963 and returned to work in the family business. "I was absolutely miserable," he recalled because he was allergic to cigarette smoke, lint, and cotton dust. "Our mill, and all the [bedspread and scatter rug] mills in Dalton, looked like the movie *Norma Rae,* where the ladies would . . . go in to work with blonde or black hair and come out with white." The dust-filled air of a cotton textile plant became intolerable for Julian.

At this point, soon after coming home from college, Julian became interested in alternative career paths. Queen got into the carpet business as a result of Julian's dissatisfaction with cotton dust and a fortuitous circumstance. A friend of Julian's offered to sell him some Kodel polyester carpet yarn at a good price. The friend said, "I can assure you that there's nothing wrong with the yarn; however, this customer is very picky. We'll sell you the yarn at half-price." Julian convinced his father that he really wanted to be in the carpet business, away from the cotton lint. So Queen moved into the manufacture of broadloom carpet. In addition to the lint problems, Julian admitted that in terms of efficiency, "we never were good scatter rug manufacturers. It is so much harder to make scatter rugs and/or novelties. There's a lot more labor involved than a bigger item like carpet. Carpet seemed to be a breeze compared to the scatter rugs."

Julian bought the carpet yarn, but Queen had no wide tufting machines designed for producing carpet. Rather than investing heavily in tufting machines at this early juncture, Julian and Harry Saul took advantage of the resources available in an industrial district to produce their first carpet. "We had it commission-tufted, commission-dyed, commission-backed" by independent contractors among the small firms that proliferated in the Dalton area. Then Julian had to find a way to market his company's new product. "One of my best friends, Lamar Hennon," with whom Julian had gone to school in Dalton, "had a chain of approximately twenty retail stores called Direct Carpet. I told Lamar that I had bought this polyester yarn, and we were going into the carpet business. He had a style that he was buying from another manufacturer, and it was really selling for him. He was paying $4.85 per square yard. I asked him what he would pay me for the same carpet in jumbo 300-foot rolls," which the friend would have to inspect "since Queen had no inspection equipment. We struck a deal at $3.85, and he gave me an order for twenty rolls (four per color)."

Queen reached a turning point in 1977. Martin Processing, the company's chief yarn supplier, like other yarn processors and suppliers at that time, kept "bumping up our prices every six weeks or so without any reason," taking advantage of the weak bargaining position of most small manufacturers. "The writing was on the wall" that Queen had to do something about this jump in costs. That year, Harry and Julian called in consultant Frank Wilson for advice. Julian detailed his recent acquisitions of new equipment, including Superba machines for heat-setting yarn (crucial for shag carpets) and a new Kusters continuous dye range. Queen "was doing about $19 million a year" in volume.

Wilson listened patiently and then replied, "By the year 1982, if you're not doing $60 million volume, you'll be out of business." That was "cheering news" to Julian after ordering all the new equipment. "I said, 'Don't worry, we'll do that.' We got the equipment in, and it was all ready to go by Labor Day of 1978."

Julian Saul immediately tried to make maximum use of the cost efficiencies of the new continuous dye range, saving up orders to facilitate the longest possible production runs for a particular color. Then Queen happened on another particular look in carpeting, a new product that would play a crucial role in building Queen Carpet. "We came up with a style called Prime Time. That one style—we did two million yards a month on that thing starting in January from nothing."

The yarn used in making the Prime Time style also had a unique story. "Chevron used to sell yarn here in the States and they made it in Puerto Rico." One of Julian Saul's neighbors, Bob Moore, just happened to be a salesman for Chevron yarns. "Just to show you what a small town it is—his daughter was babysitting for us so I called to tell her I was on my way to pick her up." Moore said to Saul, "'I've got something to show you.' So he brings this piece of carpet to me and he said, 'We've developed this yarn and we want you to try it. We'll just give you a sample.'" Now, Saul knew that Chevron had developed a reputation for poor-quality yarn production in Puerto Rico, but Moore talked him into trying it. "So we tried it and it was the worst stuff you've ever seen." Moore apologized and sent Queen "this new product . . . it was the most gorgeous thing you've ever seen." Julian started with an order of 100,000 pounds a week. "Then it was 150,000, then it was 200,000. Anyway, with this Prime Time and four other styles that went along with it, we were running."

"I was having to ration the carpet out" by 1979, Julian Saul recalled. "Our volume jumped from nineteen to twenty-nine million" during the second half of 1978. "The next year our volume jumped from twenty-nine to sixty-nine. The next year from sixty-nine to ninety-nine. The next year from ninety-nine to 129. The next year from 129 to 169. We were going up in increments of thirty and forty million dollars a year. Basically, all from this one look which was a multicolored cut loop. If you saw it today you'd say it was garish and you wouldn't have it in your house." But, as Julian Saul told *Textile World* in 1998, "Prime Time built this place."[10]

Prime Time was, according to Julian Saul, the "number one thing that got us going." A close second, he insisted, was Harry Saul's use of tax-free municipal industrial revenue bonds to finance the company's expansion. "During the Jimmy Carter years when interest rates were twenty-one and twenty-two percent and some of our competitors were paying four above prime, we never paid over nine or nine and one-quarter for the money. That really got our company going."

Queen took full advantage of fortuitous changes in federal rules for industrial revenue bonds. IRBs had been used extensively, particularly by southern states, in the 1950s and 1960s as inducements to outside industry. Such financing became a staple of the "selling of the South" industrialization strategy pursued by southern communities. Municipalities issued IRBs to finance plant construction and expansion. Facilities were then leased to industrial customers, who repaid the bonds from their revenues. Thus the bonds were secured by the industrialists' future sales. The interest rate paid on such bonds was typically below the prevailing interest rate on commercial loans because income from municipal bonds was free from federal taxation. While communities all over the United States used such financing to encourage industrial growth, the South made the greatest use of IRBs. James C. Cobb found that "in the period 1956–1968, Alabama, Arkansas, Georgia, Kentucky, Mississippi, and Tennessee were responsible for 87% of all industrial development bond issues and 60% of the dollar value of such bond sales." And the total value of such funding ballooned from around $200 million in 1965 to more than $1.39 billion in 1967.[11]

The rapid growth of industrial bonds combined with the South's use of those bonds to induce firms to move or build new plants in the South rather than elsewhere prompted intense scrutiny and mounting criticism in the 1960s. Finally, in 1969, Congress placed a limit of $5 million on tax-free IRB issues, which dramatically reduced the use of IRB financing. Searching for ways to open up lower-cost credit to small and medium businesses in the midst of the inflation and high interest rates of the 1970s, Congress reconsidered its position. Federal lawmakers raised the limit on IRB tax-free issues to $10 million in 1978. Within just two years, local governments were issuing more than $8 billion annually in IRBs.[12]

Harry and Julian Saul took full advantage of the new rules to secure low-cost financing for Queen's dramatic expansion in the 1980s, illustrating a sometimes overlooked aspect of the IRB controversy. While Cobb correctly emphasized the industrial piracy that could result from using IRBs as inducements, the Queen experience reminds us that IRBs were not used exclusively to encourage industries to change locations. Some local governments—such as Dalton's—used bonds to finance homegrown industry. Queen was a prime example of a local firm with deep roots in the community that profited from the use of this form of subsidy to industry.

Using creative financing, Julian Saul pursued a strategy of vertical integration similar to that of Shaw Industries. Within a decade after the introduction of Prime Time, Queen had become a fully integrated manufacturer, encompassing all phases of the production process from fiber extrusion and yarn processing to dyeing and finishing. By the 1990s, Queen operated five yarn-spinning plants—three in Georgia, one in South Carolina, and one in Arizona. Queen embarked on its own acquisition campaign in the early 1990s. In 1990, Julian Saul purchased Patcraft Mills, the creation of northwest Georgia carpet legend I. V. Chandler. Patcraft became the linchpin of Queen's commercial carpet efforts. Queen added Cumberland Mills in 1992.[13]

Queen took a giant step forward in 1994 with its purchase of Tuftex Industries, the largest carpet mill on the West Coast. Tuftex focused on the medium to higher end of the market spectrum, whereas Queen had primarily sold in the low to medium price range of the carpet market. The addition of Tuftex's $135 million sales boosted Queen's projected annual revenues to around $600 million and kept the company "in the race to be one of the megamills of the next century," according to analyst Frank O'Neill. Julian Saul also noted that this acquisition made Queen "the only major Eastern mill with local manufacturing facilities in the West."[14]

Harry Saul, Queen's president, and son Julian, the company's executive vice president, essentially functioned as co-CEOs through the 1970s and 1980s. The father and son developed a working relationship, but Julian hinted that he and his father did not always see eye to eye. "It's difficult to work in a family business, but the relationship between Dad and myself is unique," the younger Saul observed in a 1988 interview. "It's not that Dad and I don't have arguments, we do. But in the end, we always seem to reach an agreement that we feel is good for the company."[15]

Bob Shaw knew the Saul family well. Queen Chenilles had shared a building with Clarence Shaw's Star Dye Company. Buddy Sewell clearly recalled young Julian Saul running through both plants as a child. Star dyed most of Queen's rugs, robes, and spreads in the 1950s. Bob Shaw developed a friendship with both Harry and Julian. He offered his perspective on the relationship between the Sauls, father and son, perhaps not too dissimilar from his own relationship with his father: "Julian's vision was bigger than Harry's vision. Harry started in the chenille business before Julian had gotten there, but it was like most places—he was looking for survival. And that was about all Queen did up until the time they hit 'Prime Time'—the one fabric that just made Queen." That phenomenon—hitting on a particular look or product—was common in the Dalton area. "The same thing with Salem; they hit one fabric. And if you weren't careful, you thought you knew what was going on because you had one magic product." Many companies proved to be one-hit wonders, but Queen "survived it. Julian built the business from a little bitty business. And Harry was still very active up until five or six years ago," just a year or so before he died in 1994. Harry had grown up during the Great Depression, and "he probably didn't understand going into debt" on the scale that Julian did, commented Bob Shaw.[16] Julian Saul pressed hard to forge ahead with ambitious and expensive expansion and integration plans; Harry reluctantly went along, seeking the lowest-cost financing for his son's plans.

Queen's sales topped $720 million in 1995. At that point, Bob Shaw approached Julian Saul about the possibility of a merger. This came just as Shaw was entering the retail market. Julian declined, chiefly because he was very skeptical about the retail venture, and told Bob as a friend not to enter the retail market. However, Julian said to keep the idea in mind if the retail move did not work out or if Shaw decided to abandon the scheme.[17]

Saul's instincts proved correct, and Shaw exited the retail market in 1998. In the interim, Queen had profited from Shaw's losses at Home Depot and other retail outlets. Bob Shaw again approached Saul about a merger. Julius Shaw characterized the acquisition of Queen as perhaps the best in Shaw's history and reflected on the motivations of both sides. "Two companies had really benefited from our move into retail," Julius Shaw observed. "I think Mohawk had benefited the most, and Queen had benefited the second most." Queen's "business was so good that they were doing a lot of business on the outside," subcontracting and commission tufting. Queen "could only produce about 85 percent of what their orders were, so they were going outside for some tufting, dyeing, and yarn processing. They were getting ready to make large capital expenditures to put in more equipment; they were going to have to spend 70, 80, or 100 million dollars to keep up with the demand. When we went out of retail, we went to them and said, 'Number one, the game has changed, and we are probably going to be back with a lot of these retailers. Number two, why spend capital dollars to increase the capacity of the industry? We've got all the capacity you need.' That was exactly right, and Julian saw the benefit. He and Bob cut the deal in one week. It was the biggest deal in carpet history, and it was done in one week. We closed the deal on October 6, 1998, and had the benefit of Queen's numbers for the fourth quarter."[18]

Bob Shaw and Julian Saul confirmed the ease with which the deal had been made. "Total trust—that's really what made it easy for Queen and Shaw to get together. We had known the Saul family for fifty years, and they had known us for fifty years. We didn't have to guess whether they were honest or not, and they didn't have to guess whether we were honest. We could do things with a handshake rather than trying to detail a ten-page contract."[19]

Shaw acquired Queen for about $470 million in cash, stock, and "other considerations" in August 1998. As a result of the deal, members of the Saul family became substantial owners of Shaw stock. The Shaw and Saul families controlled nearly a third of the company's shares, a remarkable concentration of family ownership for a $4 billion company. Members of the Shaw family owned about 16 percent of the company's stock, while Saul family members now controlled about 14 percent.[20]

Therefore, the Shaw-Queen merger was also a Shaw family–Saul family merger. Business history scholars often wax eloquent about the cooperative spirit that seems to animate localized industrial districts such as Dalton. Bob Shaw saw it differently. He did not look on the Dalton district as a haven of trust and cooperation. The industry was built in part by local folks who had known each other for decades, but it was also built by newcomers. The Barwicks and others came in from other places; "they were not all Daltonians." For "the bedspread business, that was true. But for the carpet business, it was really the Sauls and the Shaws" who had deep roots in Dalton. "The rest of 'em were carpetbaggers," Shaw joked.[21]

It was only fitting, from Shaw's point of view, that these two remaining founding families join forces. A few months after the acquisition, the close relationship between the two families was confirmed in a series of personnel moves. Shaw Industries named Julian Saul as its president in January 1999.[22]

The long friendship between the Shaw and Saul families speeded the acquisition along, but the meshing of business philosophies helped make for a smooth transition. Among Shaw's competitors, none followed the vertical integration, low-cost production strategy as faithfully as Julian Saul and Queen Carpet. Julius Shaw echoed the universal sentiment among Shaw's top management, making a clear connection between the acquisition of Queen Carpet and a renewed emphasis on Shaw's venerable "low-cost production" strategy: "We've come back home, so to speak, to our core competencies. We've never felt better about who we are."[23]

New company president Julian Saul agreed with Julius Shaw's assessment. Shaw's vice president of communications "has a saying about getting back to core competencies or getting back to basics. And that's what we're doing," Saul insisted in a 1999 interview. "We want to be a carpet manufacturer and be the best that we can be."[24]

The phrase "core competencies" entered the Shaw lexicon in 1998, along with an acronym—EVA, or Economic Value Added. The failure of Shaw's bold moves of the mid-1990s had prompted a reassessment of the company's goals and strategies. The notion of core competencies emerged from a new school of business theory in the 1960s—strategic management. Advocates of strategic management argued that it was through the establishment of competitive advantages or core competencies (or both; the terms are not mutually exclusive) that a firm could earn economic rent—that is, earnings over and above the cost of the capital employed.[25]

Though the EVA concept did not last as a guiding principle at Shaw, the experiment highlighted both the company's long-term strengths and short-term difficulties. Shaw management had found ways to gain greater than average returns on investment during the company's history, and perhaps this was what attracted the company to the concept. Yet the concept could also lead to an excessive emphasis on producing those high returns in too short a time frame, particularly within the environment of a publicly traded firm whose stock price depended on constant improvements over the previous quarter's results. Nevertheless, the experiment itself testified to the flexibility of Shaw management. The more basic concept of seeking above-average returns on investment, however, remained a bedrock value at Shaw Industries.

The trick, of course, is to find capital investments that can outperform the average; that is, investments that can command an economic rent. Given the classical economists' emphasis on equilibrium and the tendency of rates of return to converge over time, how can a firm command rent? Firms could accomplish this by establishing core competencies (to use Prahalad's and Hamel's phrase)—building linked networks of skills within the firm—or by establishing competitive advantages (the term made popular by Michael Porter)—staking out unique methods of production, marketing, brand-name recognition, monopoly, and so on. In essence, by finding, or creating, a competency or ability or other advantage that is not easily available to competitors, a firm could escape the diminishing returns that classical economists argued must follow "perfect competition." John Kay, writing for London's *Financial Times*, summarized the concept of core competency in the following way: "the key distinction is between distinctive capabilities and reproducible capabilities. Distinctive capabilities," or core competencies, or competitive advantages, "are those characteristics of a company which cannot be replicated by competitors, or can only be replicated with great difficulty, even after these competitors realise the benefits which they yield for the originating company."[26]

Can core competencies be created through strategic planning? Throughout the 1970s and 1980s, many consultants argued in the affirmative. Led by Harvard's Michael Porter, a variety of consultants urged companies to adopt formal "strategic planning" methods. For Porter, successful strategies, including distinctive capabilities, could be built through a process of rational planning. Porter even identified a handful of generic strategies that businesses might pursue. Others, like Henry Mintzberg, argued that successful strategies more often resulted from intuition than planning. Mintzberg contended that good strategies emerged from "a creative process of synthesis." Formal planning, while valuable, could not alone produce successful strategy, and certainly no generic model could provide an executive with any degree of comfort. Successful strategies required intuition and creativity, an ability to recognize emerging patterns before they become obvious to all.[27]

Did Shaw Industries possess a clear competitive advantage over rivals? The answer must almost certainly be yes. Many management consultants, however, might have a difficult time identifying that advantage precisely. Shaw's strategy seems simple enough—pursue vertical integration and control of your own destiny, cut costs, promote efficiency. Shaw's competitive advantage emerged from the company's emphasis on "low-cost production." The strategy depended on the constant improvement of the company's plant and equipment. All the equipment Shaw used, however, was readily available to all its competitors, as were the business methods. Was Shaw's competitive advantage merely temporary, soon to be duplicated by competitors? Was it a product of careful planning or the result of keen insights at various critical points? Could the company's competitive advantage be maintained as the reins of management passed to new people?

Only time would tell. After forty years in the carpet industry, Bob Shaw's company continued to outperform its rivals. The low-cost production philosophy was deeply ingrained in Bob Shaw and his management team, and it permeated the organization. Shaw Industries might not be as adept at consumer marketing or managing the vagaries of international currency markets as other firms, but Shaw had developed an advantage over its American competitors. It seemed that no other firm could produce and deliver carpeting for the U.S. mass market at as low a cost as Shaw Industries. As the founder and only CEO the company had known moved closer to retirement early in the twenty-first century, Bob Shaw probably saw the adoption of Economic Value Added as a way to institutionalize, at least in part, his guiding principles. Shaw management had clearly used the EVA concept for four decades by intuition. Perhaps the concept could be formalized and passed on to a new generation of leaders.

Bud Shaw often repeated the saying that "in a land of the blind, the man with one eye is king." Warren Sims believed that Bud Shaw's aphorism summed up the secret of Shaw Industries' success. Bob and Bud Shaw and the management team they assembled exhibited a remarkable ability to see patterns and identify trends ahead of most competitors. Shaw's strength had always been people rather than planning or process. Bob Shaw had always minimized the importance of long-range planning. He insisted that his company was built in a series of stages as one block was placed on top of another.

Vance Bell summed up the prevailing view of Bob Shaw among members of his management team. Shaw's perspective embodied "a different approach to the business. He insisted on running the company a certain way, with integrity. He built a very strong organization. But he was a driver. He was extremely competitive, probably the most competitive person I've ever seen. He was a risk-taker, and that was probably one of the biggest reasons we grew. He was the biggest risk-taker around here. Most of those decisions have been good. Some of them haven't been so good, but the long-term batting average was very good."[28]

Just as important as an ability to see patterns was Bob and Bud Shaw's commitment to building a lasting institution. The Shaws never considered selling the business in its rapid growth phase, as most of their contemporaries and competitors eventually did. Shaw Industries never shied away from large capital expenditures or new debt as long as those risks led in the direction of greater efficiency in the long run. Bob Shaw never allowed the company to become simply a "cash cow."

Assembling and retaining a talented team of individuals who shared common values—as much as any other single factor, this may have accounted for Shaw Industries' successful rise. The ranks of Shaw's top management proved remarkably stable. Bob Shaw turned to people he knew, people who had proven themselves. All his associates mentioned loyalty as one of his chief defining characteristics. He appreciated receiving it and reciprocated. And he displayed a keen eye for talent. Norris Little was perhaps the best example of a key figure in the company's growth and development who was brought in from outside. Soon after the Queen merger, Bob Shaw made Julian Saul the president of Shaw Industries. Saul and Shaw shared similar management philosophies, as both men knew well before the merger, including a similar "gut-level" understanding of EVA before it was a management trend.[29]

While always on the lookout for outside talent, Shaw was also careful to cultivate young talent and promote from within. Vance Bell and Randy Merritt perhaps best exemplified that trend. Bell and Merritt were among Shaw's earliest trainees. Bell rose through the ranks to become executive vice president for operations by 2001. Merritt followed a similar path. He excelled in sales and demonstrated initiative. Merritt helped develop commercial carpet sales in the 1980s, then took over all sales and marketing for the Philadelphia division. Eventually Merritt asumed responsibility for all sales and marketing functions in the residential segment. Merritt was named executive vice president for corporate sales and marketing, establishing a firm position in the inner circle of top management. The rise of Bell and Merritt exemplified the strength of Shaw management in identifying and rewarding talent and initiative. "The trainees who came in [25–30 years ago] are now running the company," Bob Shaw observed.[30]

Beyond management personnel, Shaw also developed a solid relationship with its workforce. Shaw Industries' single greatest challenge in the area of labor relations in the 1990s and beyond may have been the increasing diversity of its workforce. In this the firm was certainly not alone. The *Wall Street Journal* noted the trend in an August 2001 front-page story. By that time, Georgia's "carpet capital" had become "a case study in a phenomenon sweeping the American interior." During the preceding decade "more than three million Mexican workers, most of them illegal, swarmed over the border to fill gaping labor shortages." From meat-processing plants in Kansas to poultry-processing factories in Arkansas and Georgia, Latinos searching for a better life expanded their job searches beyond the traditional destinations.[31]

The most important labor-market trend in northwest Georgia since the 1980s has been the change in the ethnic composition of the workforce. Dalton became a magnet for Latino immigrants during the late 1980s, and the attraction increased throughout the 1990s. The consolidation of the industry combined with demographic trends and a resurgence of demand in the 1990s to stretch a historically tight labor market in the Dalton district to the breaking point. Hispanic workers, chiefly from Mexico, helped local mill owners solve the labor problem, at least temporarily.

Whitfield County's white population grew slightly in the 1980s and then declined in the 1990s. While the county's total population grew at a healthy 15 percent (higher than the national average), the growth rate lagged behind the state average of 26 percent. A closer look at the numbers revealed two striking trends. The "official" Hispanic population rose from just over 2,000 in 1990 to more than 16,000 in preliminary numbers from the 2000 census. Hispanics officially constituted only about 5 percent of Whitfield County's population in 1990. By the beginning of the twenty-first century, at least 22 percent of Whitfield County residents were Hispanic. Census numbers probably undercounted the Hispanic presence in Dalton as elsewhere in both 1990 and 2000, but the trend was irrefutable. The student body in Dalton's kindergarten program passed a milestone in 2000—in that year, just over half the students were Hispanic. Whitfield County ranked fifth in the nation in the proportional growth of the Hispanic population during the 1990s. Whitfield County had a higher proportion of Hispanics in its population than any other Georgia county by 2000. The increasing number of signs in Spanish, the growth of Hispanic-owned businesses, the creation of an adult soccer league with more than forty teams, and the conversion of a local radio station to a Spanish-language format provided ample tangible evidence of the cultural transformation of this small southern town.[32]

The other major trend was less obvious. While the total population of Whitfield County grew in the 1990s at a pace slightly ahead of the national average, the white, non-Hispanic population of Whitfield declined from almost 67,000 in 1990 to about 60,000 in 2000. A corresponding rise in white population in surrounding counties suggested a limited "white flight" syndrome. Another piece of the explanation for the population trends probably involved Dalton's increased emphasis on education and staying in school (dating from the mid-1980s) and Georgia's new Hope scholarship program, which paid for college tuition and books for Georgia high school graduates who maintained at least a B average. Many young people from older families moved up and out of the area, seeking opportunities beyond manufacturing.

These demographic changes intersected with labor-market trends. Mill owners had long complained of a labor shortage, no doubt partially due to the high degree of concentration of the industry in northwest Georgia. It appears that mill owners' fears for the survival of the industry in Dalton, so much in evidence in the mid-1990s, had at least some basis in fact. The historically tight labor market in the northwest Georgia carpet district seemed to be driving up wages. The increasing pressure on the local labor market was masked to an extent by the recession of 1991. Dalton-area workers felt the sting of layoffs and reductions in hours as mills cut production. Coming out of the recession, however, the mills faced stiff competition for a limited labor supply. Total employee compensation in the carpet and rug industry rose almost 10 percent per year in 1993 and 1994; unit labor costs grew as well. Productivity declined for most of the 1990s while average hourly wages rose, reflecting the tight labor market.[33]

From the worker's perspective, the labor market appeared to be operating as it should, with wages increasing as demand outstripped supply. Mill owners, for their part, complained about the difficulty they encountered in finding reliable workers. Management continued to try to substitute capital for labor with limited success throughout the 1990s. As Bill Lusk observed, however, the great breakthroughs in the history of the industry had been tufting and continuous dyeing. Each had opened the possibility for dramatic increases in productivity. Tufting technology had experienced no revolutionary changes since the 1950s, he noted, only incremental increases in speed. These increases were substantial, yet there was a limit to how much the machines could be speeded up in the short run. A few manufacturers wondered aloud, and more did so in private, about the future health of the carpet industry in northwest Georgia in the face of the mounting "labor problem" in the 1980s and early 1990s.

Immigration proved to be the answer to the dilemma. Hispanic workers had first appeared in the Dalton area in 1969, working on a dam construction project. A few Latino workers made their way into the carpet mills in the 1970s, yet by the early 1980s, Dalton still had a tiny Hispanic population. A larger number of Hispanic laborers, primarily Mexicans, made their way to Dalton in the late 1980s as news of available jobs in the carpet industry filtered back home through kinship networks. The recession of 1991 slowed the rate of immigration briefly, but the trickle of Hispanic workers became a wave by the mid-1990s as the industry recovered from the recession and consolidated further. As Hispanic workers came into the Dalton district in greater numbers, the increases in compensation costs slowed to a level mill owners would have described as more manageable, and the "labor shortage" eased, though it certainly did not disappear.

The immigration of the 1990s signaled the emergence of new destinations for Latino migrants. Two University of Monterrey sociologists found that Georgia became "the single most important destination for those making their initial move from Mexico" after 1987. Hispanic immigrants had traditionally been filtered through "gateway states" such as Texas and California. After the passage of the Immigration Reform and Control Act (IRCA) in 1986, which gave amnesty to some two million undocumented immigrants, and the emergence of anti-immigrant movements in California, migrants often bypassed the older gateways and began casting a wider net when searching for opportunity.[34]

The passage of IRCA coincided with another phenomenon. In the mid-1980s local educational leaders made a concerted effort to reduce high school dropout rates in Dalton and surrounding school systems. The carpet mills had long offered steady manufacturing jobs, many of which required few skills, to young people, often enticing them to drop out of school. Many came to believe that too many of northwest Georgia's youths were trading their long-term futures for short-term consumption (a car, an apartment of their own). To the extent that these stay-in-school campaigns and related educational efforts succeeded, more Dalton-area teenagers attended college and prepared for different kinds of jobs. Given the patterns of change in population numbers for the

Dalton area in the 1990s and looking at the changing composition of the work-force, it seems reasonable to conclude that an increasing number of Dalton-area families used the carpet mills as a way to finance college for children; more and more of those children apparently moved up and out. The labor shortage for carpet mills such as Shaw, however, worsened.

Mill executives were quick to praise the newcomers. "The Hispanics have been a salvation of our carpet industry," observed Charles Parham, Queen Carpet's vice president of manufacturing, in a 1998 interview. Parham lauded Hispanic laborers as "energetic, anxious to do a good job," and like virtually all other mill executives who have spoken publicly, he observed that "they have an enviable work ethic." *Textile World* writer Walter Rozelle found that "you don't engage someone in conversation for long about the Hispanic population before the subject of work ethic surfaces."[35]

Shaw Industries and other carpet firms began employing a growing number of Hispanic workers in the 1990s. At some mills, the proportion of Hispanic workers may have exceeded a third by the end of the decade. Julius Shaw observed that his company experienced a rapid growth in Hispanic workers as well. "Our work force went from basically 0 percent Hispanic in 1990 to 12 percent by 2000," and the trend continued.[36]

A demographic shift of these proportions inevitably brought some tension. But a contributor to the leading liberal journal the *Nation* actually compared Dalton favorably to metropolitan Atlanta counties and California in describing northwest Georgia's response to immigration. Californians initiated anti-immigrant legislation at the state level in the late 1990s, and Atlanta suburbs passed ordinances requiring that commercial signs be printed predominantly in English. In Dalton, University of California at Berkeley professor David Kirp wrote, "the welcome wagon is out." As early as 1997, Dalton-area carpet mills began offering English classes to Hispanic employees, and many, including Shaw Industries, added to that a series of Spanish-language classes for managers and supervisors. Shaw's Spanish classes also included an emphasis on the culture of Hispanic Americans in an effort to help supervisors reduce tensions between Latino and Anglo workers on the shop floor.

The response among northwest Georgia natives was not universally positive. In the mid-1990s "angry whites launched an organization called Citizens Against Illegal Aliens," Kirp reported. This task force commanded enough influence in its early days to convince local leaders and the Immigration and Naturalization Service to open a joint Dalton police department and INS office, to be funded by local taxes. The task force was intended to crack down on illegal immigration, but it had faded away within five years. The office still

existed at the beginning of the twenty-first century, but after a few highly publicized raids in 1995 and 1996, it had faded into relative obscurity. Kirp characterized Citizens Against Illegal Aliens as "a spent force" by 2000.

Dalton's "welcome wagon" seemed to overshadow the protests. Prosperity
was a partial explanation; the long-term emergence of Dalton as the "carpet
capital" of the world and the short-term boom that followed the 1991 recession
combined to produce a microscopic unemployment rate in Whitfield County.
Even the massive influx of Latinos in the 1990s did not directly cost jobs for Anglo citizens, though it probably helped slow wage growth. As long as there were
jobs or opportunities for everyone, the protests against illegal immigration
could be controlled.

Prosperity alone was not the sole reason for Dalton's relative *tranquilidad*.
If that were so, Kirp noted, California would be a more inviting place for immigrants. Kirp emphasized "the social uses to which that prosperity has been
put" and credited "the vision of the politicians and executives from Carpet
who effectively run the town." Over the years, Dalton's mill owners had sought
social stability for their industrializing community. In the 1960s, this meant
crushing a textile union organizing campaign and maintaining maximum
flexibility for management within the carpet district. Kirp probably was un-
aware of this aspect of the story, and it is one that most of the *Nation*'s readers
would have found troubling. Kirp did mention that Dalton's carpet executives
decreed that there should be no trouble with school integration in the 1960s,
and the process worked as smoothly as anywhere in the South. He did not
mention that the extremely small African American population of the area
(Whitfield County historically had a black population that made up no more
than 5 percent of the total) probably played a role in minimizing tensions, but
the larger point he made was certainly correct. The carpet industry "established a multimillion dollar endowment for the local hospital, paid for new
parks, and helped underwrite the building of a new high school." There is little
doubt that Dalton benefited from the concentration of the carpet industry.
The mill owners and executives have used their influence to "smooth out the
social landscape" in a variety of ways.[37]

The best example might be Dalton's Georgia Project, and Shaw Industries'
CEO played a role in the creation of this innovative initiative. The idea for the
Georgia Project originated with venerable local attorney Erwin Mitchell. His
daughter, a teacher in Dalton's public schools, brought her father to her class-
room one day in 1996. Mitchell was appalled. "I couldn't believe I was in Dalton," he recalled. "It was a foreign land." Mitchell did not react by joining the
anti-immigrant chorus of Citizens Against Illegal Aliens. He responded to the

monumental transformation sweeping over his community by looking for ways to smooth out the process. Mitchell saw that a multicultural community was "the way of the future," as he put it. "The growth of our community," he observed in 2000, "is going to be Hispanic, not white." He well understood that many of the immigrants were undocumented, but that was beside the point. The trend had become irreversible, he contended, and community leaders agreed. To attract this burgeoning number of Hispanic workers and yet not educate their children was a recipe for disaster. And clearly, English-speaking teachers in Dalton's classrooms could not adequately educate Spanish-speaking immigrant children. Mitchell conferred with carpet industry leaders, and a possible solution emerged.

Shaw Industries had developed contacts in Mexico, particularly in Monterrey, through the company's joint venture with Alfa. While Shaw's other international ventures foundered in the 1990s, the Mexican venture proved an exception. Just after the North American Free Trade Agreement (NAFTA) became effective on January 1, 1994, Shaw negotiated a deal with the Mexican conglomerate Grupo Alfa. Alfa's diverse holdings included Mexican carpet manufacturer Terza. The Shaw-Alfa joint venture sold carpet throughout Mexico, Central America, and South America. Though volume remained low compared to the U.S. carpet market (approximately $91 million), the joint venture nevertheless proved profitable. Shaw developed good relations with its Latin American partners.[38]

Bob Shaw helped make initial contacts between Erwin Mitchell and the university community in Monterrey, Mexico. With Shaw's help, Mitchell worked out an exchange program with the University of Monterrey. Dubbed the Georgia Project, the program brought native Spanish speakers from Monterrey to Dalton to serve as teachers and role models in Dalton's public schools and as "cultural liaisons" with the Hispanic community. The project also sent Dalton teachers to Mexico for summer institutes to work on their Spanish. The program was funded in part by the local school system, a federal grant, and private donations.[39]

A *Wall Street Journal* reporter observed in 2001 that "countless textile and apparel factories have fled the South for cheap labor in Mexico." In contrast, "Dalton's biggest producers have closed operations in other regions, choosing to hunker down even deeper in their familiar north Georgia hills." The concentration of the carpet industry in Dalton aided local officials in initiating a creative program such as the Georgia Project. More than a hundred carpet mills lay within Dalton's city limits and paid property taxes—led, of course, by Shaw Industries. Whitfield County ranked far ahead of the Georgia average in per capita retail sales, and by the end of the 1990s mill workers, many of whom were Hispanic, paid sales taxes on those purchases. Dalton's schools spent more than $7,400 per student in 1999, far above the Georgia state average. California, by contrast, had similar "multicultural" demands on its educational system and an economic boom in the 1990s as well, yet per student spending in the Golden State amounted to only $5,414, well behind Georgia's Carpet Capital.[40]

The Georgia Project soon began to receive national attention. In 1998, the project was named a semifinalist in Harvard University's "Innovations in American Government" program. Partners for Livable Communities honored Erwin Mitchell and Monterrey partner Olivia Villarreal-Solano as "bridge builders" in January 2000 for their efforts to promote cultural diversity. In the summer of 2001, the National Education Association gave Mitchell its George J. Sanchez Memorial Award for achievements that improve educational opportunities for Hispanics.[41]

The Georgia Project meshed with the efforts of Shaw and other mills to increase bilingual communication in the workplace. Mitchell made no secret of his ambitious goal for his community in the long run. "The aim of our school system," he insisted, "is to make it possible for every student to become bilingual by the time of graduation." Dalton had not become any sort of multicultural utopia, and Mitchell and others understood that much remained to be done. Yet at the beginning of the twenty-first century the city of Dalton, its people, and its business community seemed to be managing a massive social transition better than other sections of the country.[42]

Shaw Industries' management continued to look to the future rather than rest on past laurels. Three efforts particularly reflected the company's commitment to moving forward. Disposing of old carpets made from nonbiodegradable artificial fibers became a serious waste management issue in the 1990s. Ironically, the growth in demand stimulated by the introduction of cheaper synthetic fibers helped create the waste problem. Shaw also reacted to the flattening of the carpet demand curve by exploring other products. In addition, the company began experimenting with new concepts in labor-management relations.

Many manufacturers began exploring the potential for recycling carpet wastes in the 1990s. Carpet manufacturers traditionally gave little attention to issues of environmental responsibility and sustainable development. That began to change in the 1990s, and Shaw Industries took a leadership role. Beginning in the mid-1990s, Shaw moved toward "greener" manufacturing processes. By 2001, Shaw produced twice as much carpet per gallon of water, helping to address the problems of excessive water usage and water pollution long associated with the Dalton carpet industry. Among numerous other initiatives, Shaw developed a new polyolefin backing material, EcoWorx, which used 40 percent less raw materials per square yard than comparable products made with PVC. EcoWorx was also reusable in the backing process, and face yarns could be readily separated for recycling as well. Such initiatives brought outside recognition. Shaw received a Governor's Award for Pollution Prevention from the state of Georgia for EcoWorx, placing first in the large industry category in 1999. Shaw Industries officials seemed convinced that recycling and other environmental efforts were both good for the community and could have a beneficial impact on the company's profits through waste reduction. Shaw's perennial emphasis on efficiency meshed, in some ways, with increasing public concern for the environment. Shaw's Contract Group also initiated a program to encourage commercial customers to recycle their old carpet. Under the program, Shaw Industries removed old carpet and shipped it to a recycling facility for use in other products. Shaw also began using recycled plastics—such as old soda bottles—to produce polyester yarn. By 1996, Shaw's standard residential-grade polyester carpets were made with 100 percent recycled fiber.[43]

The boom market that helped create the waste problem ran out in the 1990s. As the *Wall Street Journal*'s James Haggerty observed in the spring of 1998, "carpet makers are finally facing up to an uncomfortable truth: the American dream no longer requires wall-to-wall carpeting." Carpet had once held a position of unchallenged dominance in the American floor covering market. By 1997, carpet's market share had dipped from 80 percent to 58 percent. Though carpet was still king on America's floors, its position was much less secure. Most significantly, carpet seemed to offer little in the way of growth potential. Consumers increasingly shifted their dollars to hardwood floors, laminated flooring, and ceramic tile.[44]

The significance of this shift in consumer tastes was not lost on Shaw management. Shaw's retail venture came in some measure as a reaction to a declining market. Shaw first sought to combat sluggish sales by cutting out yet another layer of middlemen, as the company had done before. With the end of the retail experiment, however, Shaw looked to expand its product line. In 1999, Shaw began distributing laminates and tiles. In January 2000, Shaw introduced a line of hardwood flooring at the Surfaces trade show in Las Vegas, Nevada. Shaw contracted with other manufacturers for these hard-surface products but used its own trucking and distribution facilities to market the new product lines. Shaw and its chief competitor, Mohawk, used the distribution systems they had developed for carpeting to sell hard-surface products. "Carpet companies are no longer just carpet companies," First Union Securities' John Baugh observed. "Shaw and Mohawk have built up considerable distribution expertise because of their roots in the carpet business, and now they're leveraging that."[45] Shaw's bid to "leverage" its distribution expertise represented a return to a core competency as well.

Shaw Industries also experimented with updating its approach to manufacturing. Already a leader in manufacturing efficiency, Shaw management continued to seek new ideas. In 1991, Shaw started up a new plant to produce carpet tiles in Cartersville, Georgia. Carpet tiles, squares of carpeting that can increase design flexibility, had become an increasingly important product in the commercial arena, such as in corporate offices and institutional settings. The commercial segment of the carpet market, though still much smaller than the high-volume residential segment, had grown significantly during the 1990s. While large mills such as Shaw, Mohawk, and Beaulieu had achieved near total domination of the residential market, smaller firms still competed effectively in the highly segmented commercial area by identifying specialized niches. Specialized products for many commercial applications tended to be lower-volume but higher–profit margin items; economies of scale were less important. James Jarrett, Shaw's director of manufacturing for the contract carpet unit, explained in a 1999 interview that the company decided to implement a team manufacturing approach to enhance their ability to compete with small firms in these niche areas. "Smaller mills have to be more creative and niche oriented," Jarrett explained, "so we have to remain flexible and react quickly to market changes." Jarrett acknowledged "that it's tough when you're as big as we are, but it's how we have to be if we are going to be successful."[46]

In implementing the team concept, Shaw "purposely didn't transfer any people from other plants," Jarrett recalled. "We hired people who we thought could learn the business and work within a team-based environment." Shaw's manufacturing teams consisted of ten to twenty workers. Team coordinators tracked safety, quality, production scheduling, and a number of other categories of data. Traditionally in carpet manufacturing, workers learned one job and continued to perform that task. The team approach encouraged workers to learn new skills through on-the-job training. The capstone experience in the training regimen concept was to have a worker teach a newly acquired skill to another employee. The approach worked so well that by 1995 the company was looking for ways to expand the concept to other facilities.[47]

Shaw also increased its commitment to continuing education for its "associates." During the initial generation of development in the tufted carpet industry of north Georgia, high levels of literacy and technical proficiency were unnecessary for most workers. The stakes began to go up in the 1970s with continuous dyeing. Particularly in the 1980s, however, Shaw and other manufacturers invested in new computer-controlled tufting machines and other equipment. As Shaw and other companies moved increasingly into the extrusion of polypropylene and other synthetic yarns, an increasing number of jobs in the mills required a higher degree of literacy and math skills; some of the new jobs required technical skills as well. Shaw had for years offered high school equivalency courses on-site in many of its manufacturing plants to encourage workers to improve basic skills. Two colleges in the Cartersville area and one in Dalton began offering certificates in Applied Manufacturing Technology in the late 1990s. Shaw invited instructors to teach courses in those programs in Shaw plants. Tuition for each course was covered by Georgia's Hope scholarship program.[48]

Shaw Industries also embarked on a new effort to build brand-name recognition in the new century. Shaw partnered with popular former fashion model Kathy Ireland. Ireland had launched a line of home furnishings, including furniture and lighting, a few years earlier. Shaw had already introduced area rugs licensed by Ireland, but, of course, the high-volume area in the carpet industry continued to be the market for residential "wall-to-wall" carpeting. A Kurt Salmon Associates report on the Kathy Ireland brands showed that 42 percent of women aged eighteen to forty-nine had heard of and purchased a Kathy Ireland branded product. Other carpet manufacturers had already achieved some success with celebrity product licensing. Shaw management hoped that brand recognition would translate to increased sales. Ireland joined Shaw officials at the Surfaces trade show in early 2001 to introduce a new line of broadloom carpets. Ireland explained that she had worked closely with Shaw designers in developing the new product lines, especially in the area of color. The solid-color carpets in the Kathy Ireland line came in ninety shades. The new lines were intended to "provide solutions for families, especially those with busy moms," Ireland observed. This move represented only one piece of an ambitious new strategy.[49]

Shaw Industries had stumbled during the mid-1990s, but the company rebounded strongly at the end of the decade. As Shaw entered a new century, the company reclaimed the high ground it had occupied in the early 1990s. In *Textile World*'s ranking of the fifty most influential people in the textile industry during the twentieth century, Bob Shaw placed tenth, just ahead of Burlington Mills founder J. Spencer Love and longtime WestPoint and Dan River CEO Joseph Lanier Jr.

Shaw also placed first in the textile industry on *Fortune*'s list of the most admired companies in U.S. industry. *Fortune* surveyed more than 10,000 executives and analysts to rate the top 500 firms among the 1,000 largest U.S. companies in eight categories, including quality of management, financial soundness, employee talent, and long-term investment potential. Shaw led the seven firms represented in the textile sector. The company also received impressive rankings when compared to the rest of the overall "most admired" 500. Shaw's score in the category "quality of management" placed the company at 162nd, well in the second quintile of American big business. Shaw placed in the upper 40 percent of American big business in "financial soundness" (number 178) and "long-term investment value" (number 196). Shaw placed in the upper half of the 500 in all but two categories ("social responsibility," number 325, and "innovativeness," number 266).[50]

Shaw Industries had become, in management's phrase, "a world-class corporation." Management consultants had tried to convince Bob Shaw to move the company's headquarters to Atlanta, to a setting more suitable for a *Fortune* 500 firm. Shaw steadfastly refused, clinging to the communities of northwest Georgia that had spawned his industry, especially Dalton. "I'll admit that maybe attracting people to live in Dalton, Georgia, is probably a little harder than attracting people to live in Atlanta. But I think there are advantages and disadvantages—and if you put your foundation deep enough, they can't move it. We've put our stake pretty deep in the ground right here."[51]

In spite of Shaw Industries' best efforts at the end of the 1990s, the company's stock price never fully recovered. Trading at $17 per share in late 1999 (still undervalued from the company's perspective), Shaw's stock dipped to about $13 by June 2000. Bob Shaw traveled to Omaha, Nebraska, that month to negotiate for reinsurance protection in a possible upcoming merger. Shaw went to Omaha because it was the home of Berkshire-Hathaway, the holding company of legendary investment guru Warren Buffett. Berkshire's portfolio included insurance companies that offered the services Shaw expected to need. As the meeting was breaking up, Shaw took what might have been a shot in the dark aimed at solving Shaw Industries' nagging stock market dilemma. "Mr. Shaw asked Mr. Buffett if he might like to make a direct investment in Shaw," according to the *Wall Street Journal.* Buffett was initially noncommittal.[1]

Why would Bob Shaw propose selling a large stake in the company to a single investor who would then have the power to alter strategy and policy for Shaw Industries? Had the founders given up on their idea of building an institution that would last? Had they begun to consider selling out?

The answer is complex. As the 1990s ended, Shaw faced an investing community indifferent to solid but unspectacular companies. Although Shaw had restored profitability after a relatively short period of struggle and showed promise for future earnings growth, most investors were mesmerized by the lure of easy money in high-tech stocks after 1995. Investment analysts spoke of a "new economy" dominated by information and technology companies. Old ideas about reasonable returns, many analysts advised, should be scrapped in favor of more optimistic ones. As the Dow-Jones Industrial Average surpassed 11,000 in the late 1990s, some giddy analysts talked about changing rules and gushed over the prospects of "Dow 36,000" (within 3–5 years), "Dow 40,000" (by the year 2016), or even "Dow 100,000" (by 2020).[2] Shaw Industries was a classic "old economy" company engaged in manufacturing a basic element of home furnishings. Like most other "old economy" stocks, Shaw's share price languished even as the company quietly continued to earn solid returns.

Perhaps the answer was simply to withdraw from the public markets altogether. Shaw had reaped great benefits from the stock exchange since going public in 1971, but the environment had changed by the mid-1980s. The hostile-takeover and leveraged-buyout mania of the 1980s followed by the tech boom of the 1990s had led to an ever-increasing emphasis on short-term results for "old economy" companies. Shaw's strategy had always been based on long-term considerations. The rising returns produced by the stock market during the past twenty years seemed, to a greater degree year by year, to increase pressure on corporate management to produce spectacular results every quarter. "New economy" companies seemed to be immune from those pressures. Indeed, high-tech firms seemed to many observers to be immune from the traditional rules that governed business success in the late 1990s; years after successful initial public offerings, many (notably Internet bookseller Amazon.com) had not earned a dime in profits by 1999. Federal Reserve chairman Alan Greenspan famously characterized the behavior of investors in the 1990s with the phrase "irrational exuberance." The run-up in stock prices from the early 1980s to the end of the century was not supported by any corresponding increase in corporate earnings. Greenspan and others feared that the stock boom was based more on hope (or greed) than logic.[3]

Warren Buffett agreed. He had become an icon of long-term investing by the 1990s. Observers often joked that if you asked Buffett when the proper time was to sell a stock, his reply was always "never." Starting small in the 1950s, Buffett built his holding company, Berkshire-Hathaway, into a Wall Street powerhouse in the 1990s. Buffett invested in classic "old economy" companies long before the term became fashionable, and he held on to these companies. By the 1990s, he was the largest single stockholder in Coca Cola (about 8 percent) and sat on that Georgia-based company's board. He also held a controlling interest in a host of other companies, including GEICO Insurance, the Nebraska Furniture Mart, and other enterprises.

Buffett had purchased Berkshire-Hathaway itself in May 1965. At the time, Berkshire was a struggling textile manufacturer producing commodity synthetic cloth. Buffett built Berkshire into an investment firm that owned stock in a variety of other companies, originally principally insurance and reinsurance companies but increasingly firms in other fields. Buffett's investing acumen won him a legion of followers. Berkshire's stock price—reflecting the collective value of the firm's portfolio—reached stratospheric levels in the 1990s, rising from $18 per share in 1965 to around $70,000 in mid-2001.[4]

In building his fortune, Warren Buffett had resisted the takeover mania of the 1980s and the high-tech boom of the 1990s. He had invested in some takeover targets in the 1980s but resisted entering into bidding wars. He simply took advantage of the feeding frenzy over, for example, RJR-Nabisco to make some short-term profits. Buffett became deeply troubled by the hostile takeovers and leveraged buyouts financed by junk bonds. He summarized his view of corporate raiders and their argument that they were only creating value for shareholders in a 1998 address to the management of ABC/Cap Cities, another of his holdings. By loading target firms with debt, raiders converted equity to debt. The massive interest payments on those debts were tax deductible. Buffett argued that this conversion of equity into debt only left a larger burden to be borne by the average taxpayer. "[T]hey talk about creating value for shareholders. They aren't creating value—they are transferring it from society to shareholder," Buffett insisted. "That may be a good thing or a bad thing, but it isn't creating value—it's not like Henry Ford developing the car or Ray Kroc figuring out how to deliver hamburgers better than anyone else. . . . In the last few years, one [company] after another has been transformed by people who understood this game. That means every citizen owes a touch more of what is needed to pay for all the goods and services that the government provides."[5]

Buffett's biographer, Roger Lowenstein, summarized the investment philosophy of the "sage of Omaha" in similar terms. Buffett had a "prejudice for what was enduring" and "defined investing as an attempt to profit from the results of the enterprise, as distinct from the [share] price action." Leveraged buyout (LBO) artists, in Buffett's view, "did not really qualify as 'investors.'" Buffett defined "creating value" as "adding to the sum of socially useful or desirable products and services." Raiders and LBO artists merely "transferred assets from one pocket to the next," and profited from share prices artificially inflated by the buyout and the tax breaks.[6]

Buffett developed a penchant for acquiring controlling interests in undervalued companies that produced good cash flow and turned a profit. He tended to require that the company's existing management remain in place and retain a stake in ownership. Buffett then let the experienced managers manage, free of the day-to-day, short-term concerns about stock prices and beating the predictions of Wall Street analysts. Berkshire's subsidiaries retained their company names and identities. It was this approach that made a deal with Buffett attractive to Bob Shaw. A direct investment from Buffett could remove Shaw from the Wall Street expectations game yet leave the company essentially intact as a local institution. It was, in a sense, a way to sell the company without losing control. For three decades, Shaw Industries had its outstanding shares spread among thousands of investors in the public markets. Berkshire-Hathaway would now replace those myriad investors.

So when Buffett responded in a noncommittal fashion, Bob Shaw didn't drop the matter. Upon returning to Dalton, he sent Buffett a packet of information about Shaw Industries. A few days later, Bob Shaw and Shaw president Julian Saul returned to Omaha to discuss a direct investment by Buffett. The investment wizard played his cards close to the vest, still refusing to make a direct investment. As Shaw and Saul were leaving, however, he "asked if they minded Berkshire buying shares on the open market." Of course, they did not mind, and Buffett began buying Shaw stock.[7]

The deal seemed to be in the making when Flooring America, Shaw's largest customer, filed for Chapter 11 bankruptcy protection. Buffett notified Shaw Industries that any talks about a direct investment would have to be put on hold. The CEO persisted, however, speaking with Buffett three times by phone in late July. "By August 16," as *Wall Street Journal* reporters put it, "Mr. Shaw was close to reeling in Mr. Buffett." On August 25, Shaw and vice-chairman Norris Little visited Buffett in Omaha again. At that meeting, Buffett offered to buy 80 percent of Shaw Industries' stock for $19 per share, a premium of more than 50 percent above its current Wall Street price. Bob Shaw and Julian Saul would maintain a stake (5 percent each) in the company for a time and continue to run Shaw Industries.[8]

Shaw announced the proposed deal on September 6, 2000. The board of directors approved the sale in October. Shareholders gave final consent to the deal in January 2001. Shaw Industries soon became a subsidiary of Berkshire-Hathaway and ceased to be a publicly traded company in its own right. Shaw Industries would retain its company name and significant management autonomy, however. The institution that Shaw management had long spoken of endured. Julius Shaw summarized the deal in just these terms. "We think this is a unique opportunity to partner with one of the finest companies in America—Berkshire Hathaway," he told the press when the deal was announced. "The history of Berkshire is that they continue to operate their companies with existing management. That certainly was attractive to us." Wall Street analysts agreed that the $19 per share represented a premium for Shaw stockholders that was unlikely to be matched in any other way. SunTrust Equities' Keith Hughes observed that "Warren Buffett has an excellent reputation of buying undervalued companies and helping them succeed. These types of stocks have been largely forgotten by Wall Street and it's tough to come up with a way that the price of Shaw's stock would have risen to this level any time soon."[9]

For Buffett, the Shaw deal symbolized a new strategy. He believed that the construction industry would be a significant growth area in the future. To that end, he acquired not just Shaw Industries but several other enterprises that manufactured building materials. As Buffett put it in his 2001 annual letter to stockholders, "we have embraced the 21st century by entering such cutting-edge industries as brick, carpet, insulation, and paint. Try to control your excitement."[10] That was precisely the point. Shaw Industries' products were not glamorous. They were, however, staples of American consumption. Carpets certainly added to the "sum of socially useful or desirable goods." Shaw Industries—in the broad sense, including the company's direct and indirect ancestors such as Clarence Shaw and Cabin Crafts—had played a large role in making carpet an affordable commodity for middle-class and working-class families. Shaw Industries would continue to focus on producing carpets at the lowest possible cost for the largest possible market. The task of maintaining the company's leadership in the industry would increasingly fall to new people in the twenty-first century.

Introduction

1. Cobb, *Selling of the South.*
2. Wright, *Old South, New South,* 251–57.
3. Schulman, *From Cotton Belt to Sunbelt,* 139, 165–66.
4. I follow Charles Sabel and Jonathan Zeitlin (as best I can) in arguing that "human life is intelligible only as narration—a story with a beginning, middle, and meaningful end." Sabel and Zeitlin, "Stories, Strategies, Structures: Rethinking Historical Alternatives to Mass Production," in Sabel and Zeitlin, *World of Possibilities,* 11.
5. Krugman, *Geography and Trade,* 5, 129.
6. Ibid., 60–61.
7. Ibid., 9.
8. See Wright, *Old South, New South,* 124–55.
9. The description of the early days of bedspread tufting is drawn from Patton, *Carpet Capital,* 84–88.
10. Flamming, *Creating the Modern South,* 44–45.
11. See the United States Historical Data Census Browser at <http://fisher.lib.virginia.edu/census/>, accessed 13 Dec. 2001.
12. Reg Burnett, RBI Carpet Education Manual, 1994, distributed at Reg Burnett International (RBI) seminar, April 1994, in the possession of the author.
13. Patton, *Carpet Capital,* 76–77.
14. Reynolds, *Innovation in the United States Carpet Industry,* 43–46.
15. Blackford and Kerr, *Business Enterprise in American History,* 292–93.
16. Hobsbawm, *Age of Extremes,* 268–69.
17. A classic description of the rise of what many have called "Fordism" and its decline in the post–1973 years is Piore and Sabel, *Second Industrial Divide.*
18. Philip Scranton, "'Have a Heart for the Manufacturers!' Production, Distribution, and the Decline of American Textile Manufacturing," in Sabel and Zeitlin, *World of Possibilities,* 310–43.
19. Blackford and Kerr, *Business Enterprise in American History,* 292.
20. Harold G. Vatter, "The Position of Small Business in the Structure of American Manufacturing, 1870–1970," in Bruchey, *Small Business in American Life,* 159–61.
21. Ibid., 161.
22. This brief description of the industry is drawn from Patton, *Carpet Capital,* chapters 1 and 2.

One. Beginnings

1. See Ayers, *Promise of the New South*, especially 96–97.
2. Elbert Shaw, interview by Randall Patton, 2 March 1999, Shaw Industries History series.
3. J. C. (Bud) Shaw, interview by Randall Patton, 11 April 1998, Carpet History series; Robert E. (Bob) Shaw, interview by Randall Patton, 19 Aug. 1999, Shaw Industries History series.
4. *Dalton Daily Citizen-News*, 10 Feb. 1964.
5. Jack Turner, interview by Randall Patton, 9 March 1999, Shaw Industries History series.
6. Ibid.; J. C. (Bud) Shaw, interview by Randall Patton, 1 May 2001, Shaw Industries History series.
7. Bud Shaw, interview, 1 May 2001.
8. Julian McCamy, interview by Randall Patton, 29 Oct. 1999, Shaw Industries History series.
9. Turner, interview.
10. "American Inventive Genius: Fred Westcott," *Modern Floor Coverings*, n.d., clipping found in Cabin Crafts scrapbooks, Crown Archives.
11. Ibid.
12. Ibid.
13. Ibid.
14. Bob Shaw, interview.
15. Bud Shaw, interview, 11 April 1998.
16. Bob Shaw, interview.
17. Bud Shaw, interview, 11 April 1998; Warren Sims, interview by Randall Patton, 15 Aug. 1994, Carpet History series.
18. Sims, interview.
19. Ibid.
20. Bob Shaw, interview.
21. Elbert Shaw, interview.
22. Ibid.
23. Buddy Sewell, interview by Randall Patton, 16 June 1999, Shaw Industries History series.
24. Ibid.
25. Ibid.
26. Ibid.
27. Ibid.
28. Ibid.
29. Ibid.
30. Ibid.
31. Ibid.
32. John Kirk, interview by Randall Patton, 6 June 2001, Shaw Industries History series.
33. Ibid.

34. Sewell, interview.
35. Ibid.
36. Flamming, *Creating the Modern South,* 121.
37. Minchin, *Hiring the Black Worker,* 3.
38. Ibid.; Sewell, interview.
39. Ibid.
40. Sims, interview.
41. Sewell, interview.
42. *Dalton Daily Citizen-News,* clipping found in Cabin Crafts scrapbooks, n.d. [probably 1967], Crown Archives; McCamy, interview.
43. Otis Payne, interview by Randall Patton, 18 June 1999, Shaw Industries History series.
44. Ibid.
45. Turner, interview.
46. Payne, interview; Turner, interview.
47. Payne, interview.
48. McCamy, interview.
49. "Cabin Crafts, Inc.," *Westpointer* 3, no. 3 (1956): 3–4.
50. Payne, interview.
51. Ibid.
52. Roger McNamara, interview by Randall Patton, 11 May 1999, Shaw Industries History series.
53. Sidney Felker, interview by Randall Patton, 16 June 1999, Shaw Industries History series.
54. Payne, interview.
55. *Textile World,* May 1962, 56–62.
56. Clipping, probably from *Floor Covering Weekly,* n.d. [most likely early 1960s], found in Cabin Crafts scrapbooks, Crown Archives.
57. *Chattanooga News Free Press,* 18 Oct. 1962, Crown Archives.
58. WestPoint Pepperell, "Carpet and Rug Division Sales Policy Manual: Company History," 11 May 1987, Crown Archives.
59. Bud Shaw, interview, 11 April 1998.

Two. Making the Transition

1. Buddy Sewell, interview by Randall Patton, 16 June 1999, Shaw Industries History series.
2. Ibid.
3. Robert E. (Bob) Shaw, interview by Randall Patton, 19 Aug. 1999, Shaw Industries History series.
4. J. C. (Bud) Shaw, interview by Randall Patton, 11 April 1998, Carpet History series.
5. Ibid.; Bob Shaw, interview.
6. *TTMA Directory,* 1965, 187–90, Tufted Textile Manufacturers Association Papers.
7. Max Beasley, interview by Bart Threatte, 11 May 1994, Carpet History series; *Carpet and Rug Industry Review,* 1993, Carpet and Rug Institute Papers.

8. Sewell, interview.
9. Bud Shaw, interview, 11 April 1998.
10. David L. Carlton, "Entrepreneurship and Industrialization: The Case of North Carolina," paper presented at the Business History Conference, 6 March 1999, paper in the possession of the author.
11. Flamming, *Creating the Modern South,* 320–21.
12. Ibid.
13. Bud Shaw, interview, 11 April 1998.
14. Julius Shaw, interview by Randall Patton, 9 Sept. 1999, Shaw Industries History series; Bud Shaw, interview, 11 April 1998.
15. Bob Shaw, interview.
16. *Home Furnishings Daily,* 5 Oct. 1960; Bud Shaw, interview, 11 April 1998; Warren Sims, interview by Randall Patton, 15 Aug. 1994, Carpet History series.
17. *Textile World,* Jan. 1965, 81; Bud Shaw, interview, 11 April 1998.
18. Sewell, interview.
19. Ibid.
20. Bud Shaw, interview, 11 April 1998.
21. Bob Shaw, interview; Sims, interview.
22. Sewell, interview; Bob Shaw, interview.
23. Patton, *Carpet Capital,* 207–8.
24. Walter Hemphill, interview by Randall Patton, 24 May 1999, Shaw Industries History series.
25. Ibid.
26. Ibid.
27. Ibid.
28. Ibid.
29. Ibid.; Bob Shaw, interview.
30. Hemphill, interview.
31. Ibid.; Sewell, interview.
32. John Kirk, interview by Randall Patton, 6 June 2001, Shaw Industries History series.
33. Ibid.
34. Ibid.; Elbert Shaw, interview by Randall Patton, 2 March 1999, Shaw Industries History series.
35. Kirk, interview. Kirk's recollections of the early days of Star Finishing were supported by Elaine Mozingo, longtime secretary to Bob Shaw.
36. Kirk, interview.
37. Patton, *Carpet Capital,* 123–48.
38. Ibid., 314–15. See also McDonald, "Textile Workers and Unionization." McDonald provides a wealth of data based on a survey of more than two hundred Dalton carpet mill workers. His analysis indicates that work in a carpet mill was generally less physically demanding than other areas of textile labor. It would be wrong to characterize McDonald as anti-union on this basis, however; his sympathies clearly rested with organized labor.

39. Patton, *Carpet Capital*, 150–59.
40. U.S. Bureau of the Census, *Census of Manufactures*, 1963 and 1967.
41. TTMA "Newsletter," 22 Aug. 1962, Tufted Textile Manufacturers Association Papers.
42. Ibid.
43. Kirk, interview.
44. Ibid. Independent studies confirmed the anecdotal evidence about labor turnover. See Plice, *Manpower and Merger*.
45. Raymond Roach, interview by Randall Patton, 23 May 1994, Carpet History series; Willie Hicks, interview by Linda Williams, 17 April 1996, Carpet History series; Minchin, *"What Do We Need a Union For?"*
46. *Textile World*, Oct. 1962, 106–8.
47. Ibid.
48. RBI Carpet Education Manual, Reg Burnett International, n.d., in the possession of the author.
49. *Textile World*, Oct. 1962, 106–8.
50. Ibid.
51. Hemphill, interview.
52. *Dalton Daily Citizen-News*, 30 Jan. 1963.
53. Warren Sims, interview by Randall Patton, 15 Aug. 1994, Carpet History series; Bill Lusk, interview by Randall Patton, 2 Sept. 1999, Shaw Industries History series.
54. Lusk, interview.
55. *Chattanooga Times*, 11 March 1963.
56. *Dalton Daily Citizen-News*, 20 March 1963.
57. Sims, interview.
58. *Dalton Daily Citizen-News*, 20 March 1963.
59. Data on workplace accidents and injuries are available from the Bureau of Labor Statistics through its website at <www.bls.gov/iif/home.htm>, accessed 13 December 2001.
60. *Dalton Daily Citizen-News*, 29 Sept. 1963.
61. Sims, interview.
62. Julius Shaw, interview.
63. Bud Shaw, interview, 11 April 1998.
64. Julius Shaw, interview.
65. Sims, interview.
66. Ibid.
67. Ibid.
68. Ibid.
69. Ibid.
70. Ibid.
71. Ibid.
72. Ibid.

Three. A Philadelphia Story

1. Warren Sims, interview by Randall Patton, 15 Aug. 1994, Carpet History series; Robert E. (Bob) Shaw, interview by Randall Patton, 19 Aug. 1999, Shaw Industries History series; Ken Jackson, interview by Randall Patton, 12 May 1999, Shaw Industries History series.

2. "The Philadelphia Carpet Story," pamphlet published by Revonah Spinning Mills, Hanover, Pennsylvania, 1960, copy found at Carpet and Rug Institute, Dalton, Georgia.

3. Ibid.

4. Ibid.; Lisa Solomon, "Philadelphia Carpet Company," research paper in the possession of the author.

5. *Floor Covering Weekly*, 16 Dec. 1957.

6. "Philadelphia Carpet Story."

7. Spright Holland, interview by Randall Patton, 30 Jan. 1999, Shaw Industries History series.

8. *Floor Covering Weekly*, 4 Feb. 1963.

9. *Home Furnishings Daily*, 6 June 1963.

10. Ibid.

11. Holland, interview.

12. Bob Foltz, interview by Randall Patton, 16 May 1999; Shaw Industries History series.

13. *Home Furnishings Daily*, 10 June 1963.

14. *Home Furnishings Daily*, 19 Sept. 1963.

15. *Southern Textile News*, 23 Nov. 1963; Travis (Dusty) Rhodes, interview by Pat Taylor, 17 Dec. 1993, Carpet History series.

16. Holland, interview.

17. Ibid.

18. Jack Turner, interview by Randall Patton, 9 Mar. 1999, Shaw Industries History series.

19. Sims, interview.

20. Bob Shaw, interview; Bill Lusk, interview by Randall Patton, 2 Sept. 1999, Shaw Industries History series; J. C. (Bud) Shaw, interview by Randall Patton, 11 April 1998, Carpet History series; Julius Shaw, interview by Randall Patton, 9 Sept. 1999, Shaw Industries History series.

21. First National Bank of Atlanta to J. C. Shaw, 12 Dec. 1967.

22. Bud Shaw, interview, 11 April 1998; Robert Harlin, interview by Randall Patton, 6 May 2001, Shaw Industries History series.

23. "Prospectus: 575,000 Shares Shaw Industries, Inc., Common Stock," Drexel Firestone, 14 Oct. 1971.

24. Bob Shaw, interview.

25. "Stockholder List for Philadelphia Holding Company," 25 Feb. 1969, Warren Sims Papers.

26. This brief analysis is the author's, based on his interpretation of comments from an

interview with Robert Harlin and drawn from a variety of indirect, off-the-record comments and from the author's "reading between the lines." If this assessment is inaccurate, the responsibility lies solely with the author.

27. Lusk, interview; Sims, interview.
28. J. C. (Bud) Shaw, interview by Randall Patton, 1 May 2001, Shaw Industries History series; Holland, interview.
29. Holland, interview.
30. Walter Hemphill, interview by Randall Patton, 24 May 1999, Shaw Industries History series.
31. Norris Nielsen, "Shaw Industries, Inc.: J. C. Bradford & Co. Regional Research Report, January 17, 1972."
32. Holland, interview.
33. "Associations of the Carpet and Rug Industry in the United States Leading to the Carpet and Rug Institute," n.d., [probably 1970], Carpet and Rug Institute, Dalton, Georgia. On CRI and government regulation, see Patton, *Carpet Capital*, 236–46.
34. Gary N. Mock, "Early Development of Continuous Carpet Dyeing," *Textile Chemist and Colorist*, 30, no. 8 (Aug. 1998), 66.
35. E. T. Barwick, interview by Tom Deaton, 8 April 1980, Carpet History series.
36. *Floor Covering Weekly*, 5 Feb. 1968; *Textile Industries*, Feb. 1968; both clippings from CRI's E. T. Barwick Clipping File.
37. Bob Shaw, interview.
38. Former Barwick Mills president A. J. Paton, quoted in *Business Week*, 19 May 1975, 59–60.
39. "Prospectus," Drexel Firestone; Hemphill, interview.
40. Lusk, interview.
41. Ibid; Bob Shaw, interview.
42. "Prospectus," Drexel Firestone.
43. *Home Furnishings Daily*, 23 April 1969; *Textile World*, Nov. 1966, 109–13; *Textile World*, Oct. 1968, 102–5.

Four. The Emergence of Shaw Industries

1. William C. Lusk to Shaw Industries stockholders, telex, 24 April 1972.
2. Warren Sims, interview by Randall Patton, 15 Aug. 1994, Carpet History series.
3. Shaw Industries, "Notice of Annual Meeting to Shareholders," 22 Oct. 1980.
4. Drexel Firestone to the Board of Directors, Philadelphia Holding Company, 25 March 1971; stock offering announced in *Home Furnishings Daily*, 26 Aug. 1971.
5. Drexel report, 25 March 1971.
6. Ibid.
7. Ibid; Kurt Salmon Associates, "Tufting's Unrealized Profit Potential," *Textile Industries*, May 1969, 55–65.
8. Norris Little, interview by Jim Engstrom, 19 April 1995, Carpet History series; Robert E. (Bob) Shaw, interview by Randall Patton, 19 Aug. 1999, Shaw Industries History series.

9. Blackford and Kerr, *Business Enterprise in American History,* 299–300.

10. Norris Nielsen, "Shaw Industries, Inc.: J. C. Bradford & Co. Regional Research report," 17 Jan. 1972.

11. Robert W. Kirk, "The Carpet Industry: Present Status and Future Prospects," University of Pennsylvania, Wharton School of Finance and Commerce, Industrial Research Report no. 17, 1970, 20–24.

12. Bill Lusk, interview by Randall Patton, 2 Sept. 1999, Shaw Industries History series; Bob Shaw, interview.

13. Little, interview.

14. Ibid.

15. Ibid.

16. Ibid.

17. Ibid.

18. Ibid.

19. Ibid. Little's assessment is consistent with the views of mainstream business historians. See Blackford and Kerr, *Business Enterprise in American History,* 299–300; Bert Lance, quoted in *Atlanta Constitution,* 13 Jan. 1975.

20. Norris Little interview from *In the Loop* (Shaw Industries newsletter), Aug.–Sept. 2001. Julius Shaw underlined Little's importance to the company in the same issue, as did current vice president for administration Carl Rollins and J. C. Shaw in informal conversations with the author.

21. Shaw Industries, press release, 30 Sept. 1972.

22. Drexel Firestone, "Progress Report," Aug. 1972.

23. Lusk, interview.

24. Drexel Firestone, "Progress Report."

25. Ibid.

26. Ibid.

27. Mock, "Early Development of Continuous Carpet Dyeing," 67.

28. Ibid.

29. Ibid., 69.

30. Little interview, *In the Loop.*

31. Roy Johnson, quoted in *Carpet and Rug Industry,* July 1973, 10–12.

32. Shaw Industries, press release, 3 Dec. 1973; Walter Hemphill, interview by Randall Patton, 24 May 1999, Shaw Industries History series.

33. Flemming, "Northwest Georgia Carpet Finishing Industry," 25.

34. Chernow, *Titan,* 150.

35. Hobsbawm, *Age of Extremes.*

36. CRI, *Carpet and Rug Industry Review,* 1993, 8–9.

37. *Atlanta Constitution,* 13 Jan. 1975, clipping in Warren Sims Papers.

38. Shaw Industries, Annual Report, 29 July 1974; Interim Report, 3 Oct. 1974; Bill Lusk to McDonald and Little public relations firm, 30 Oct. 1974.

39. Shaw Industries, Interim Report, 22 April 1975; press release, 23 Jan. 1976; Interim Report, 23 Jan. 1976.

40. Sims, interview.

41. Robert E. Shaw's remarks summarized by Richard Hoffmann in *Home Furnishings Daily*, 18 Feb. 1976, 17.
42. Ibid.
43. Sims, interview; Warren Sims, "A Unified Leadership for a Growing Company," Shaw Industries, Annual Report, 1978.
44. Norris Little, interview by Randall Patton, 5 May 1999, Shaw Industries History series.
45. Shaw Industries, draft Interim Report, 27 Jan. 1978, and handwritten note appended to the report.
46. Bob Shaw, interview.
47. "Minutes of the Meeting of the Board of Directors of Shaw Industries, Inc.," 27 April 1977; J. C. (Bud) Shaw, interview by Randall Patton, 11 April 1998, Carpet History series; Spright Holland, interview by Randall Patton, 30 Jan. 1999, Shaw Industries History series.
48. Sims, interview.
49. Ibid.; J. C. (Bud) Shaw, interview by Randall Patton, 1 May 2001, Shaw Industries History series.
50. Bob Shaw, interview.
51. "Minutes of the Annual Meeting of the Directors of Shaw Industries, Inc.," 26 Oct. 1977.
52. Ibid.
53. Sims, interview.
54. *Atlanta Constitution*, 23 May 1997, 3E, and 3 June 2000, 2F; Post Properties, press release, *PR Newswire*, 31 May 2000, accessed through LexisNexis Academic Universe, <www.lexisnexis.com>, 15 Jan. 2001.
55. "Minutes of the Executive Committee Meeting of Shaw Industries, Inc.," 30 Nov. 1977.
56. Ibid.; Holland, interview; Enid G. Colp, "Shaw Changes Marketing with Command Post Switch," *Retailing Home Furnishings*, 2 Jan. 1978.
57. "Minutes of the Executive Committee of the Board of Directors of Shaw Industries, Inc.," 25 Jan. 1978.
58. "Minutes of the Executive Committee of Shaw Industries, Inc." 29 March 1978.
59. Julius Shaw, interview by Randall Patton, 9 Sept. 1999, Shaw Industries History series.
60. Ibid.
61. Ibid.
62. Ibid.
63. Ibid; Julius Shaw column, *In the Loop*, Aug.–Sept. 2001; memorandum from Carl Rollins, Shaw vice president for administration, to Randall Patton, 9 July 2002.
64. Buddy Sewell, interview by Randall Patton, 16 June 1999, Shaw Industries History series.
65. Ibid.
66. Ibid.; Shaw Industries, Annual Report, 1976.

Five. Survival of the Fittest

1. Richard Eldredge to CRI Board of Directors, 19 Feb. 1979, CRI Papers.
2. *Merrill Lynch Market Review,* 5 Dec. 1983.
3. "House Committee on Banking Hears CRI Testimony," *CRI Newsletter,* 8, no. 12 (22 Dec. 1981), Warren Sims Papers.
4. Ibid.
5. "Private Pension Funds: New Source of Housing Finance?" *Federal Home Loan Bank Board Journal* 15, no. 11 (Nov. 1982), 9; "Will Pension Funds Invest in Residential Mortgages?" *Institutional Investor,* 16, no. 8 (Aug. 1982), 119.
6. Minutes of a Special Meeting of the Executive Committee of Shaw Industries, Inc.," 27 May 1981.
7. Warren Sims, interview by Randall Patton, 15 Aug. 1994, Carpet History series; Chuck Reece, "Carpet King," *Georgia Trend,* Aug. 1990.
8. Vance Bell, interview by Randall Patton, 6 May 1999, Shaw Industries History series.
9. Ibid.
10. Ibid.
11. Ibid.
12. Ibid.
13. Ibid.
14. Ibid.
15. Ibid.
16. Elbert Shaw, interview by Randall Patton, 2 March 1999, Shaw Industries History series.
17. Ibid.
18. Ibid.
19. Ibid.
20. Ibid.
21. *Sales and Marketing Management,* 16 Jan. 1984, 19.
22. Bell, interview.
23. Ibid.; Julius Shaw, interview by Randall Patton, 9 Sept. 1999, Shaw Industries History series.
24. *Sales and Marketing Management,* 16 Jan. 1984, 19; Julius Shaw, interview.
25. Bell, interview.
26. *Forbes,* 31 Dec. 1984, 147.
27. Julius Shaw, interview.
28. Ibid.
29. Bell, interview.
30. *Atlanta Journal-Constitution,* 17 March 1985; Reg Burnett, interview by Randall Patton, 5 May 1999, Shaw Industries History series.
31. *Atlanta Journal-Constitution,* 17 March 1985.
32. "Minutes of the Executive Committee of Shaw Industries, Inc.," 31 March 1982; Bill Lusk, interview by Randall Patton, 2 Sept. 1999, Shaw Industries History series.
33. Lusk, interview.

34. "Minutes of the Executive Committee of Shaw Industries, Inc.," 26 May 1982.
35. Shaw Industries, press release, 16 Dec. 1983; *Textile World,* June 1985.
36. Burnett, interview; *Textile World,* June 1985.
37. Lusk, interview.
38. Walter Hemphill, interview by Randall Patton, 24 May 1999, Shaw Industries History series.
39. *Floor Covering Weekly,* 29 April 1985.
40. Julius Shaw, interview.
41. *Carpet and Rug Industry Review, 1993, 7.*
42. Robert E. (Bob) Shaw, interview by Randall Patton, 19 Aug. 1999, Shaw Industries History series.
43. Sims, interview; Bell, interview.

Six. Leadership in a Maturing Industry

1. Julius Shaw, interview by Randall Patton, 9 Sept. 1999, Shaw Industries History series.
2. This discussion of DuPont is based on Luck, Ferrell, and Lucas, "Case C-1," 315–19; Bette Collins, "Stainmaster," case study, Graduate School of Business Administration, University of Virginia, 1989, 2–3. The second study was prepared with the assistance of DuPont.
3. Collins, "Stainmaster."
4. Ibid.
5. *Textile World,* Jan. 1987, 75; *Flooring,* July 1987, 8.
6. Frank O'Neill, "Has the American Carpet Industry Entered into a New Era of Consumer Marketing?" *Carpet and Rug Industry,* Oct. 1988, 7–8.
7. *Atlanta Constitution,* 10 Aug. 1987.
8. Quoted in Alalmo, "Robert Shaw's Terms of Controversy."
9. Julius Shaw, interview.
10. Ibid.
11. Ibid.
12. Ibid.
13. Ibid.
14. Ibid.
15. Bill Lusk, interview by Randall Patton, 2 Sept. 1999, Shaw Industries History series.
16. Robert E. (Bob) Shaw, interview by Randall Patton, 19 Aug. 1999, Shaw Industries History series; Lusk, interview.
17. *Wall Street Journal,* Southeast ed., 30 Sept. 1987.
18. Anderson, *Social Consequences of Economic Restructuring,* 51–52.
19. Ibid., 53; *Investor's Daily,* 22 June 1990, 1.
20. See Burrough and Helyar, *Barbarians at the Gate.*
21. Ibid., 140–42.
22. Pete Engliardo, "A Textile Maker That's Not Following the Pattern," *Business Week,* 18 Nov. 1985, 47.

23. Lusk, interview.
24. Ibid.
25. Ibid.; Kerry Hannon, "Full Speed Ahead and Damn the Stock Market," *Forbes,* 25 Jan. 1988.
26. Lusk, interview.
27. Ibid.
28. Warren Sims, interview by Randall Patton, 15 Aug. 1994, Carpet History series.
29. Julian McCamy, interview by Randall Patton, 29 Oct. 1999, Shaw Industries History series.
30. Hannon, "Full Speed Ahead."
31. Bob Shaw, interview.
32. Frank O'Neill, "The Top 25," *Carpet and Rug Industry,* June 1988, 12–14.
33. Michael Berns, "Carpet Mill Anemia," *Carpet and Rug Industry,* Jan. 1989; Michael Berns, "The Shaw Factor," *Carpet and Rug Industry,* Oct. 1989.
34. Berns, "Shaw Factor." This brief summary of Berns's views is drawn from Patton, *Carpet Capital,* 274–75.
35. Randy Merritt to Philadelphia sales force, 31 Oct. 1989, memo in the files of Shaw salesman Eric Duncan.
36. "Shaw Inter-Office Memorandum," 22 March 1993; Shaw quoted in *Atlanta Journal,* 16 May 1990.
37. "History of E&B Carpet Mills," typescript, n.d., from the files of Bobby Mosteller; *Dallas Morning News,* 10 July 1966.
38. Sims, interview.
39. *Modern Textiles,* Feb. 1966, from Bobby Mosteller clipping file; *Barron's,* 27 June 1966.
40. Lusk, interview.
41. *Business Week,* 20 Feb. 1989, 134.
42. Julius Shaw, interview.
43. Lusk, interview.
44. *Wall Street Journal,* Southeast ed., 12 June 1991; Chuck Reece, "Carpet King," *Georgia Trend,* Aug. 1990, 13.
45. *Wall Street Journal,* Southeast ed., 12 June 1991.
46. Bob Shaw, interview.
47. Lusk, interview; *PR Newswire,* 7 June 1989.
48. Reg Burnett used the phrase "aggressive pricer" to describe Salem in the *New York Times,* 30 May 1992, 35.
49. Julius Shaw, interview.
50. Ibid.
51. Ibid.
52. North Carolina Employment Law Letter, April 1996.
53. Shaw Industries, press release, 23 July 1993.
54. *Chemical Market Reporter,* 247, no. 11 (13 March 1995): 22.
55. Vance Bell, interview by Randall Patton, 6 May 1999, Shaw Industries History series; Lusk, interview.

56. *Chemical Week,* 26 April 1989, 19 July 1989.
57. Bell, interview.
58. Lusk, interview.
59. Bell, interview.
60. Ibid.
61. Warren Sims, "Shaw Industries, Inc., Business Philosophy," Jan. 1990, Warren Sims Papers.
62. George Williams, Robert Reeves, and Scott Barland, "Shaw Industries: A Strategic Analysis," report compiled for Strategic Management course, Kennesaw State College, School of Business, paper in the possession of the author; Little interview, *In the Loop.*
63. *Atlanta Constitution,* 24 Aug. 1987, D1.
64. Ibid.
65. Anne Gentry, interview by Linda Williams, 6 April 1996, Carpet History series.
66. Pat Brock, interview by Linda Williams, 5 April 1996, Carpet History series.
67. Sims, "Business Philosophy."
68. Ibid.; Sims, interview.
69. *Dalton Daily Citizen-News,* 27 Jan. 1990, 1A.
70. Ibid., 3A.
71. *Dalton Daily Citizen-News,* 18 Feb. 1990, 6A.
72. David S. Hill to Warren Sims, 11 Feb. 1992, Warren Sims Papers.
73. Federal News Service, 3 Aug. 1992, accessed through LexisNexis Academic Universe, <www.lexisnexis.com>.

Seven. Difficult Times

1. Frank O'Neill and Bobbie Carmical, "The Relentless Rise of Shaw Industries," *Floor Focus,* Oct. 1993, 18; Reg Burnett, interview by Randall Patton, 5 May 1999, Shaw Industries History series; Robert E. (Bob) Shaw, interview by Randall Patton, 19 Aug. 1999, Shaw Industries History series.
2. Shaw quoted in Carmical, "The Man Behind Shaw Industries," *Floor Focus,* Oct. 1993, 37. Shaw's analysis of the relative merits of the Chinese and Russian roads to a market economy echoes in some respects that of Eric Hobsbawm in *The Age of Extremes,* esp. chapter 16, "End of Socialism," 462–99.
3. Shaw Industries, press release, 16 Nov. 1992.
4. Carpet Institute of Australia, Ltd., "The Australian Carpet Industry," <www.carpetinstitute.com.au/ln004/cial1.nsf>, accessed 2 January 2002.
5. Shaw Industries, press release, 23 Aug. 1993, 4 Nov. 1993.
6. Bartlett, *Carpeting the Millions,* 191–93. See also Attfield, "Tufted Carpet in Britain," 205–16.
7. Bartlett, *Carpeting the Millions,* 192–97.
8. Ibid., 200–201.
9. *Economist,* 20 Aug. 1977, 88.
10. *Financial Times,* 28 April 1988, "Survey" section, VI.

11. *Financial Times,* 21 June 1996, 21.
12. Janice Kirby, "Growth in Global Markets: European Update," *Carpet and Rug Industry,* Aug. 1993, 12.
13. "Shaw Industries, Inc.—History," Gale Business Resources, <www.galenet.com>, accessed 19 Jan. 2001.
14. Burnett, interview.
15. Phil Owen, "Carpets International: Three Years Later," *Textile World,* March 2000, Carpet and Rug section.
16. "EC Pulls Rug from Carpet Factory," *London Daily Telegraph,* 15 Dec. 1994, 27, accessed through LexisNexis Academic Universe, <www.lexisnexis.com>, 10 Jan. 2001.
17. "450 Job Losses Announced by US-Based Carpet Multinational," Universal News Services, 6 Dec. 1996, accessed through LexisNexis Academic Universe, <www. lexisnexis.com>, 10 Jan. 2001.
18. Mike Nahan, "Feltex Ready to Quit," *Victoria Herald Sun,* 24 Nov. 2001, 84, accessed through LexisNexis Academic Universe, <www.lexisnexis.com>; Schumpeter, *Capitalism, Socialism, and Democracy,* 82–85.
19. *Financial Times,* 5 March 1998, 27 (mini-booms), 21 June 1996, 21 (falling carpet sales); Bill Lusk, interview by Randall Patton, 2 Sept. 1999, Shaw Industries History series.
20. Bob Shaw quoted in Ed Lightsey, "King of Carpet," *Georgia Trend,* 1 April 1999, 16.
21. Phil Owen, "Carpets International: Three Years Later," *Textile World,* March 2000, 35–37.
22. Bob Shaw, interview.
23. Ibid.; *Wall Street Journal,* Southeast ed., "Heard in the Southeast," 8 Feb. 1995, S2.
24. Bob Shaw, interview.
25. Jonathan Trivers, quoted in *Kansas City Star,* 2 July 1996, D1.
26. Julius Shaw, interview by Randall Patton, 9 Sept. 1999, Shaw Industries History series.
27. Ibid.
28. Ibid.
29. Bob Shaw, interview.
30. Ibid.
31. Lusk, interview.
32. Bob Shaw and Frank O'Neill, quoted in *Atlanta Journal-Constitution,* 15 Dec. 1995, 5H.
33. The named individuals were quoted in *HFN* [*Home Furnishing News*], 29 Jan. 1996, 20.
34. Lorraine Miller, quoted in *Wall Street Journal,* Southeast ed., 15 July 1998, S2.
35. *Wall Street Journal,* Southeast ed., 15 July 1998, S2.
36. Lusk, interview.
37. Burnett, interview. Bill Lusk echoed Burnett's views.
38. *Wall Street Journal,* Southeast ed., 15 July 1998, S2.
39. Lindsey Kelly, "Is Shaw Industries Too Big?" *Georgia Trend,* Sept. 1993, 33–34; *Atlanta Constitution,* 14 Dec. 1995.

40. *Atlanta Constitution*, 14 Dec. 1995, 6F.
41. *PR Newswire*, 27 Oct. 1997.
42. "Minutes of the Executive Committee of Shaw Industries, Inc.," 28 Nov. 1979. Attached to these minutes is a "Written Antitrust Compliance Program for Shaw Industries, Inc."
43. Julius Shaw, interview.
44. Ibid.; *Atlanta Constitution*, 23 Jan. 1998, 8H.
45. Julius Shaw, interview.
46. *Atlanta Constitution*, 24 June 1998, 1D.

Eight. A Return to Core Competencies

1. Julius Shaw, interview by Randall Patton, 9 Sept. 1999, Shaw Industries History series.
2. *Atlanta Constitution*, 24 June 1998, 1D.
3. Julius Shaw, interview; *HFN* [*Home Furnishings News*], 10 Aug. 1998, 16.
4. *HFN*, 20 July 1998, 35; *HFN*, 10 Aug. 1998, 16.
5. Unless otherwise noted, all information and quotes regarding the Saul family and Queen Carpet in the following sections are from an interview with Julian Saul conducted by Randall Patton, 3 Aug. 1993, Carpet History series.
6. Robert E. (Bob) Shaw, interview by Randall Patton, 19 Aug. 1999, Shaw Industries History series.
7. See Flamming, *Creating the Modern South*, 282–306.
8. Bobbie Carmical, "Harry Saul: A Patriarch of the Carpet Industry," *Sun Belt Floor Covering*, March 1988, 24–26.
9. Walter Guinan, quoted in Carmical, "Harry Saul."
10. Walter Rozelle, "Queen's Legacy Stays True to Form," *Textile World*, May 1998, 42.
11. Cobb, *Selling of the South*, 44.
12. Ibid., 45–46.
13. *Carpet and Rug Industry*, April 1996, 25.
14. *Atlanta Constitution*, 7 June 1994, C3.
15. Julian Saul, quoted in Carmical, "Harry Saul," 25.
16. Bob Shaw, interview.
17. Julian Saul, interview by Randall Patton, 5 March 1999, Shaw Industries History series.
18. Julius Shaw, interview.
19. Julian Saul, interview, 5 March 1999; Bob Shaw, interview.
20. Bob Shaw, interview.
21. Ibid.
22. *Wall Street Journal*, Eastern ed., 13 Jan. 1999, B9.
23. Julius Shaw, interview.
24. Julian Saul, quoted in *Flooring*, 1 Nov. 1999, 20.
25. John Kay, "Mastering Strategy," *Financial Times*, Survey ed., 27 Sept. 1999, 2–4. Kay surveys the field of management strategy, emphasizing the work of Michael Porter

and also C. K. Prahalad and Gary Hamel. Prahalad and Hamel popularized the term "core competencies" in presenting a resource-based view of strategy.

26. Ibid., 3.

27. Porter, *Competitive Strategy*. On generic strategies, see esp. 34–46. A useful brief summary of Porter's views may be found in the *Economist*, 12 Jan. 1985 (U.S. ed.), 61. See also Porter, "The State of Strategic Planning," *Economist*, 23 May 1987 (U.S. ed.), 17. Henry Mintzberg, "Mintzberg: The Insightful Manager," interview by Donna Brown, *Management Review*, Dec. 1991, 20. The quote is from Mintzberg. Mintzberg's views on planning are fleshed out at length in Mintzberg, *Rise and Fall of Strategic Planning*.

28. Vance Bell, interview by Randall Patton, 6 May 1999, Shaw Industries History series.

29. *Flooring*, 1 Nov. 1999, 20.

30. Correspondence from Randy Merritt, 9 July 2002, in the possession of the author; Malcolm Fleschner, "Pile It On," *Selling Power*, October 2001, 8–11.

31. Joel Millman and Will Pinkston, "Mexicans Move from Poverty to Suburbia in the U.S.'s Burgeoning 'Carpet Capital,'" *Wall Street Journal*, Southeast ed., 30 Aug. 2001, 1.

32. Russell Grantham, "Latinos Reshaping Georgia Mill Town," *Atlanta Constitution*, 13 May 2001, 1P.

33. Data on productivity and wages from U.S. Bureau of Labor Statistics, Industry Productivity and Labor Cost Data Tables, <www.bls.gov/bls/proghome.htm>, accessed 20 Dec. 2001.

34. Hernandez-Leon and Zuniga, "'Making Carpet by the Mile,'" 60–61.

35. Charles Parham, quoted in *Textile World*, May 1998, 13; Walter Rozelle's observations are from *Textile World*, Dec. 1998, 86.

36. Julius Shaw, quoted in *Wall Street Journal*, Southeast ed., 30 Aug. 2001, 1.

37. Kirp, "Old South's New Face," 27–30.

38. Grupo Alfa Company Profile, *Latin Finance*, 1 Dec. 1994, accessed through Lexis-Nexis Academic Universe, <www.lexisnexis.com>.

39. Erwin Mitchell, quoted in *Richmond Times-Dispatch*, 5 Sept. 1999, A8, and in Kirp, "Old South's New Face."

40. *Wall Street Journal*, Southeast ed., 30 Aug. 2001, 1; *Los Angeles Times*, 29 Dec. 1999, A1.

41. *Chattanooga Times*, 2 July 2001, B3.

42. Kirp, "Old South's New Face." Ironically, only a week before it received the NEA award, the Dalton school board voted to cut funding for a portion of the Georgia Project and focus on recruiting bilingual teachers locally. See *Chattanooga Times*, 2 July 2001, B3.

43. Marc Rice, "As Waste Piles Up, Carpet Industry Seeks Recycling Plan," Associated Press, 4 Jan. 1995, accessed through LexisNexis Academic Universe, <www.lexisnexis.com>; "New Roadbed Companion for Dirt, Sand: Carpeting," *American City and County*, Nov. 1997, 48; Robert Simpson, "Used Carpet Recycling," *Flooring*, 1 March 2000, 30; "Shaw Contract Recycling Program Is Underway," *Flooring*,

1 Nov. 1996; Georgia Department of Natural Resources Newsletter, found at <http://www.ganet.org/dnr/p2ad/newsletter/news/govpics.htm>, accessed 9 July 2002.
44. *Wall Street Journal*, Southeast ed., 31 March 1998, B1.
45. John Baugh, quoted in Patti Bond, "Georgia-Based Carpet Companies to Show Hardwood Floors," *Atlanta Journal-Constitution*, 25 Jan. 2000, D1.P
46. James Jarrett quoted in Seth Hopkins, "Shaw Takes the Floor," *Cartersville Magazine*, Summer 1999, 22.
47. Ibid., 22–23.
48. Ibid., 23.
49. *HFN*, 12 Feb. 2001, 25, accessed through LexisNexis Academic University, <www.lexisnexis.com>.
50. The rankings may be viewed at <www.fortune.com/fortune/mostadmired/>.
51. Bob Shaw, interview.

Epilogue

1. Carrick Mollenkamp and Devon Spurgeon, "A Shaw Drama: How Berkshire Deal Got Done," *Wall Street Journal*, Southeast ed. 20 Nov. 2000, C1.
2. The trend among analysts was noted in a book review in *Business Week*, 27 Sept. 1999, 62.
3. See Shiller, *Irrational Exuberance*. Greenspan's remark can be found in his speech to the American Enterprise Institute, 5 Dec. 1996, at <www.federalreserve.gov/boarddocs/speeches/1996/>, accessed 4 January 2002. Wall Street events of 2000–2001 seem to have vindicated, at least partially, this critique.
4. See Lowenstein, *Buffett*, 122–39; stock price data from Hoover's Online, <www.hoovers.com/co/>, accessed 16 Aug. 2001. Buffett never allowed stock splits, which explains, in part, the high per share value.
5. Warren Buffett, quoted in Lowenstein, *Buffett*, 273–74.
6. Ibid., 273.
7. Mollenkamp and Spurgeon, "Shaw Drama."
8. Ibid.
9. Shareholder approval, *Chattanooga Times*, 5 Jan. 2001, C1; Julius Shaw and Keith Hughes, quoted in *Chattanooga Times*, 7 Sept. 2000, A1.
10. Warren Buffett, quoted in Christopher Farrell, "Being Warren Buffett," *Business Week OnLine*, 20 April 2001, <www.businessweek.com/bwdaily/dnflash/apr2001/nf20010420_940.htm>, accessed 4 January 2002.

Manuscript Collections

Bobby Mosteller Clipping File, Chatsworth, Georgia.
Cabin Crafts scrapbooks, Crown Gardens and Archives, Dalton, Georgia.
Carpet and Rug Institute Papers, Carpet and Rug Institute, Dalton, Georgia.
Shaw Industries Records, Corporate Headquarters, Dalton, Georgia.
Tufted Textile Manufacturers Association Papers, Carpet and Rug Institute, Dalton, Georgia.
TWUA-GTA Joint Board Papers, Southern Labor Archives, Georgia State University, Atlanta, Georgia.
Warren Sims Papers, Shaw Industries, Dalton, Georgia.

Oral Histories and Interviews

Carpet History series, Kennesaw State University, Sturgis Library, Kennesaw, Georgia. Tape and transcript.
Shaw Industries History series, Kennesaw State University, Center for Regional History and Culture, Kennesaw, Georgia. All interviews by Randall L. Patton. Tape.

Newspapers and Periodicals

Advertising Age
Atlanta Journal and Constitution
Barron's
Business Week
Calhoun Times
Carpet and Rug Industry
Chattanooga News-Free Press
Chattanooga Times
Dallas Morning News
Dalton Citizen
Dalton Daily Citizen-News
Dalton News
Economist
Floor Covering Weekly
Flooring
Fortune

Georgia Trend
Home Furnishings Daily
Home Furnishings News
Investor's Daily
Los Angeles Times
Management Review
Modern Floor Coverings
Modern Textiles
New York Times
Southern Textile News
Sun Belt Floor Covering
Textile Chemist and Colorist
Textile World
Textile Industries
Wall Street Journal
Westpointer

Books, Articles, and Dissertations

Alalmo, Dan. "Robert Shaw's Terms of Controversy." *Flooring,* July 1987, 8.

Anderson, Cynthia D. *The Social Consequences of Economic Restructuring in the Textile Industry.* New York: Garland, 2000.

Attfield, Judy. "The Tufted Carpet in Britain: Its Rise from the Bottom of the Pile." *Journal of Design History* 7, no. 3 (1994).

Ayers, Edward L. *The Promise of the New South: Life after Reconstruction.* New York: Oxford University Press, 1992.

Bartlett, J. Neville. *Carpeting the Millions: The Growth of Britain's Carpet Industry.* Edinburgh, U.K.: John Donald, 1975.

Bartley, Numan V. *The New South, 1945–1980.* Baton Rouge: Louisiana State University Press, 1995.

Blackford, Mansel. *A History of Small Business in America.* New York: Twayne, 1991.

Blackford, Mansel, and Austin Kerr. *Business Enterprise in American History.* 3rd ed. Boston: Houghton Mifflin, 1993.

Bruchey, Stuart, ed. *Small Business in American Life.* New York: Columbia University Press, 1980.

Burrough, Bryan, and John Helyar. *Barbarians at the Gate: The Fall of RJR-Nabisco.* New York: Harper and Row, 1990.

Chernow, Ron. *Titan: The Life of John D. Rockefeller.* New York: Vintage, 1999.

Cobb, James C. *Industrialization and Southern Society, 1877–1984.* Lexington: University Press of Kentucky, 1984.

————. *The Selling of the South: The Southern Crusade for Industrial Development, 1936–1990.* 2nd ed. Urbana: University of Illinois Press, 1993.

Ewing, John S., and Nancy P. Norton. *Broadlooms and Businessmen: A History of the Bigelow-Sanford Company.* Cambridge: Harvard University Press, 1955.

Flamming, Douglas. *Creating the Modern South: Millhands and Managers in Dalton, Georgia, 1884–1984.* Chapel Hill: University of North Carolina Press, 1992.

Flemming, James B. "The Northwest Georgia Carpet Finishing Industry: Its Operation and Financing." Master's thesis, Stonier Graduate School of Banking, Rutgers University, 1974.

Heilbroner, Robert. *The Economic Transformation of America, 1600–Present.* 3rd ed. New York: Harcourt Brace, 1994.

Hernandez-Leon, Ruben, and Victor Zuniga. "'Making Carpet by the Mile': The Emergence of a Mexican Immigrant Community in an Industrial Region of the U.S. Historic South." *Social Science Quarterly* 81, no. 1 (2000): 58–73.

Hobsbawm, Eric. *The Age of Extremes: A History of the World, 1914–1991.* New York: Random House, 1995.

Kirp, David. "The Old South's New Face." *Nation,* 26 June 2000, 26–30.

Krugman, Paul. *Geography and Trade.* Cambridge: Massachusetts Institute of Technology Press, 1991.

Luck, David J., O. C. Ferrell, and George H. Lucas Jr. "Case C-1: DuPont 'Stainmaster.'" In *Marketing Strategy and Plans.* 3rd ed. Englewood Cliffs, N.J.: Prentice Hall, 1989.

McDonald, Joseph A. "Textile Workers and Unionization: A Community Study." Ph.D. dissertation, University of Tennessee, Knoxville, Tennessee, 1981.

Minchin, Timothy J. *"What Do We Need a Union For?" The TWUA in the South, 1945–1955.* Chapel Hill: University of North Carolina Press, 1997.

Mintzberg, Henry. *The Rise and Fall of Strategic Planning.* New York: Free Press, 1994.

Patton, Randall L., with David B. Parker. *Carpet Capital: The Rise of a New South Industry.* Athens: University of Georgia Press, 1999.

Piore, Michael, and Charles Sabel. *The Second Industrial Divide: Possibilities for Prosperity.* New York: Basic Books, 1984.

Plice, Steven S. *Manpower and Merger: The Impact of Merger upon Personnel Policies in the Carpet and Furniture Industries.* Manpower and Human Resources Study no. 5. Philadelphia: Wharton School, University of Pennsylvania, 1976.

Porter, Michael. *Competitive Strategy: Techniques for Analyzing Industries and Competitors.* New York: Free Press, 1980.

Reynolds, William A. *Innovation in the United States Carpet Industry, 1947–1963.* Princeton, N.J.: Van Nostrand, 1968.

Sabel, Charles, and Jonathan Zeitlin, eds. *World of Possibilities: Flexibility and Mass Production in Western Industrialization.* Cambridge: Cambridge University Press, 1997.

Saxenian, Annalee. *Regional Advantage: Culture and Competition in Silicon Valley and Route 128.* Cambridge: Harvard University Press, 1994.

Schulman, Bruce J. *From Cotton Belt to Sunbelt: Federal Policy, Economic Development, and the Transformation of the South, 1938–1980.* New York: Oxford University Press, 1991; reprint, Durham, N.C.: Duke University Press, 1994.

Schumpeter, Joseph. *Capitalism, Socialism, and Democracy.* Rev. ed. New York: Harper and Row, 1975.

Scranton, Philip. *Endless Novelty.* Princeton, N.J.: Princeton University Press, 1997.

Shiller, Robert. *Irrational Exuberance.* Princeton, N.J.: Princeton University Press, 2000.

Woodward, C. Vann. *Origins of the New South, 1877–1913.* Baton Rouge: Louisiana State University Press, 1951.

Wright, Gavin. *Old South, New South: Revolutions in the Southern Economy since the Civil War.* New York: Basic Books, 1986.

Italic page numbers refer to illustrations.

Little, Norris, 85–87, 90–91, 102, 138, 173, 188
Looper, Glenn, 8
Love, J. Spencer, 183
Lusk, William C., 59, 75, 85, 88, 100, 105, 113–14, 123–24, 126–28, 131–32, 157

management strategy, 171–72
Marion Manufacturing Company, 45, 74, 81
mass production model, 14–16
Maxim Group, 155
McCamy, Julian, 31, 34–35, 82, 128
McCamy, Robert, 10, 19, 20–21, 22, 31, 34–35, 38, 47, 126
McCarty, Frank, 48, 131
McCarty, John B., 24, 48, 74, 81, 131
McNamara, Roger, 36, 90
Merritt, Randy, 130, 173–74
Milken, Michael, 125
mill building crusade, New South, 5–6
Mintzberg, Henry, 172
Mitchell, Erwin, 178–80
Mohawk, 1, 6, 12, 156, 181–82
Monsanto, 120
Monterrey, Mexico, 179–80
Morrison, Stuart, 50

New Found Industries, 88
New South, 17
New York Carpet World, 155
North American Free Trade Agreement (NAFTA), 179
nylon, 11–12; BCF, 11–12, 42, 85–86, 154; staple, 11–12, 121–22

Pate, Carl, 58–60
paternalism, 26, 28–29
Payne, Otis, 32–35
pension funds, 106
Philadelphia Carpet Company, 1, 2, 6, 65, 66–77
Philadelphia Holding Company, 73–74, 81–83

polypropylene yarn, 134, 135–37, 147
Porter, Michael, 171–72
Post Properties, 99–100
Prahalad, C. K., 171, 205–6 (n. 25)
President's Emergency Council, 2
printing, 78–80, 89

Queen Carpets, 1–2, 156, 163–70

Rabun Gap, Georgia, 85
RCA, 86–87
Real Silk Hosiery, 19
recessions: years 1973–74, 92–95; years 1981–82, 104–8
regional concentrations (agglomerations), 4–5; of early woven carpet industry, 5; of tufted carpet industry, 88
residential mortgages, 105–6
Revonah Spinning Mills, 66
Rhodes, Travis "Dusty," 71
Rice, George, 81
Rockefeller, John D., 92
Rocky Creek Mills, 45, 46, 65

S & H Greenstamps, 87
Sabre Carpets, 64–65, 76
Salem Carpets, 133–35
Sapp, W. M. (Bill), 31–32, 37
Saul, Harry, 1, 2, 42, 163–69
Saul, Julian, 1, 2, 138, 163–70, 173
Schulman, Bruce, 3–4
Schumpeter, Joseph, 149
Scranton, Philip, 14
secondary backing, 36
Sewell, Buddy, 25–28, 30–31, 40, 41–42, 47, 50–51, 102–3
Shaw, Clarence, 1, 2, 10, 13, 38–39, 47; business philosophy, 30, 40–42; dyeing carpets, 41; early years, 17–20; employee relations, 25–31; illness, 39–40; Presbyterian faith, 24–25
Shaw, Elbert, 18, 25, 52, 109–10
Shaw, J. C. (Bud), 1, 2, 8, 10, 18, 39, 40, 80, 101, 118, 172–73; buys Philadelphia

Westcott, Fred, 10, 19–23, 38
Westcott, Lamar, 10, 19–23, 38, 48
Westcott Hosiery Mill, 18–19
West Point Manufacturing Company,
   34–35, 123–29
WestPoint Peperrell. *See* West Point
   Manufacturing Company

Whitener, Catherine Evans, 7, 17
Wright, Gavin, 3

yarn mills, 88, 114–16

Zimmer, Peter, 78
Zimmer printer, 78–80, 89–90